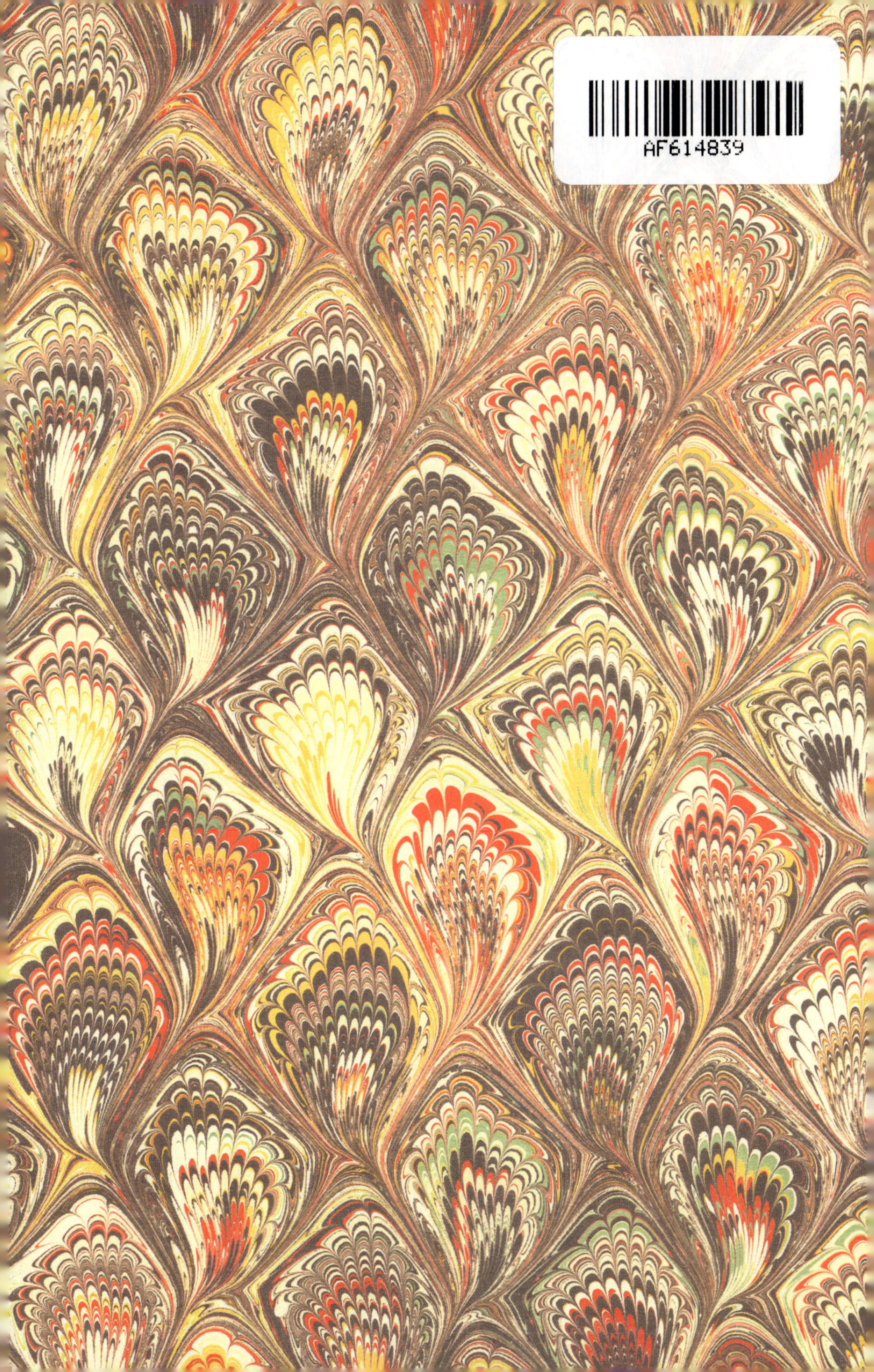

IMAGES
of America

PLATEAU VALLEY

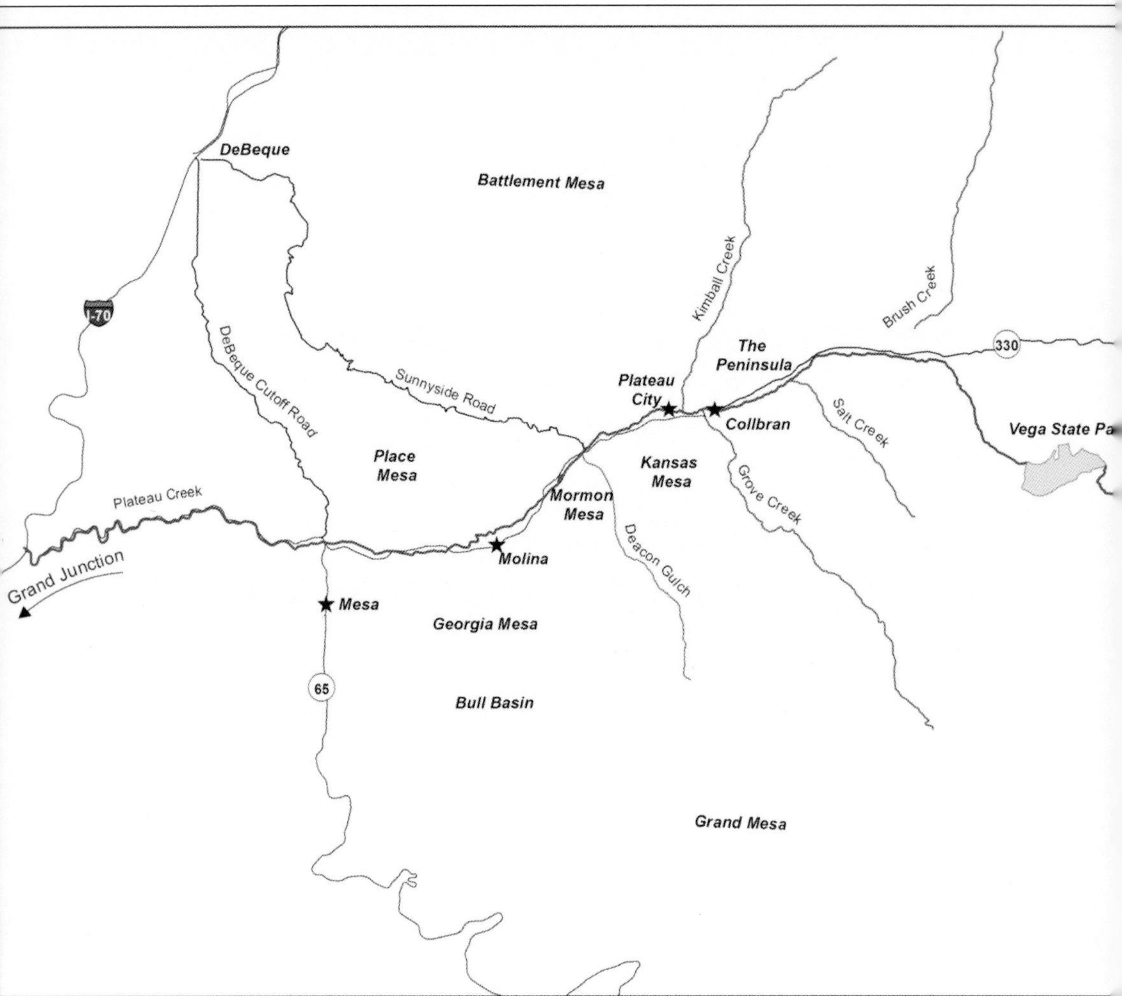

Map of Plateau Valley. This map shows the relative locations of the communities and natural features discussed in this book. (Author's collection.)

On the Cover: Charles Herbert Crane Funeral. Charles Herbert Crane died on October 8, 1918. He was a seaman on the USS *Massachusetts* and had just returned from a voyage when he contracted Spanish influenza. He died one week later of pneumonia at age 22 and received full military honors. The military escort consisted of a firing squad, a bugler, and a sergeant in charge. (Griffith family collection.)

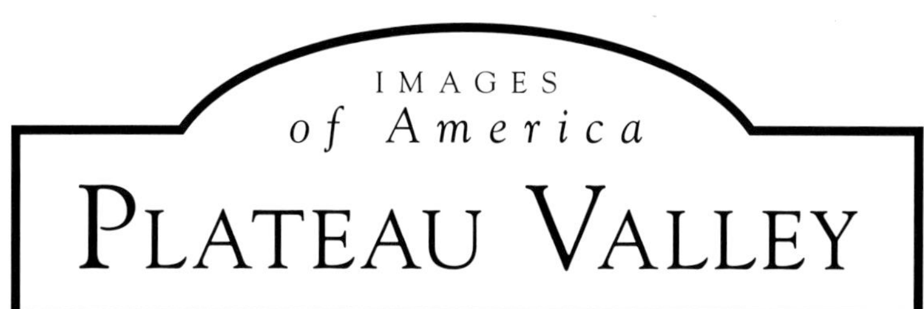

Nicole Inman

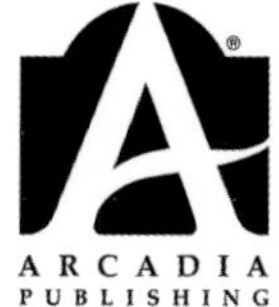

ISBN 978-1-4671-1545-2

Published by Arcadia Publishing
Charleston, South Carolina

Printed in the United States of America

Library of Congress Control Number: 2016933270

For all general information, please contact Arcadia Publishing:
Telephone 843-853-2070
Fax 843-853-0044
E-mail sales@arcadiapublishing.com
For customer service and orders:
Toll-Free 1-888-313-2665

Visit us on the Internet at www.arcadiapublishing.com

This book is lovingly dedicated to my great-grandmother Ethelle Silliman Raymond, my grandfather William "Bill" Raymond, and my mother, Jerri Inman, who all instilled in me a love of history.

Contents

Acknowledgments

First and foremost, I owe my mother, Jerri Inman, a tremendous debt of gratitude. Without her help and motivation, this book would not have been possible. My deepest thanks go also to Sylvia Spangler, Anise Kelley, and Hazel Place with the Plateau Valley Historical Preservation Society. Additional thanks go to Erin Schmitz with the Museum of the West, Lloyd Files Research Library, for her help and assistance. Several families gave generously from their collections, including Terry Griffith, Rudy and Arita Charlesworth, and Scott Walck, a generous contributor who passed away during the writing of this book. Finally, to all the others who shared their time, stories, and enthusiasm for the preservation of history, thank you.

INTRODUCTION

Plateau Valley is nestled in the shadow of the Grand Mesa, the largest flat-topped mountain in the world. The summit reaches 10,000 feet in elevation over an area that covers 800 square miles and towers more than a mile over the surrounding Gunnison and Colorado River valleys. Battlement Mesa, a smaller mesa standing at 9,000 feet in elevation, forms the northern wall of the valley.

Plateau Creek is a 50-mile-long tributary of the Colorado River. The headwaters are in northeastern Mesa County, in the Grand Mesa National Forest. The creek passes north of Vega State Park and enters Plateau Valley at Collbran, Colorado. From there, it flows west to the junction of State Highway 330 and State Highway 65, the Grand Mesa Scenic and Historical Byway. It then enters Plateau Canyon, a narrow 12-mile-long canyon of sheer rock walls.

The climate in Plateau Valley is mild, with moderate snowfall and comfortable temperatures. Summer recreation includes hunting, camping, fishing, and hiking. Winter recreation includes cross-country skiing, snowmobiling, ice fishing, and downhill skiing. Livestock ranching is still the leading industry. Hunting abounds, with deer, elk, and turkey in plentiful supply. Seven species of trout—rainbow, Colorado River cutthroat, Snake River cutthroat, brown, brook, splake, and Arctic Grayling—can be found year-round in more than 100 lakes and 25 streams. At lower elevations, lakes thaw by late April, with the lakes at the top of Grand Mesa opening up by the end of June.

Plateau Valley, with its fertile soils, has always been known for its high-quality grass and hay. In the early days, loose hay would be hauled to DeBeque, Colorado, for the livery stable and railroad trades. When horse-powered balers were brought to the valley, even more hay could be transported per load. It was in great demand outside of the valley as well as within, as it could be sold for cash or bartered for goods.

The first cattle to graze in the valley were driven in from Utah for the summer, crossing both the Colorado River and Plateau Creek. Historically, winters were more severe, and the creek ran much higher and faster, which made crossing it far more dangerous. Those early ranchers turned their cattle out onto the foothills of the Grand Mesa, a few miles up Salt Creek, Grove Creek, and the Meadows. Before 1905, cattle were allowed to graze without restriction, but after that time, reserve boundaries were established and cattle permits issued. In the fall, cattle were gathered from the forest and sorted. Those to be marketed were trailed to DeBeque, across Sunnyside. They swam the Colorado River and were loaded onto railroad cars to be shipped to Denver markets.

In 1902, the cattlemen of the area organized to form the Plateau Valley Stock Growers Association. They were able, as a group, to address and deal with problems and concerns that affected their livelihood. These issues have, over the years, included cattle rustling, predatory animals, toxic plants, and weevil-infested hay. Growers held their first annual banquet on December 3, 1912. The association is no longer active in the valley.

In 1912, the first Stray Day was held at the Flying Triangle Ranch, two miles south of Collbran on Kansas Mesa. Stray Day was the day all the ranchers gathered to collect the few stray cattle left on the mountain, sort out theirs, and take them home. In 1916, Owen Crane and Ed Jones started a new era in range history when they conceived the idea of a cattle pool and ran cattle for a number of smaller operators. A cowboy, known as a pool rider, is hired to live in the cabin at the pool corrals and look after the cattle for the summer. This system is still used today.

In the 1950s, the Plateau Valley Cowbelles Association was formed. The organization was made up of the cattlewomen of the valley. The name changed to the Plateau Valley CattleWomen, but the organization remains active in the community and state to promote the beef industry.

Cowboy Prayer

May your belly never grumble.
May your heart never ache.
May your horse never stumble.
May your cinch never break.

—Anonymous

One

Town of Collbran

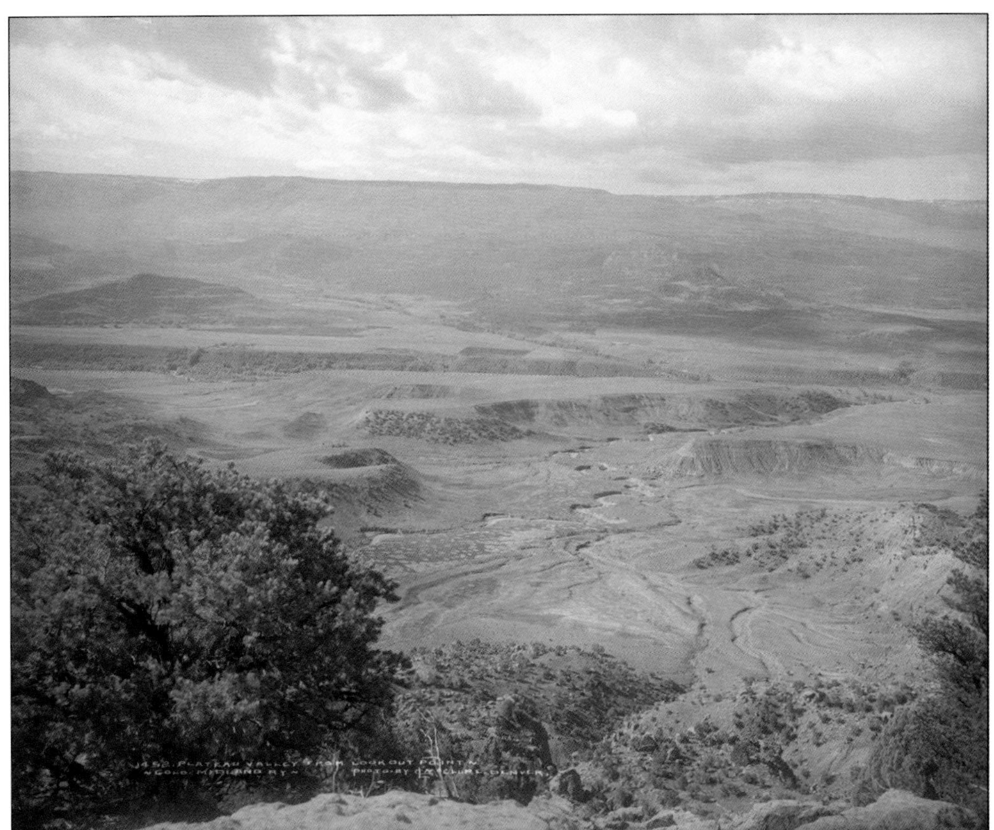

Plateau Valley from Lookout Point, c. 1910s. Pictured is the view from Lookout Point across Plateau Valley in Mesa County, Colorado, reached via the proposed Colorado Midland Railway. The image shows mesas, drainages, sage, juniper, and pinyon vegetation. (Denver Public Library, Western History Collection [Call MCC-1452].)

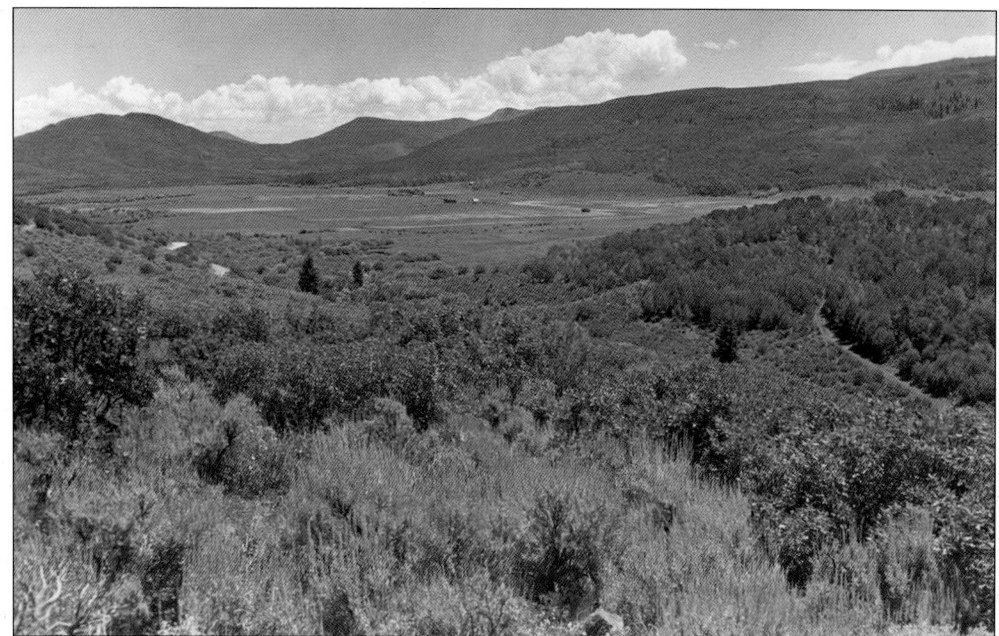

The Meadows. The George Hawxhurst family and the Horace Dunlap family came to the area by way of Ute Indian trails when the Utes' campfires were still smoldering. By 1885, most of the area of the Meadows had been homesteaded. At that time, 25 families were living there. A post office, cemetery, school, and two sawmills were soon started. Most of the settlers had moved away by 1924, and the school closed in 1936. (William H. Nelson Collection, Colorado Mesa University Special Collections.)

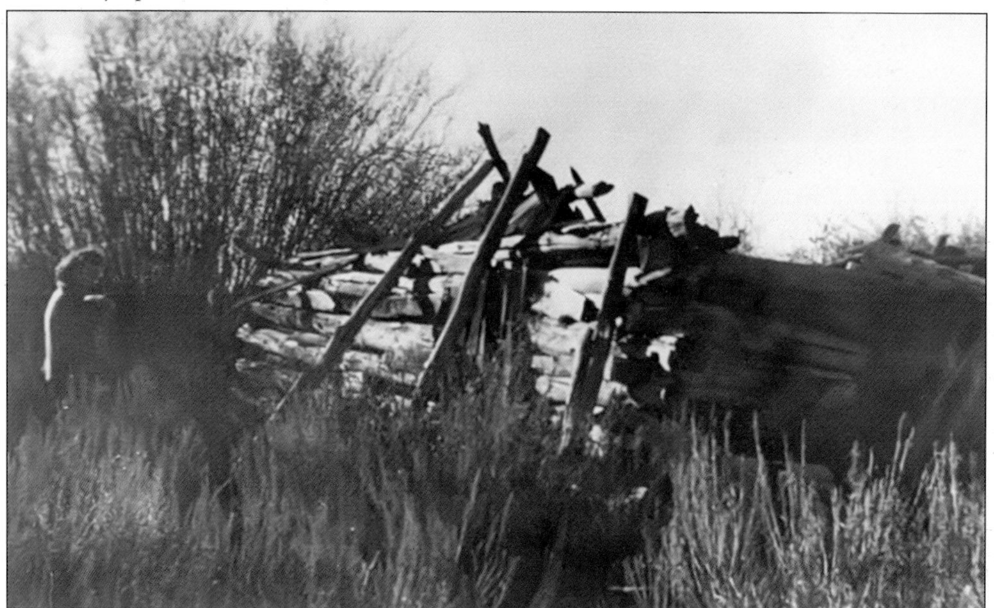

Hawxhurst Cabin. The Hawxhurst family arrived in the Meadows in Plateau Valley on October 7, 1881. There was high grass and good soil. Their cabin was constructed with hand-hewn logs and oak pegs. It measured 16 feet by 16 feet, with oiled flour sacks for windows. (Plateau Valley Historical Preservation Society.)

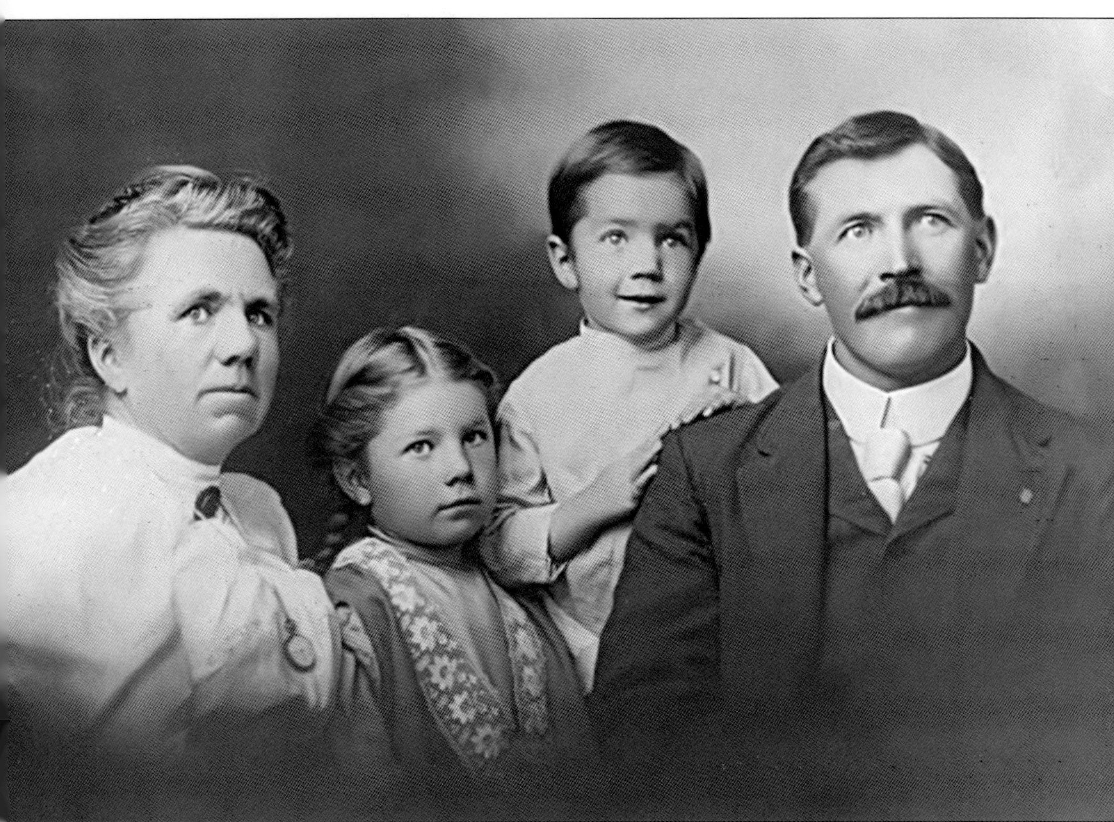

Hawxhurst Family. Pictured here from left to right are Maggie Hawxhurst, Helen Anna Hawxhurst, Harold Hughes Hawxhurst, and Alexander P. Hawxhurst. The George Hawxhurst family came to Plateau Valley with their daughter Mary and her husband, Horace Dunlap. George Hawxhurst related this story about making his way to Plateau Valley: "the big trail which leads to White River agency was fresh, and as we went down Leon Creek we came to two camps on Grove Creek and Salt Creeks, where the Indians were hiding out; and on Buzzard Creek their fires were still alive, where they had camped the night before. . . . On reaching home, we built a cabin, turned our horses out and were dead to the world for six months." (Plateau Valley Historical Preservation Society.)

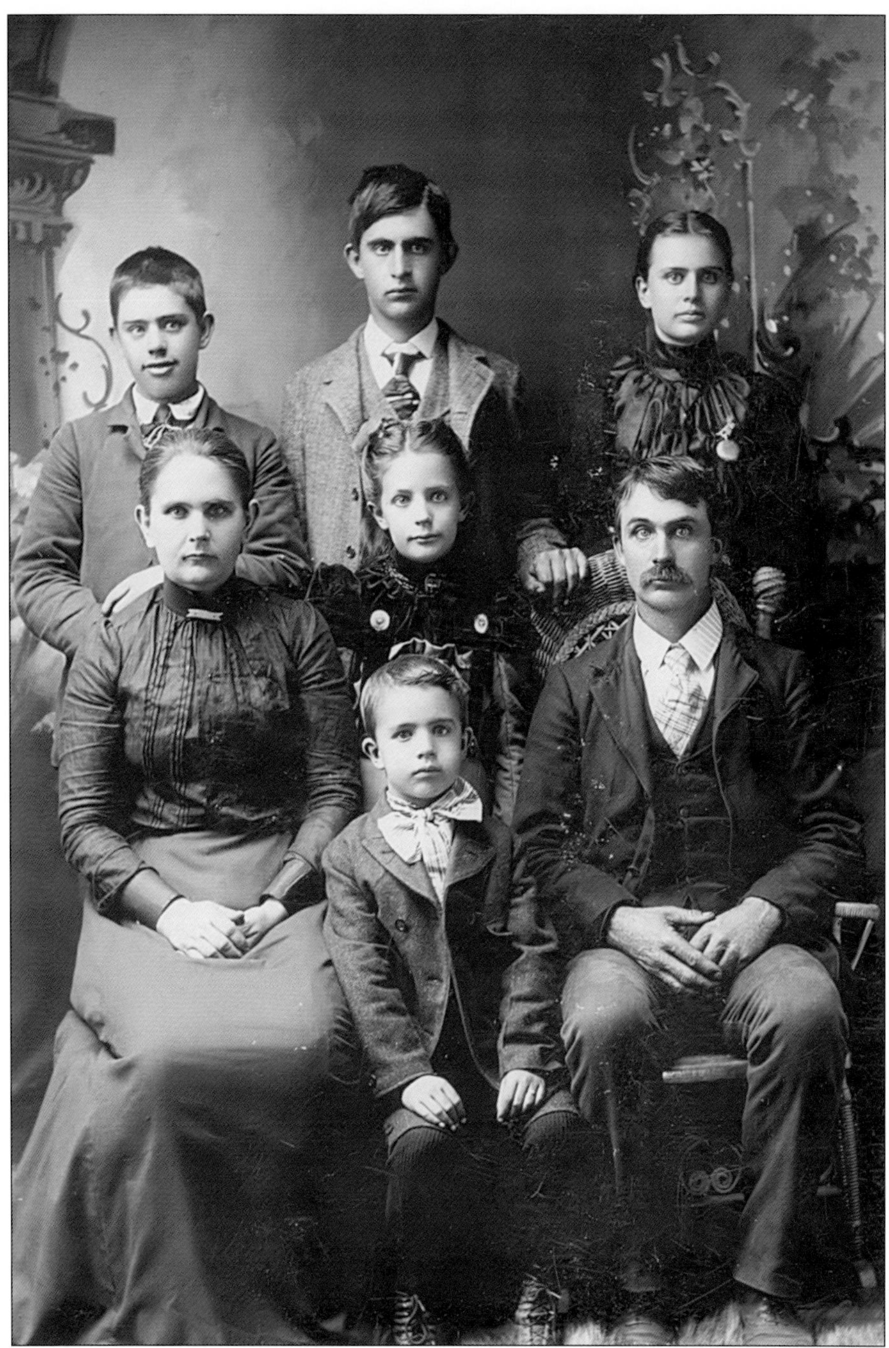

DUNLAP FAMILY, 1896. Pictured here are Horace and Mary (née Hawxhurst) and their family. Mary was the daughter of George Hawxhurst. They came with the Hawxhurst family to Plateau Valley in 1881. In 1882, Hattie Dunlap was born, the first white child born in Mesa County. Her mother, Mary, was the first white child born in the Denver area. The families were alone in the region at this time, except for the occasional traveler and George Howard's band of horse and cattle thieves, who allegedly used the valley as a hiding place for stolen stock. (Plateau Valley Historical Preservation Society.)

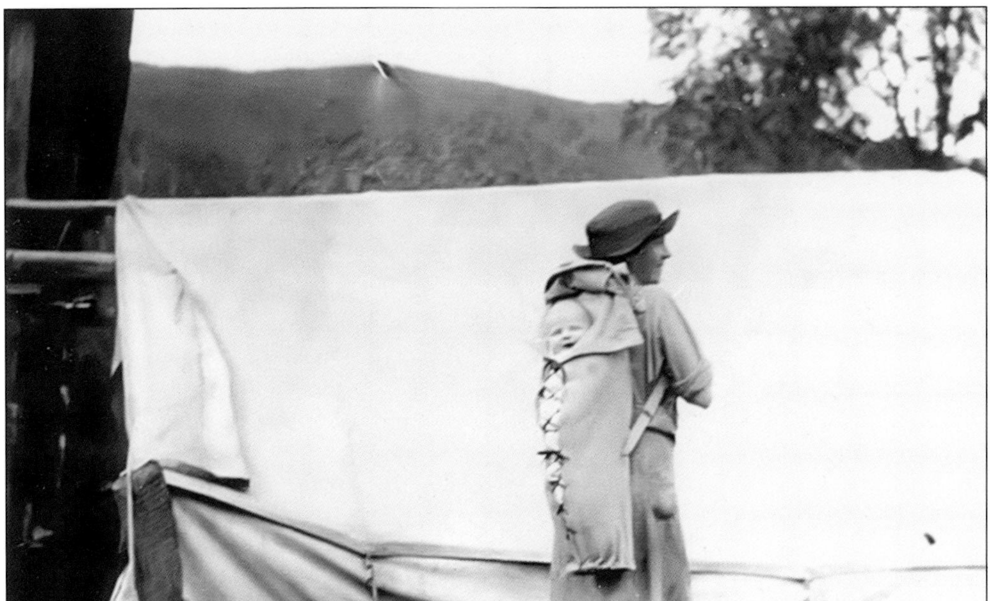

Helen Young and Daughter Donna. Helen Young composed the book *Skin and Bones*, which was based on her uncle Tom Hawxhurst's diary and numerous articles her father, Alex Hawxhurst, had written. Her daughter, Donna, saved old papers written by Ben and C.B. Pitts from the dirt and debris of the old printing office. It is considered the most complete history of Plateau Valley to date. (Plateau Valley Historical Preservation Society.)

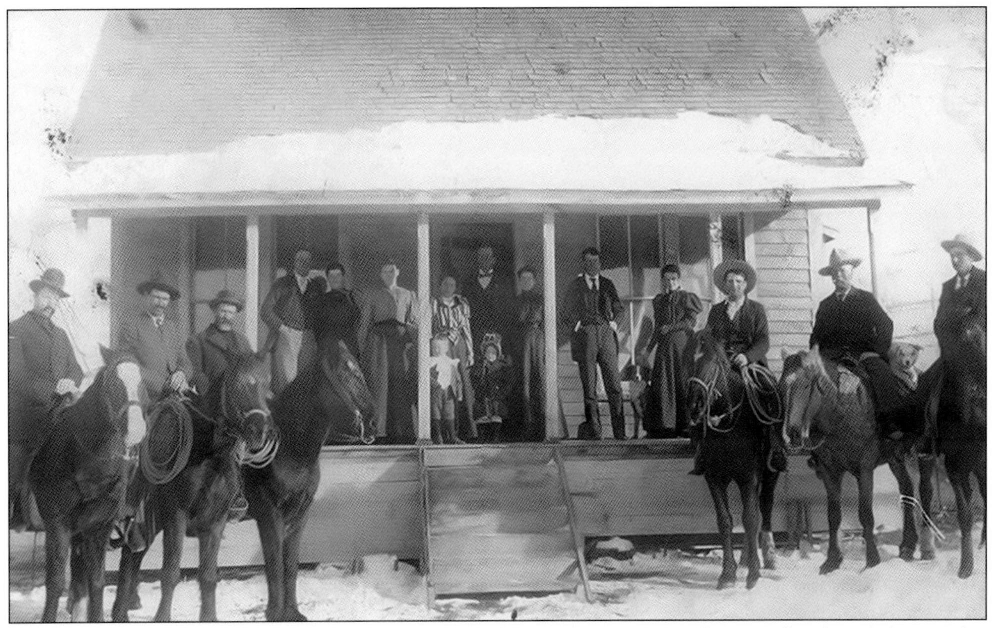

Dave and Burley Anderson Family, 1897. The Andersons are often credited with being the second family to make their way to Plateau Valley; however, their wagon broke down on the top of the Grand Mesa, and the J.P. Brown family passed around them. (Plateau Valley Historical Preservation Society.)

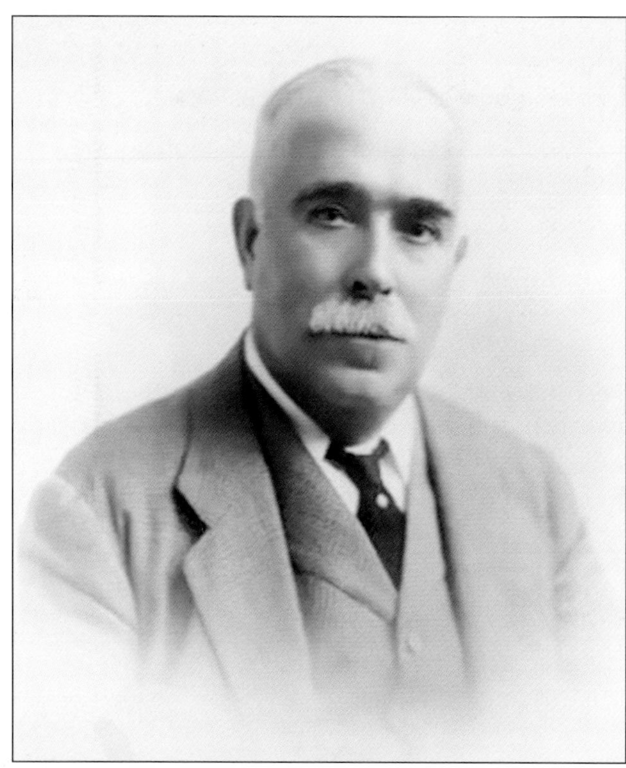

Henry Collbran. Henry Collbran was a railroad and mining operator. He was born in London, England, on December 23, 1853. He and his wife, Anabel Maurice Merrill, came to America in 1881. The town was named after him because it seemed likely he would build the Midland Railroad through Plateau Valley; however, a route along the Colorado River was chosen instead. (Plateau Valley Historical Preservation Society.)

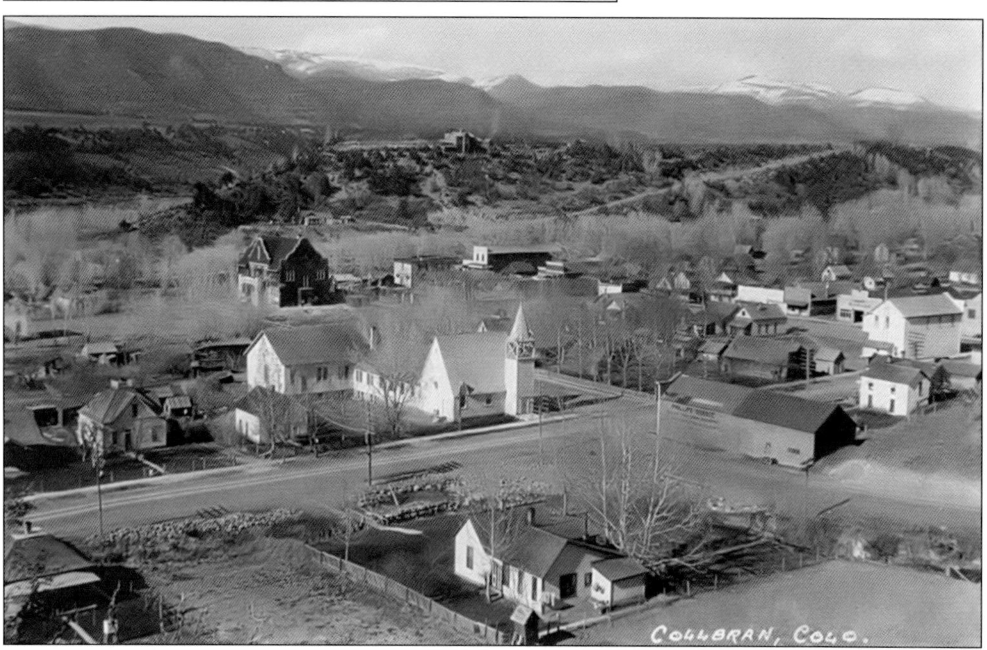

Collbran, Colorado. Collbran was first called Hawxhurst after the first family to settle in Plateau Valley. It was changed to Collbran in 1892 after Henry Collbran, a railroad man who worked to bring the Midland Railroad to Plateau Valley. The townsite was incorporated in 1908. Agriculture and hunting have been the mainstays of the economy since the town was founded. (Rudy and Arita Charlesworth.)

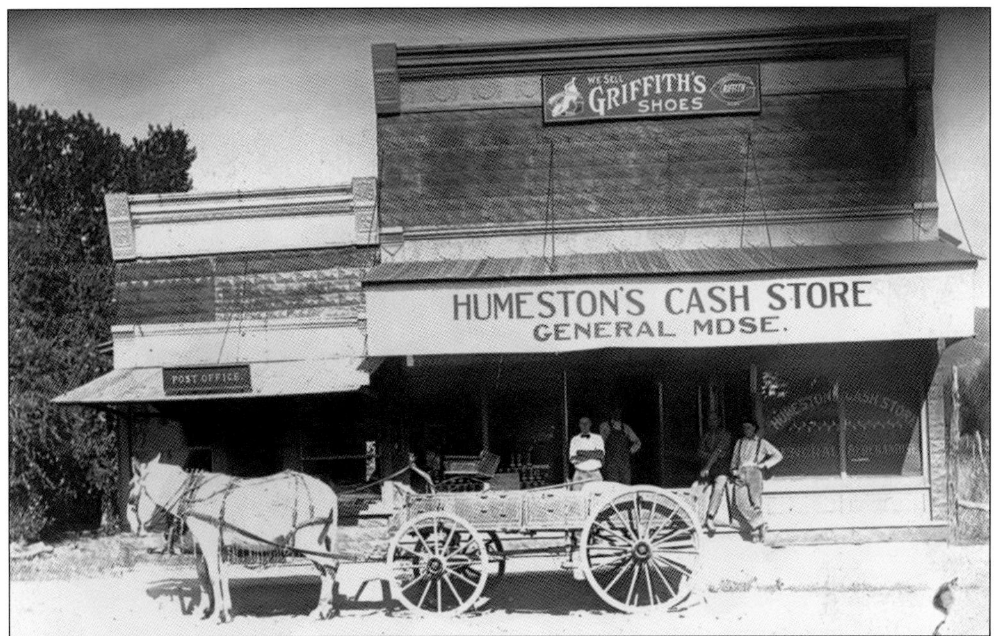

Humeston's Cash Store. Humeston's store was located on Main Street, south of Underhill's store and north of what was Lorimor Millinery Shop and later, around 1917, the post office. Loudene Humeston, daughter of store owner Del Humeston, was an icon of the Plateau Valley community. She was a teacher in Collbran for 50 years, teaching three generations of valley residents. She was a member of Collbran Congregational Church, where she taught Sunday school and played piano. She was also a member of the Order of the Eastern Star, Kappa Delta Gamma sorority, and the P.E.O. Sisterhood. (Both, Museum of Western Colorado, Lloyd Files Research Library.)

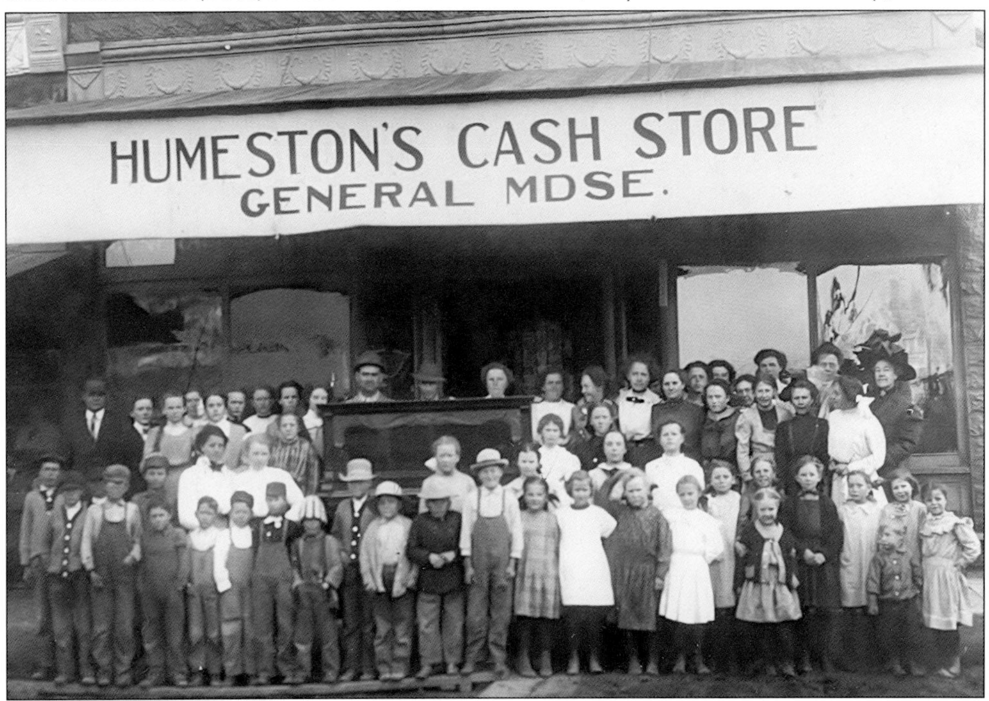

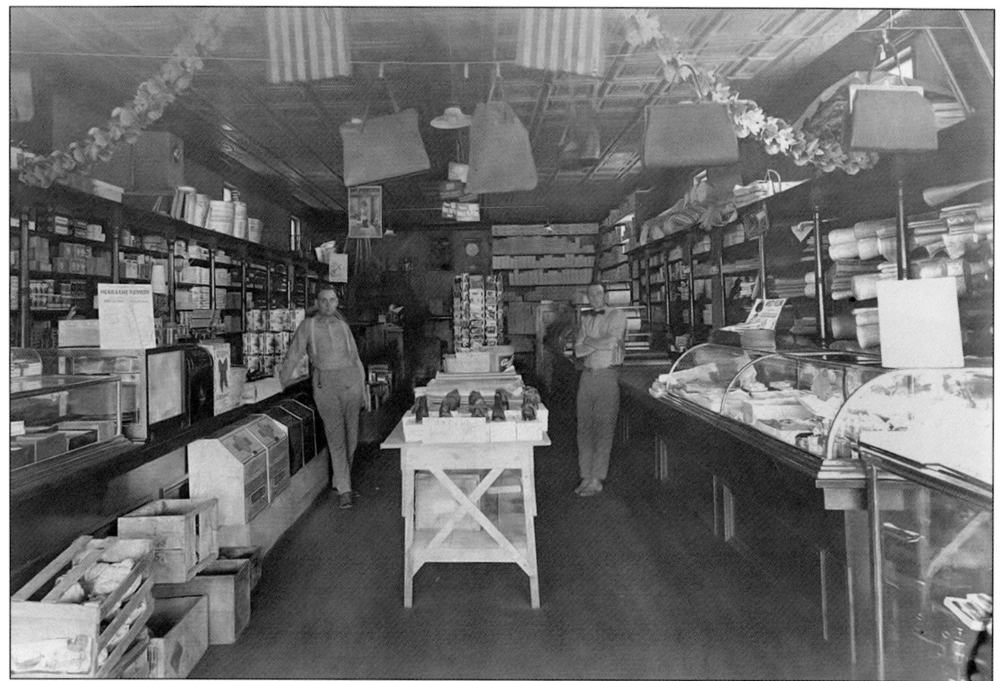

INTERIOR, HUMESTON'S CASH STORE, C. 1911. Pictured here are Del Humeston (left) and Leo Thomas. Thomas, of Humeston, Iowa, had taken a position at Humeston's store in 1911. The local newspaper also mentioned that he was coaching basketball in October 1911 and, in February 1912, was featured as leader of the choir in a production of *The New Minister*, a musical comedy. He returned to Iowa in April 1912. (Museum of Western Colorado, Lloyd Files Research Library.)

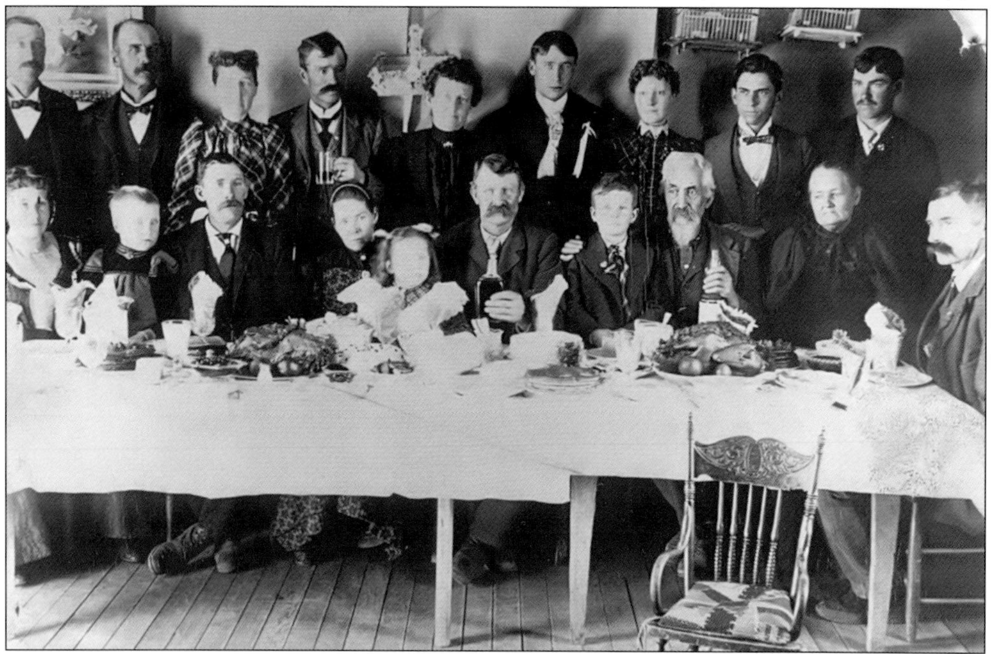

FIRST HOTEL IN COLLBRAN. The first hotel opened in Collbran in 1898. It was operated by Mr. and Mrs. Frank Snyder. (Plateau Valley Historical Preservation Society.)

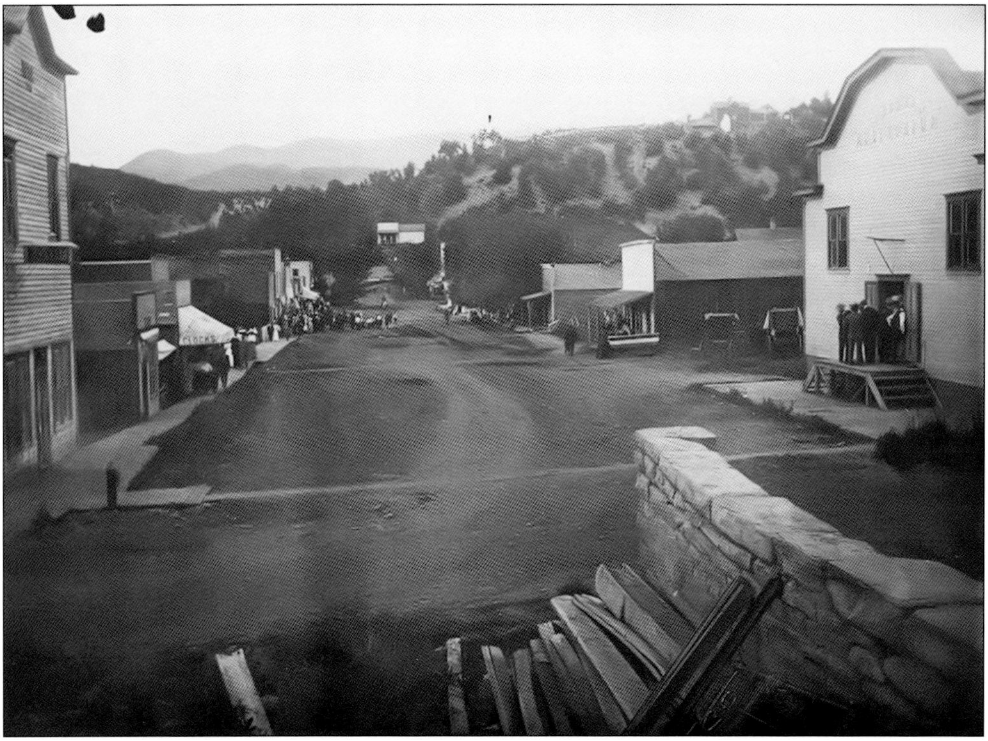

COLLBRAN'S MAIN STREET. John Alexander Fitzpatrick built the first house in Collbran. Some of the first businesses were the Big Store, built by W.M. Englehart and Parkison, the Blue Front Grocery, a barbershop, a livery barn, blacksmith shops, and a tin shop, among others. By 1903, over a hundred houses were built in addition to a church, the International Order of Odd Fellows (IOOF) hall, and other buildings. (Rudy and Arita Charlesworth.)

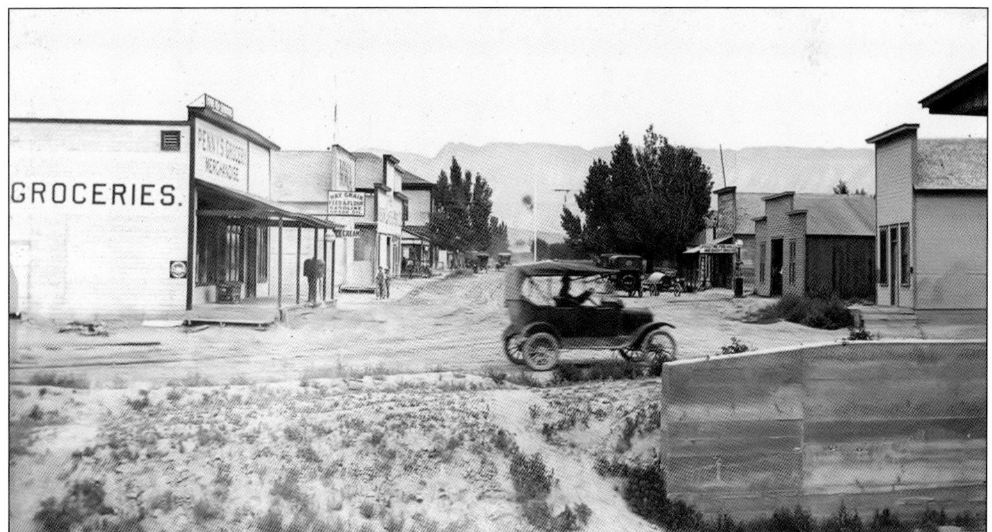

"SPEND YOUR IDLE TIME AT THE COLLBRAN PASTIME." The third building on the right is the Pastime Pool Hall and Short Orders. Advertising in the *Plateau Voice* from 1921 indicates that the store specialized in tobacco, cigars, candies, ice cream, and soda fountain drinks. W.L. Teem was the proprietor. (Rudy and Arita Charlesworth.)

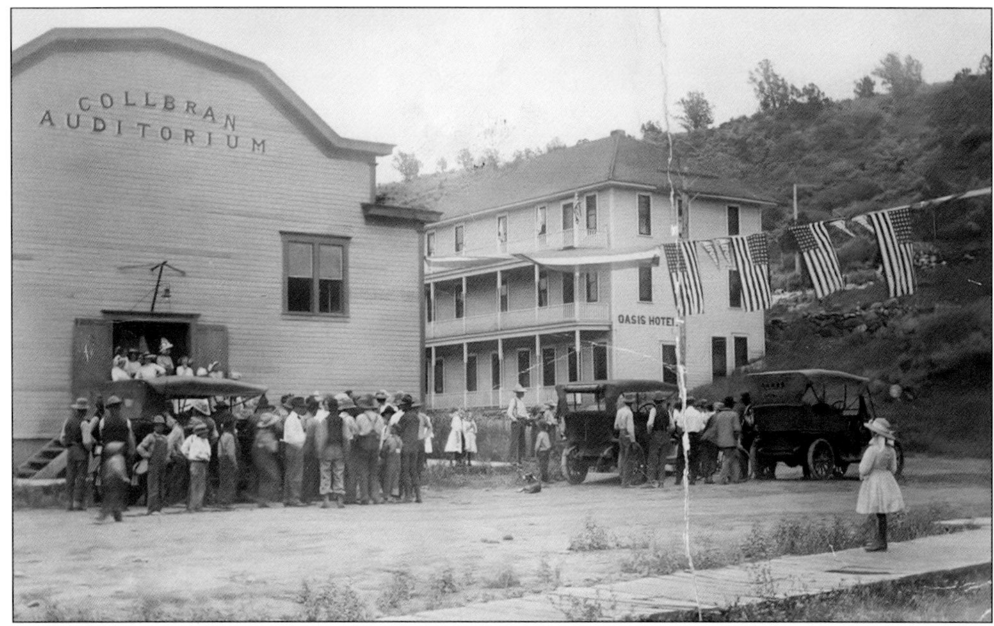

Oasis Hotel and Collbran Auditorium. The Oasis Hotel was dedicated on July 9, 1911. E.R. Jones built the hotel, which was three stories and had 20 rooms. It was fitted with gas lights, steam heat, baths, and other modern conveniences. The *Plateau Voice* reported that fire destroyed the hotel and all of its contents on July 26, 1916. (Rudy and Arita Charlesworth.)

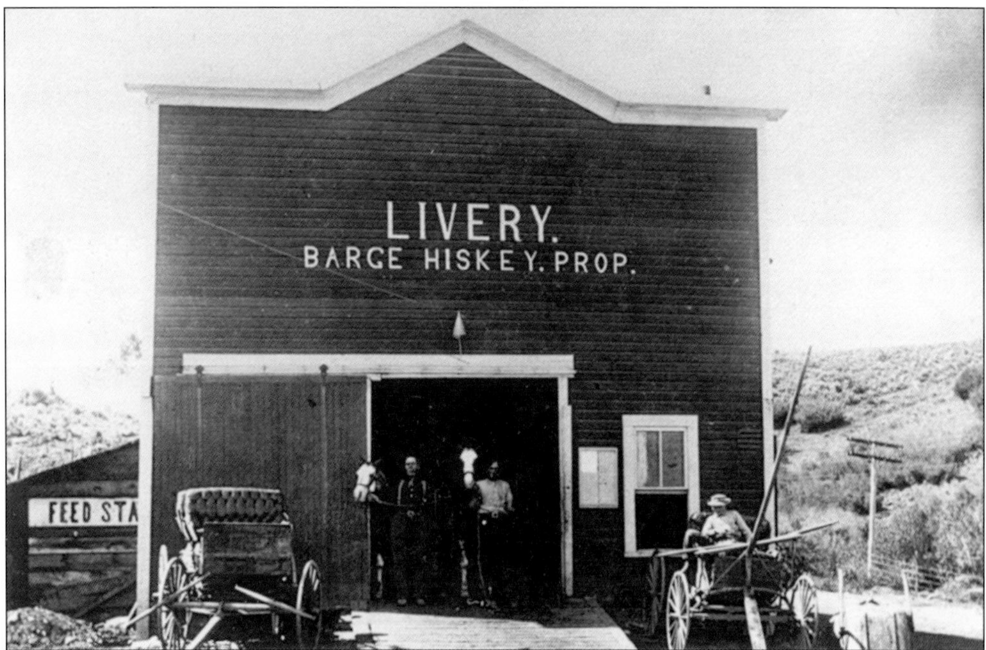

Barge Hiskey's Livery. Livery barns operated in a manner similar to automobile rental agents today. Those who came into town on a stagecoach would need to rent a horse to conduct their business while in town. Hiskey operated the livery stable until the advent of automobiles, after which he purchased the stage line operating between Collbran and DeBeque, using a modified Model T. (Plateau Valley Historical Preservation Society.)

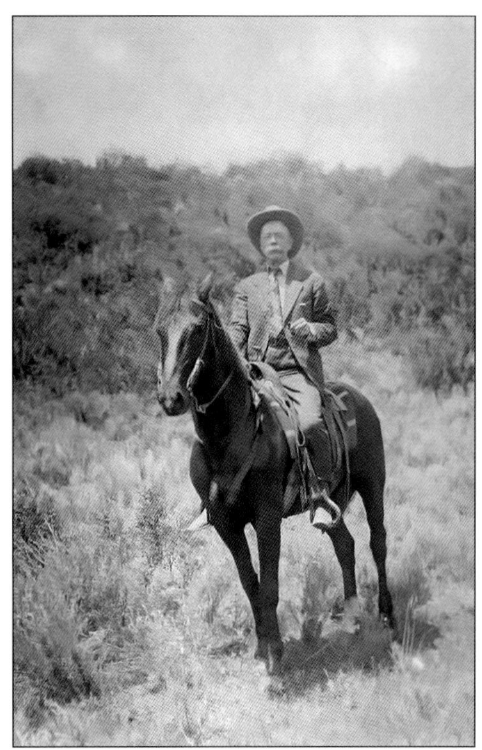

FRED TANNER, 1915. Frank and Fred Tanner ran the Miner's and Merchant's Bank in Ouray, Colorado, before coming to Collbran. *From Banknotes to Books: A History of the Stockman's Bank, Collbran, Colorado* states that Frank Tanner joined with Sam McMullin in Collbran to form the Plateau Valley Bank. When the proponents of the Stockmen's Bank filed their charter, Tanner and McMullin filed a series of lawsuits. The Stockmen's Bank prevailed and, according to the *Plateau Voice*, bought out the Plateau Valley Bank in 1916. (Courtesy Rudy and Arita Charlesworth.)

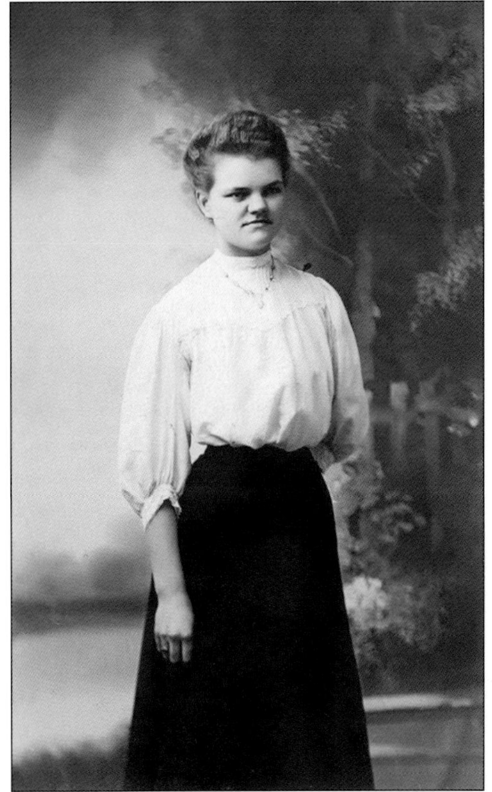

ELSIE WEBBER. Ernest H. and Eliza B. Erickson and three small girls (Elsie, Myra, and Edna) moved from Cripple Creek, Colorado, to Kansas Mesa in 1900. In the summer of 1910, Elsie was married to Hugh Webber. They moved to Ellensburg, Washington, and in 1917, widowed, Elsie returned to Collbran with her small son. After graduating from Ross Business College, she went to work at the Stockmen's Bank as a teller and bought a house in Collbran. (Rudy and Arita Charlesworth.)

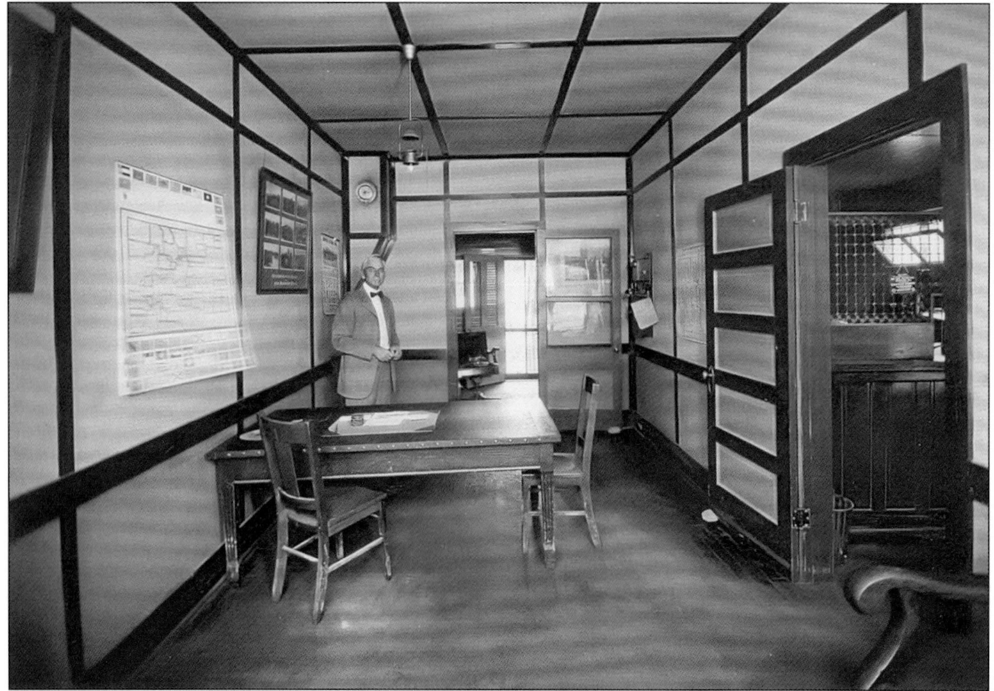

Stockmen's Bank. In 1915, D.A. Randall and John Milne, both from Grand Junction, Colorado, organized the Stockmen's Bank. They opened for business in 1916 with W.M. Porter as the cashier and J.J. Long as president. According to *From Banknotes to Books: A History of the Stockmen's Bank Building Collbran, Colorado*, the new bank prospered beyond its expectations. In 1929, plans for a new Stockmen's Bank building were drawn up. The new building was located at the same site as the old building. The old frame building, constructed in 1908, was purchased by C.C. McDaniel. The original safe from 1908 remained on site, as it was impossible to move. The new bank and vault were constructed around the safe. (Both, Rudy and Arita Charlesworth.)

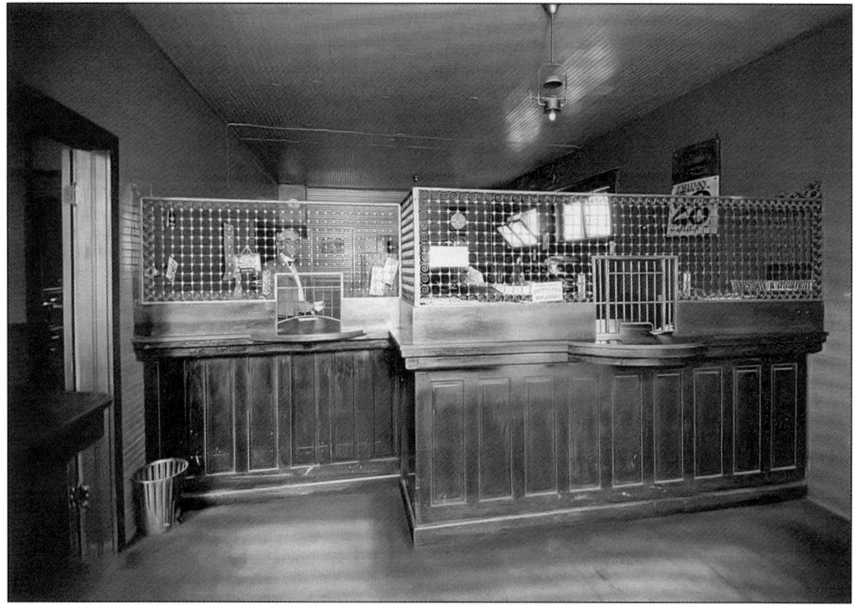

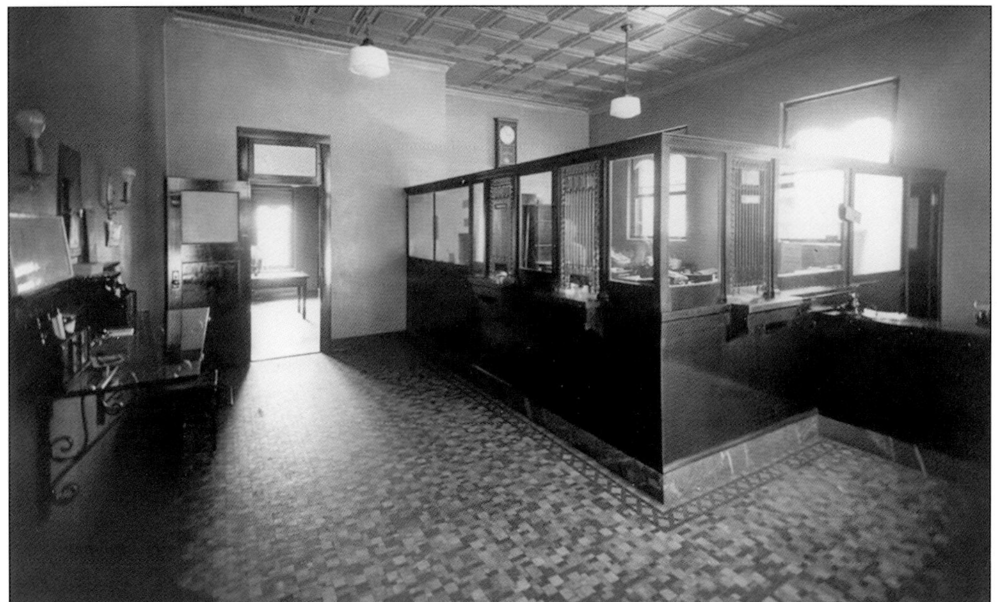

Stockmen's Bank. This is the infamous c. 1929 interior photograph of the new bank in which three ghostly figures appear. (Plateau Valley Historical Preservation Society.)

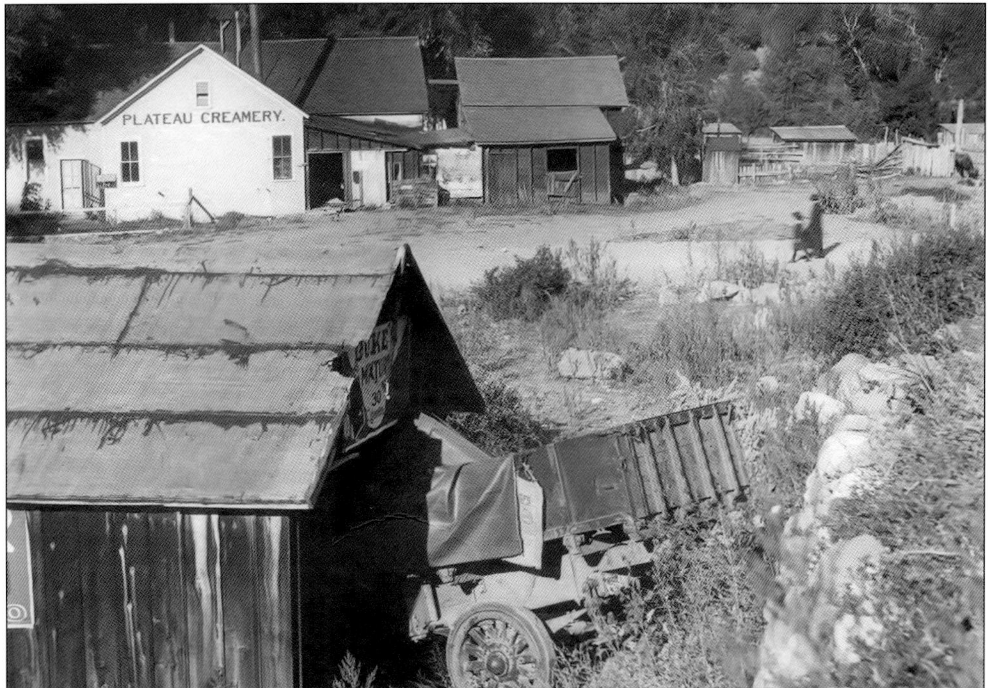

Plateau Creamery. When the first creamery building burned, it was a serious loss to Plateau Valley. The old creamery company was later dissolved and a new cooperative creamery association of about 130 producing members was formed. A new brick building was constructed. Plateau Valley was said to have been recognized as one of the best dairy sections in the state due to the even climate, cool water, high-quality alfalfa hay, bluegrass pastures, and locally raised grains. (Plateau Valley Historical Preservation Society.)

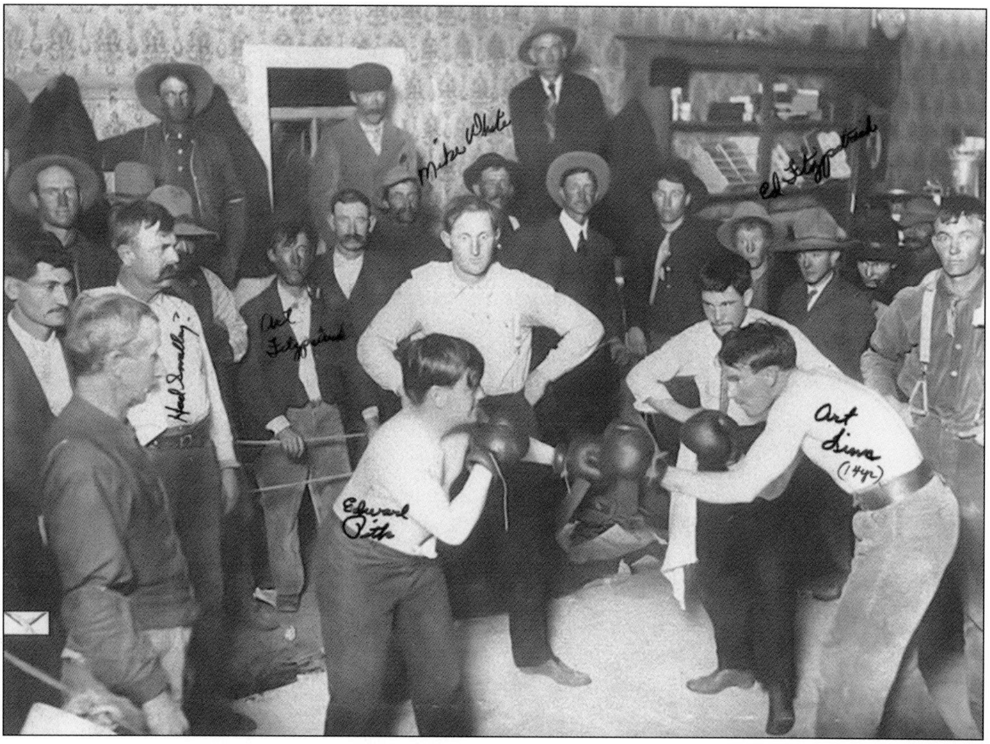

TANNER BUILDING. Local youth are seen here in a boxing match in the Tanner Building. This structure was also known as the Ziegel Building, erected in 1892 by Parkinson and Englehart. It was originally known as the Big Store and, in the 1920s, as the Tanner Building. Parkinson and Englehart sold it to T.G. Underhill, with Frank Tanner as a silent partner. The Ziegels owned it. (Plateau Valley Historical Preservation Society.)

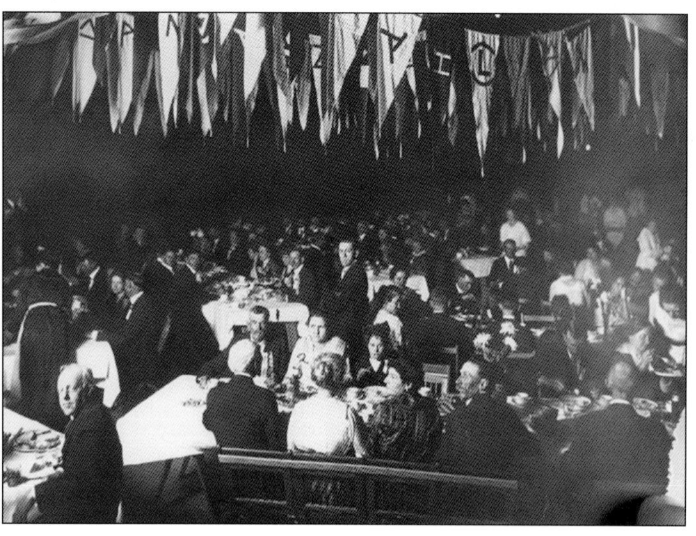

STOCKMAN'S BALL, 1912. Among those in this photograph are Joel Jackson Long, Hattie Shattuck Long, Dorothy Harnet, Mary Kenney, Dan Kenney, and Ben Pitts. It was reported that several dances, including the YT waltz and Buckhorn two-step, were named after prominent places in the area. (Plateau Valley Historical Preservation Society.)

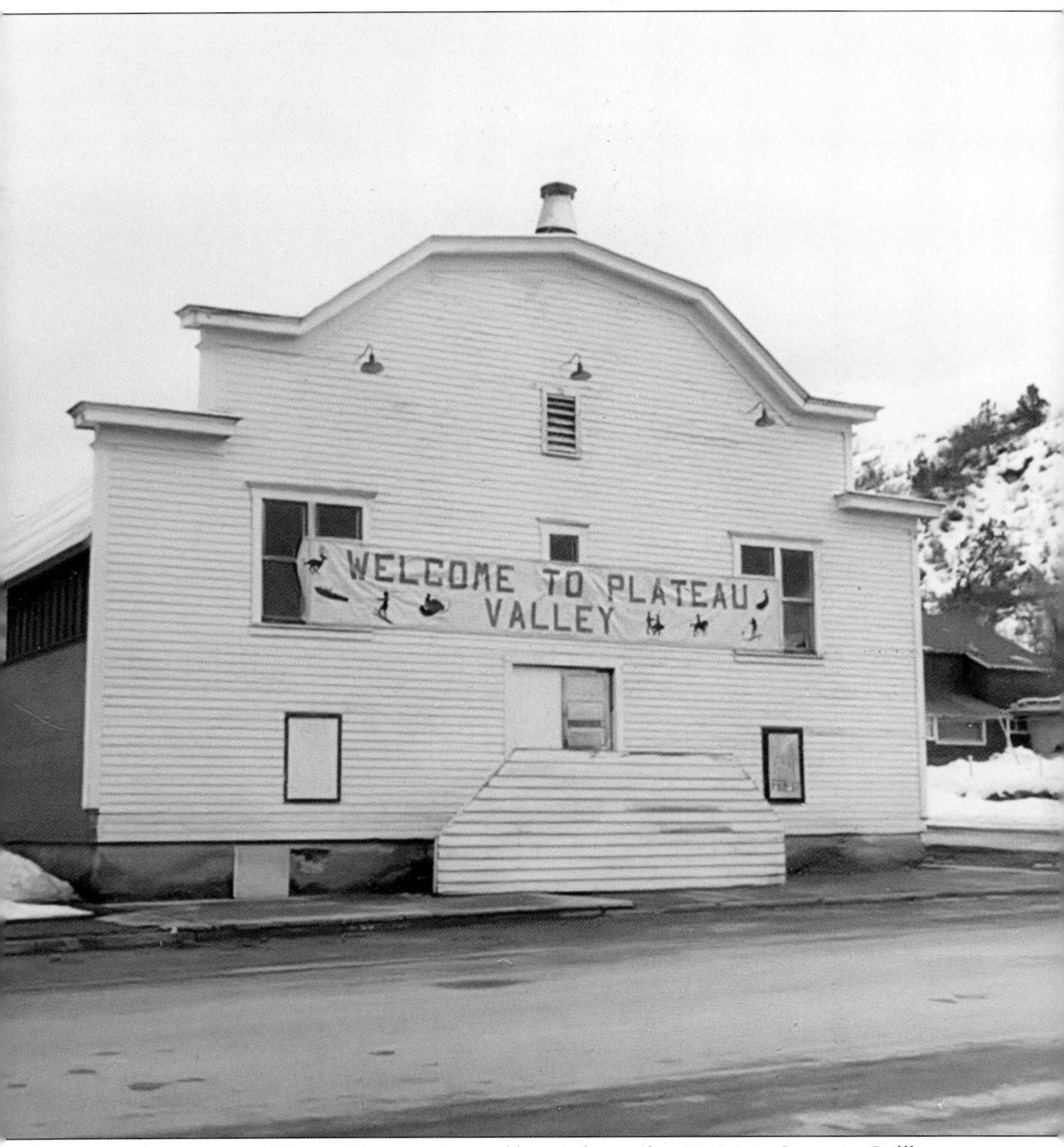

Collbran Auditorium. The auditorium pictured here is located at 102 Main Street in Collbran. Construction on the auditorium was begun for Dr. William Zinke in 1909 by E.S. Coakley, Steve John "S.A." Harris, Ernie Winston, and John Kendall. The round roof rafters were built on the ground and hoisted into place with two big hay derricks. It was one of the biggest auditoriums in any small town in the West. Before it was built, the location was the site of John Art Fitzpatrick's livery stable. (Rudy and Arita Charlesworth.)

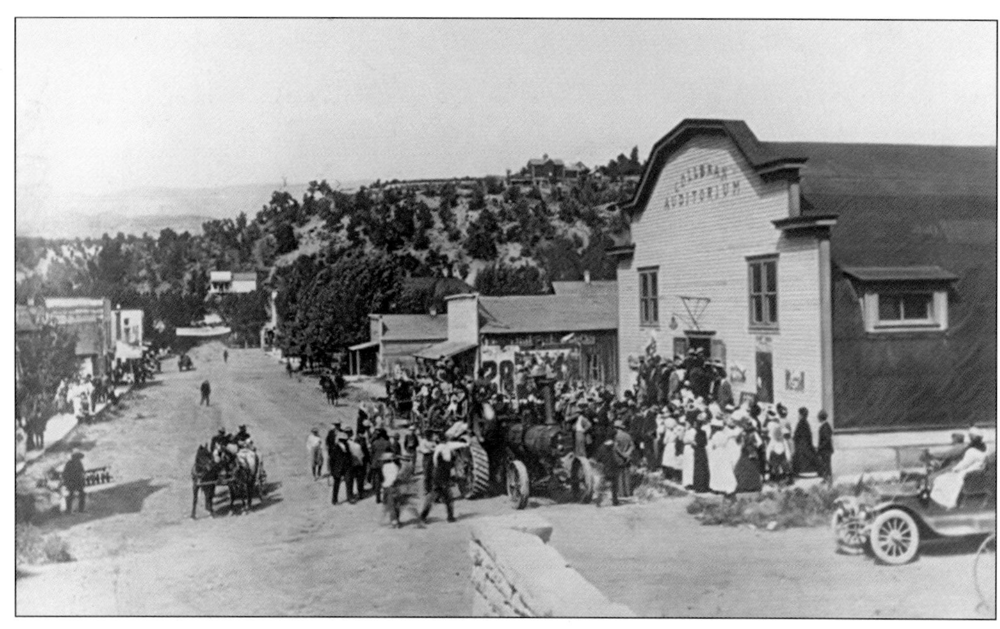

Collbran Auditorium, c. 1911. Residents are crowded around a steam engine outside the auditorium. The stage curtains were installed in 1905, and the first movies were shown in 1914. The auditorium hosted lectures, banquets, movies, product demonstrations, concerts, dances, masquerade balls, skating, plays, basketball games, Chautauquas, graduations, minstrel shows, and club meetings. (Both, author's collection.)

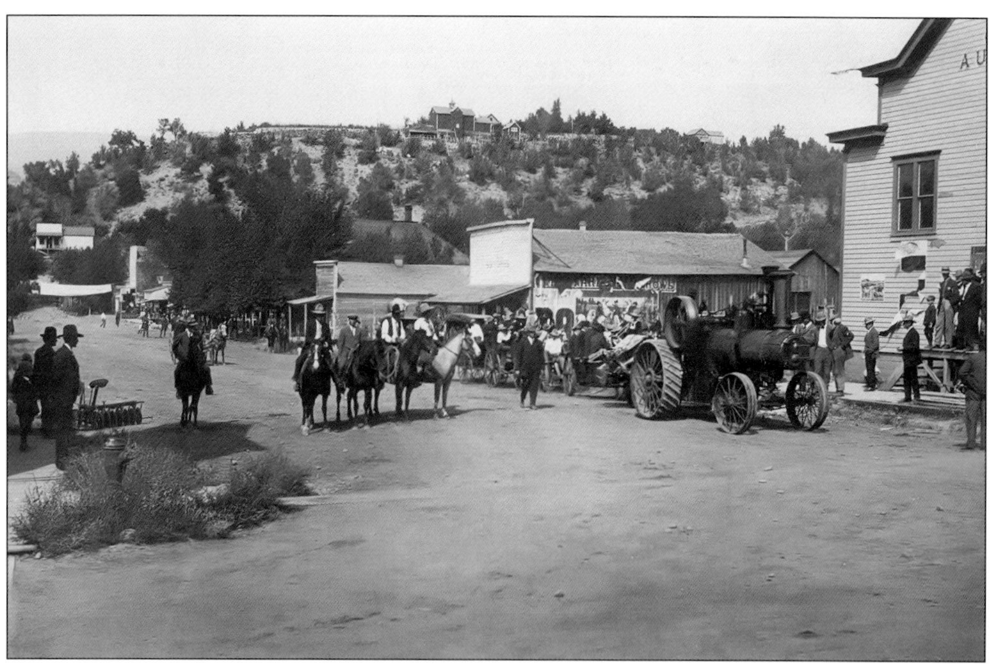

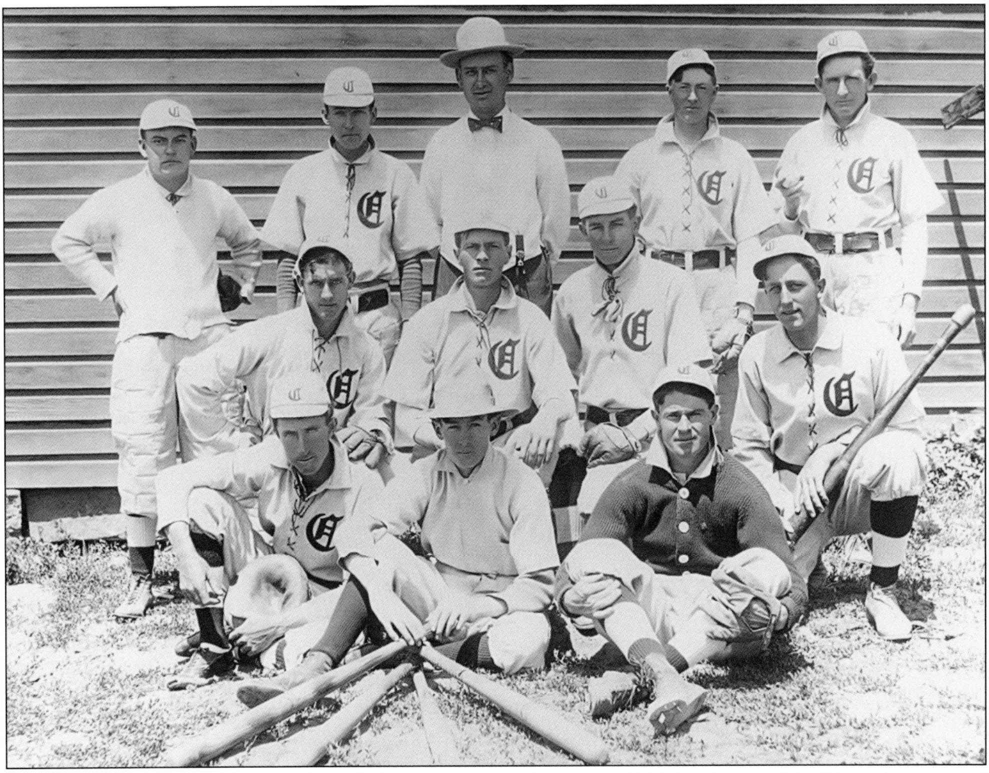

COLLBRAN BASEBALL TEAM. From left to right are (first row) Ed Henderson, Fay Tomlinson, and Tom May; (second row) Floyd "Buck" Smalley, Claude Roach, Ross Tomlinson, and Earl Dingman; (third row) Joe McGrade, Ernie Winston, Del Humeston, Fred Wilson, and Al VanCleve. (Museum of Western Colorado, Lloyd Files Research Library.)

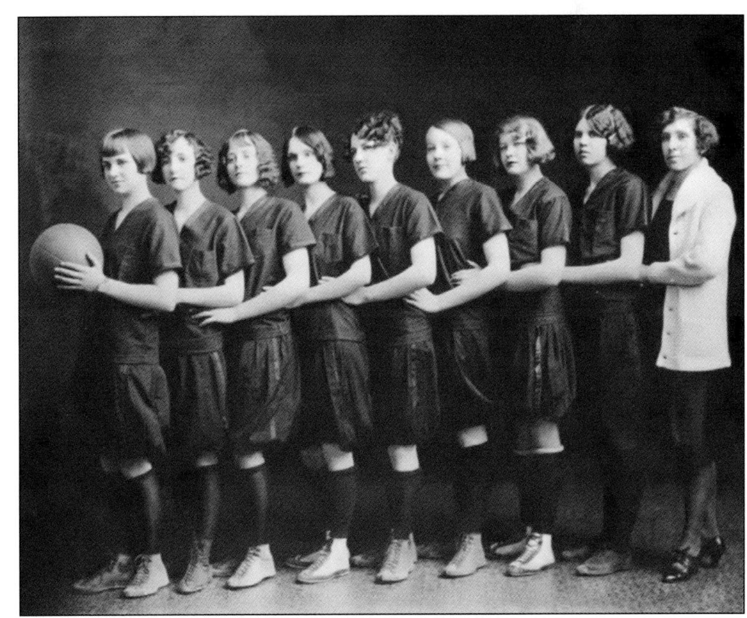

COLLBRAN UNION HIGH SCHOOL BASKETBALL, 1929. These girls are, from left to right, captain Vivian Deweese, Velma Webb, Mildred Young, Leona Maigatter, Jessy Kenny, Hazel Wulf, Bula Carson, Roberta Armour, and coach Muriel Hanks. (Plateau Valley Historical Preservation Society.)

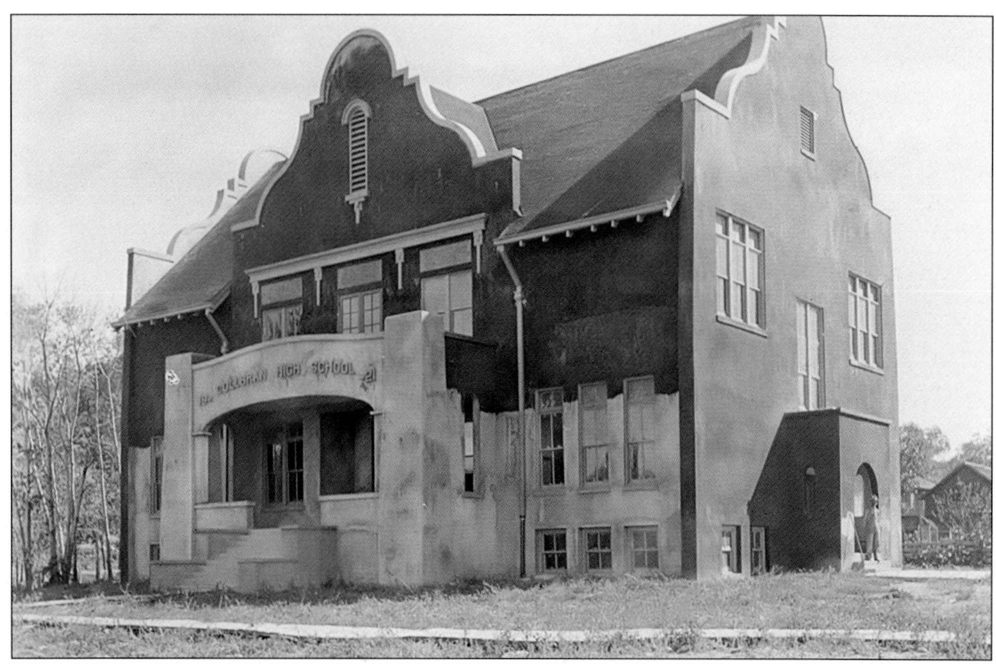

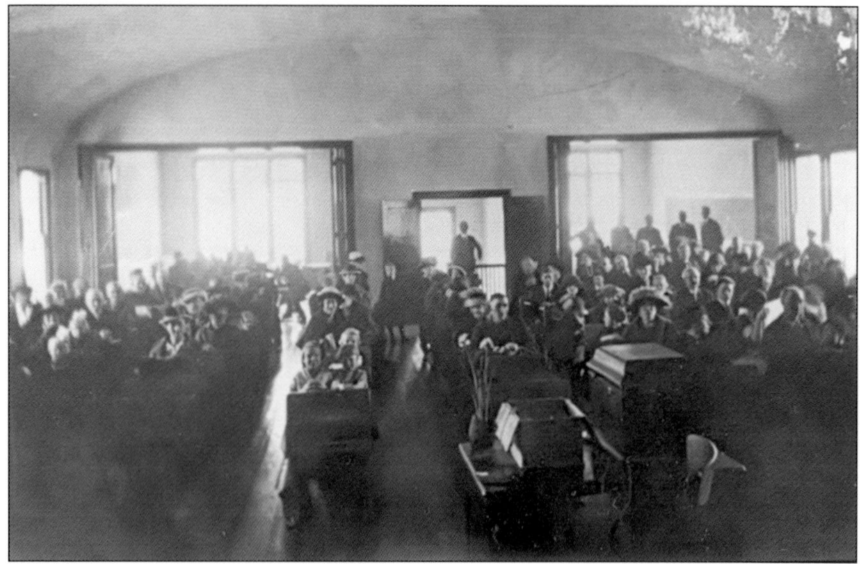

Collbran Union High School. The high school was organized in 1908. In 1917, a bond issue was put to vote for the construction of a new high school in Collbran. The proposition was put forth to issue bonds in the sum of $11,500 to secure a suitable location and erect a modern school building "of sufficient size to accommodate the union high school with a reasonable growth," according to the *Plateau Voice* of Mary 4, 1917. The dedicatory program after its construction was held on December 31, 1922. The program included music by the Collbran Orchestra and high school chorus, an invocation by Rev. W.D. Barnes, and short talks by the chairwoman, Mrs. B.F. Pitts; the secretary of the school board, Z.B. McClure; P.A. Johnson; Dr. William Zinke; and Dr. W.V. Watson. Presentation of the building to the district was made by H.P. Christensen, builder, and acceptance of the building was made by C.E. Hurd, president of the school board. (Both, Plateau Valley Historical Preservation Society.)

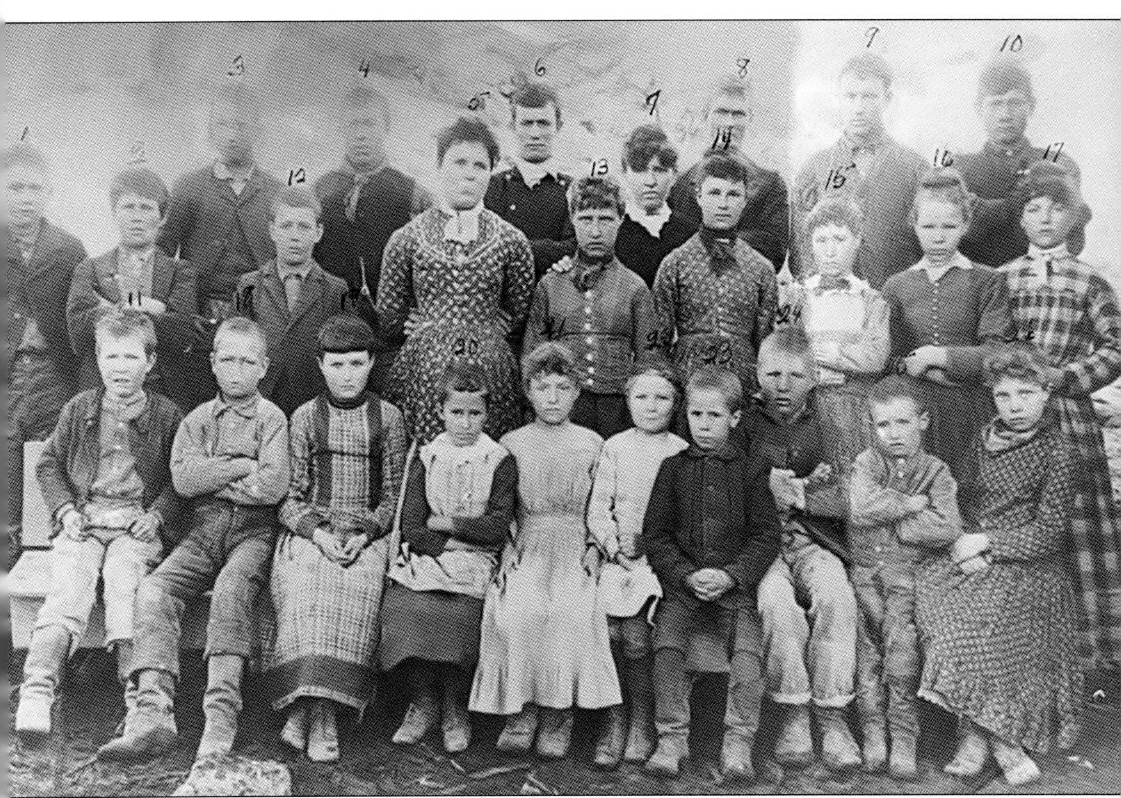

COLLBRAN SCHOOL, 1888. Hattie Long Shattuck taught at Collbran School in 1888. Pictured in numeric order are 1. George Williams, 2. Jim Kiggins, 3. Park Parkison, 4. Jack (or Zack) Kiggins, 5. Rose Kiggins, 6. Cad Carmichael, 7. teacher Hattie Shattuck, 8. Bill Mattingly, 9. Ollie Kiggins, 10. Bill Carmichael, 11. John Jones, 12. Glen Bertholf, 13. Elsie Bertholf, 14. Lilly Kiggins, 15. Gertie Fitzpatrick, 16. Melissa Snyder, 17. Arnie Mattingly, 18. Fred Bertholf, 19. Delia Kiggins, 20. Hattie Kiggins, 21. Dora Mattingly, 22. Lena Snyder, 23. Art Fitzpatrick, 24. Arthur Bertholf, 25. Barry Williams, and 26. Maud Williams. (Scott Walck collection.)

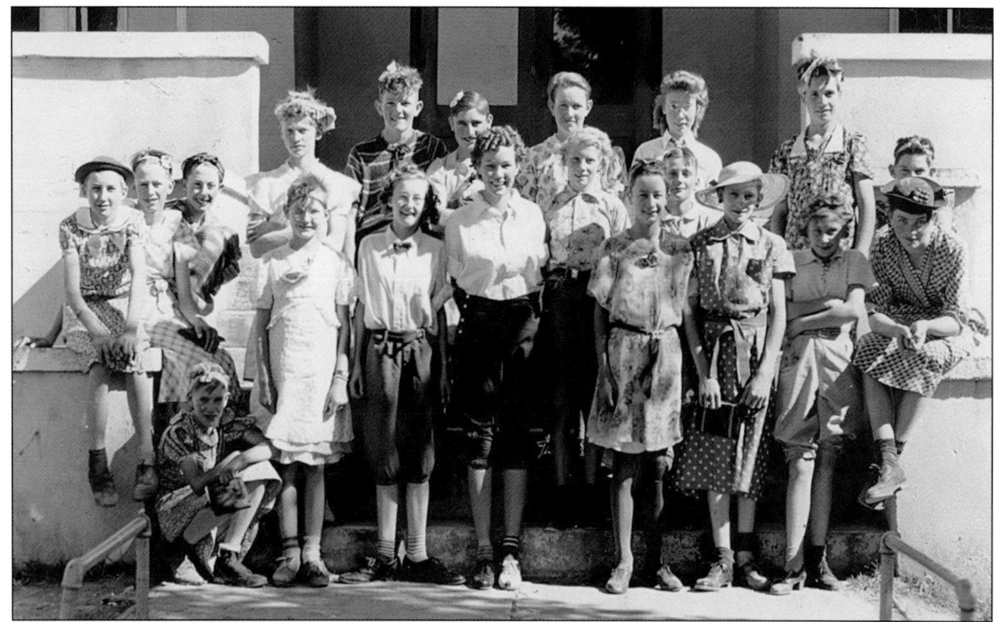

FRESHMAN INITIATION, 1939. Students of Collbran Union High School are dressed in opposite-gender clothing as a rite of initiation. Pictured are, from left to right, (first row) Calvin Fitzpatrick, Lloyd Potter, Betty Jane Strickland, Maggie ?, Jim Wilhort, Doris Smith, Clifford Hill, Parley Bloss, Pete McKee, Marjorie Stanton, and Kenneth DeWeese; (second row) Junior Brinkley, Clifford Stanton, Clifford Christensen, Roscoe Bloss, Dean Walck, Kenneth Wilson, Clifford Carnes, Ruth Segabart, Ray Brown, and Donald McKelvie. (Plateau Valley Historical Preservation Society.)

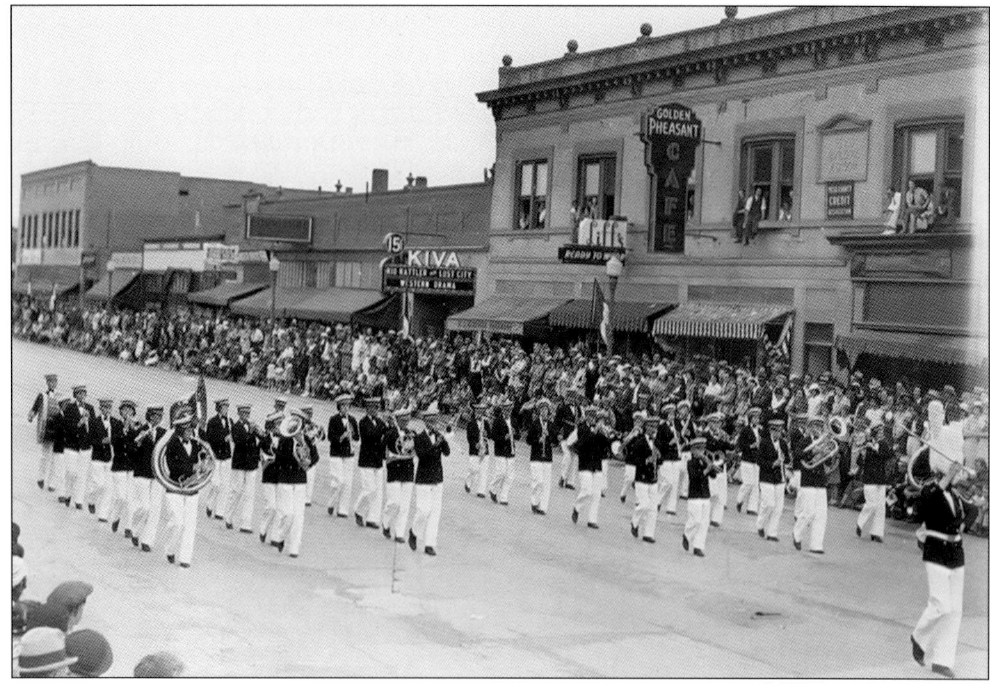

PARADE. The Collbran Union High School Marching Band took part in this April 1936 parade that traveled up Main Street in Grand Junction. (Plateau Valley Historical Preservation Society.)

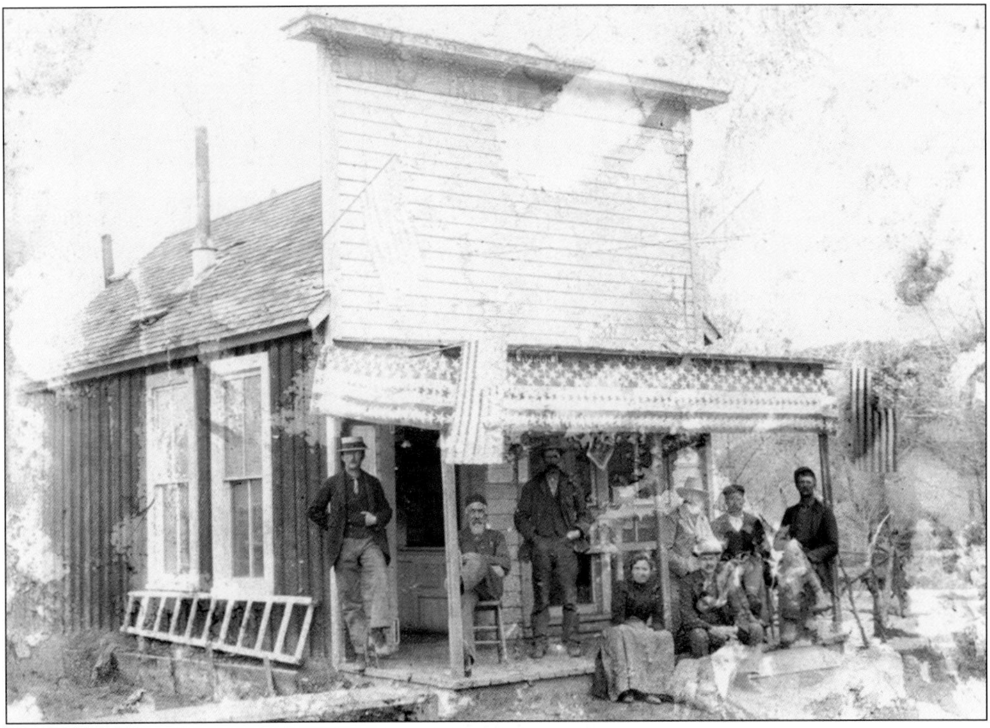

OLD COLLBRAN POST OFFICE. The old Collbran Post Office was originally known as Hawxhurst and was constructed in 1882. Postmasters included George Hawxhurst, Horace Dunlap, and George Hall. The name was changed to Collbran in 1892. Pictured here are, from left to right, Lloyd Gifford, Joe Putney, Maggie Hawxhurst, Mr. Hughes, Ned Rice, and Henry Johnson. (Henry Peck Collection, Museum of Western Colorado, Lloyd Files Research Library.)

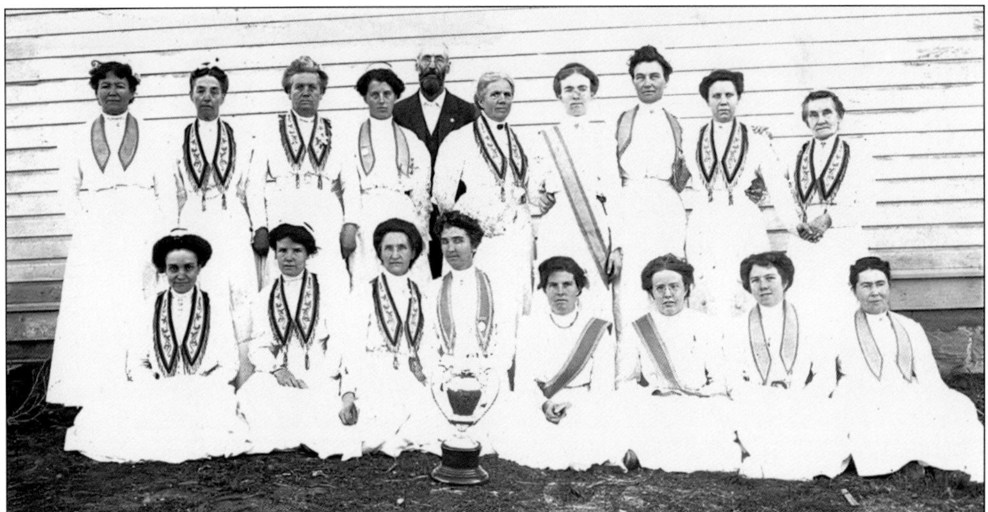

WOMAN'S SOCIETY CLUB. Pictured here from left to right are (first row) Bessie Williams Hodgson, Burley Anderson, Mrs. Sarah Phillips, Mollie (Mrs. Jim) Harris, Fran Long, Ivy Crane Rogers, Mabel Pitts Long, and Maude (Mrs. Homer) Buttrick; (second row) Mrs. Hank Tomlinson, Mrs. John Place, Mrs. Jenny Pitts, Tressa Kendall Palmer, Mr. Woods, Margaret Hawxhurst, Addie Crane Coakley, Mrs. Woods, May Labbe, and Mrs. Gregg. (Griffith family collection.)

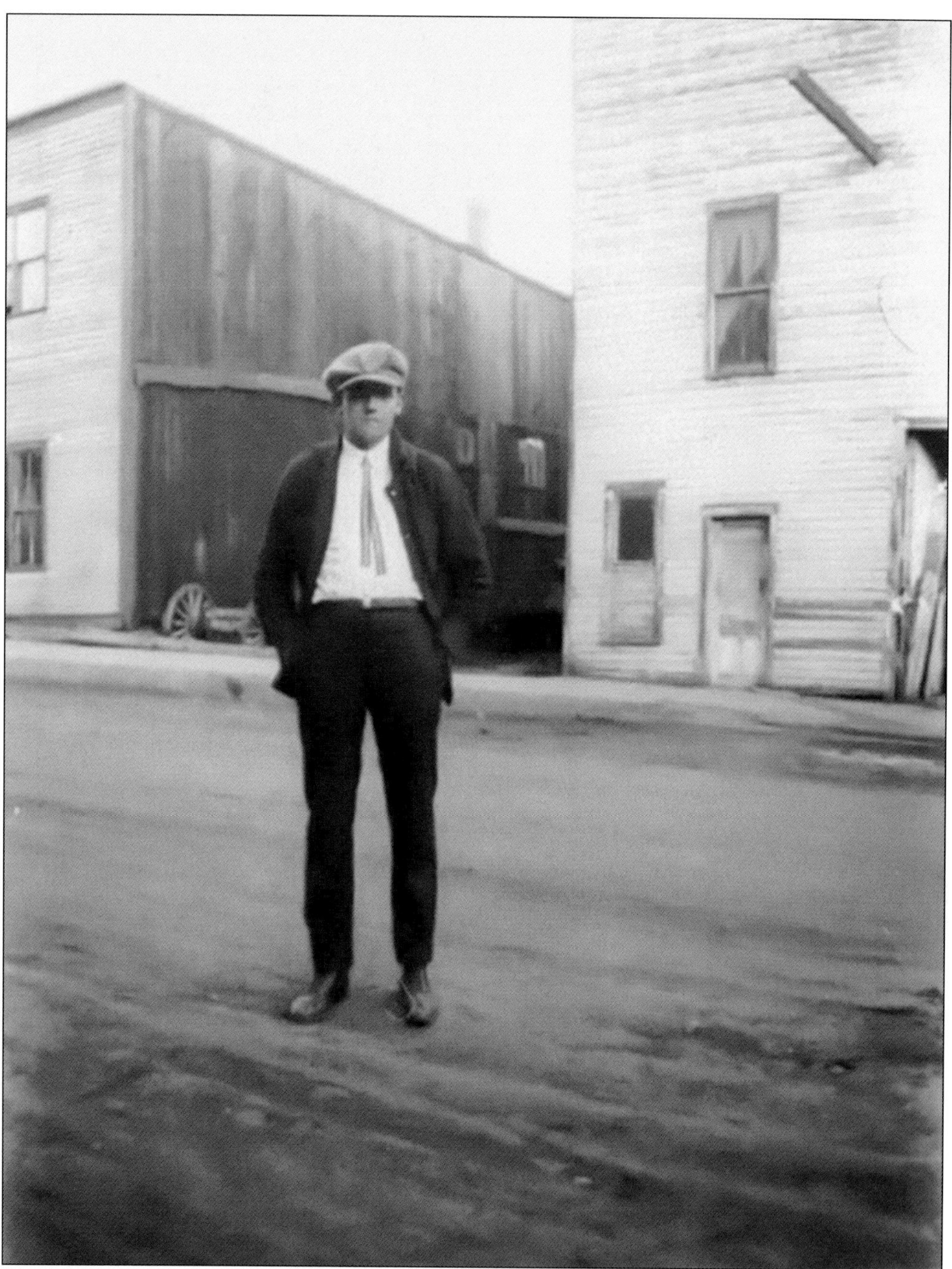

COLLBRAN, C. 1920S. Wilbur Raymond poses for a picture in Collbran. The *Plateau Valley Voice* reported in 1923: "Last Saturday Wilbur Raymond, of Kansas Mesa, was accidentally shot by his own 25-calibre rifle while it was slung to his saddle. The ball made a severe flesh wound. It appears, as *The Voice* understands, that young Raymond and a companion were up on Grand Mesa horseback. Passing under some brush the hammer of the gun caught and the rifle was discharged. The ball struck him in the fleshy portion of the thigh and penetrated downward and out at a point several inches from where it entered. It was a mighty close call for the young man, to say the least." (Author's collection.)

Dr. William Zinke. Dr. Zinke was the first doctor in Plateau Valley. He commissioned the construction of the Collbran Auditorium in 1909. (Plateau Valley Historical Preservation Society.)

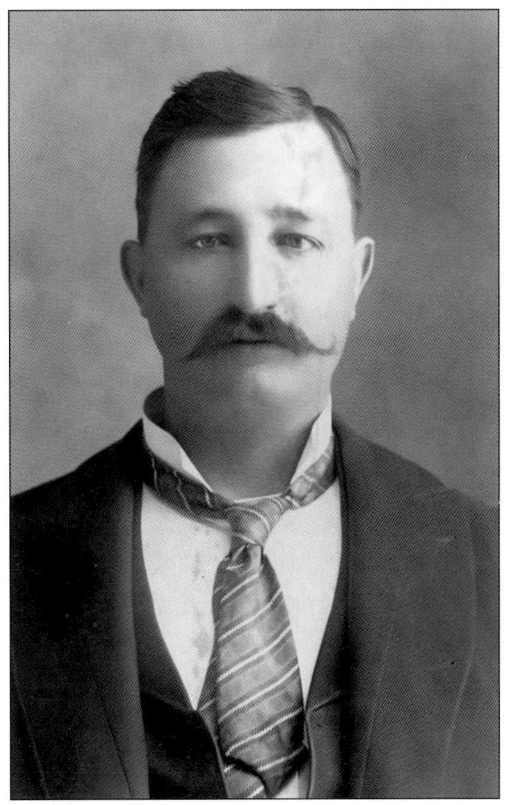

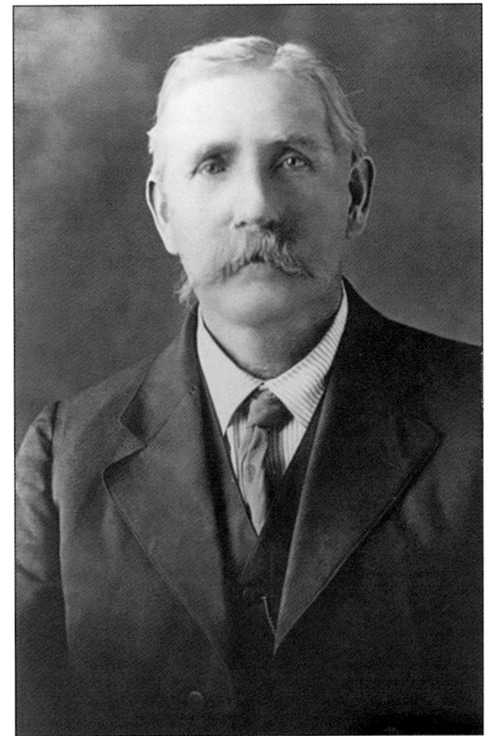

Dr. Benjamin R. Price, Dentist. The book *Skin and Bones* stated, "Dr. Price was a dearly loved dentist, kind and thoughtful to one and all. Anyone with any age is still carrying around some of his fillings." (Plateau Valley Historical Preservation Society.)

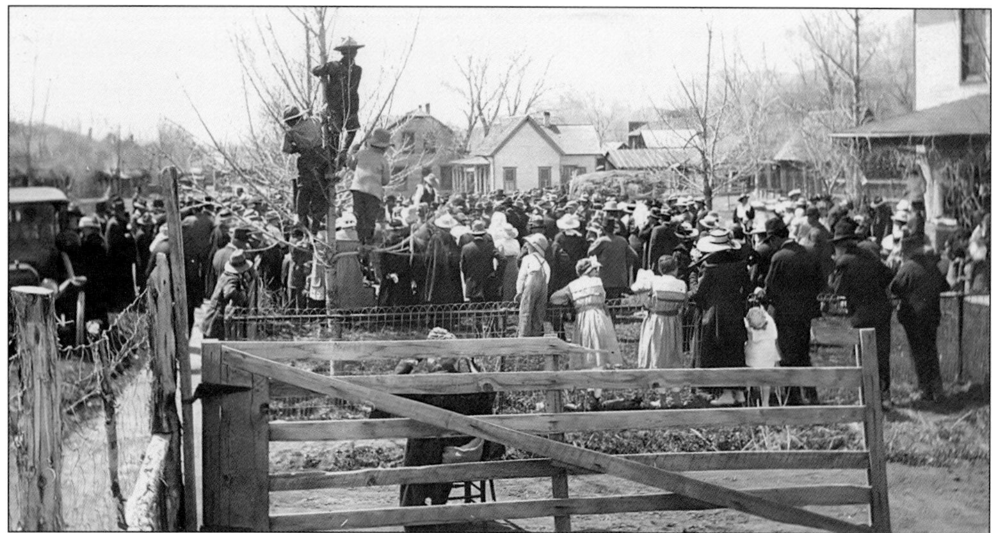

RED CROSS FAIR. The Red Cross Fair, held on April 26, 1918, netted over $1,500 according to the *Plateau Voice*. The sale included a dinner served by the Red Cross ladies. Rev. Edward B. Martin of Grand Junction delivered the opening address. Although the local residents did not know him, he made an impression upon those gathered. After a monologue by Colonel Shults, the Red Cross ladies led a parade to the lawn of the Hodgson cottage on Spring Street. (Helen Young Collection, Museum of Western Colorado, Lloyd Files Research Library.)

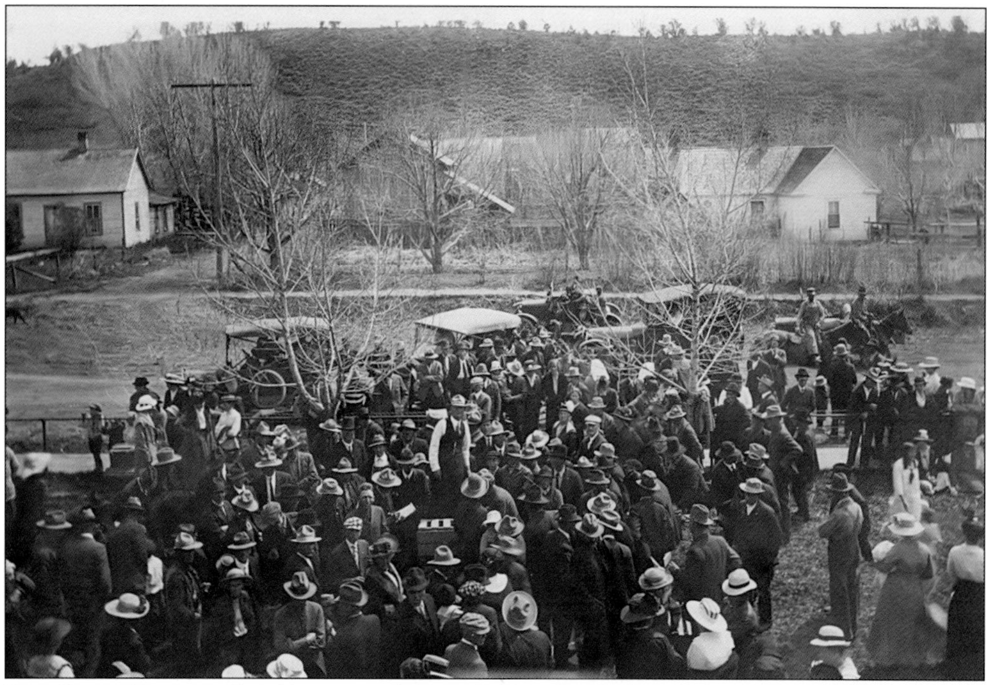

RED CROSS AUCTION. For the auction, livestock, fruits, grain, beans, potatoes, plants, ornamental shrubs, preserves, aprons, rugs, fancywork, and more were donated. One particular rooster was sold and resold a number of times, resulting in a "forty or fifty dollar increase in the Red Cross finances," according to the front-page *Plateau Voice* report of April 26, 1918. (Helen Young Collection, Museum of Western Colorado, Lloyd Files Research Library.)

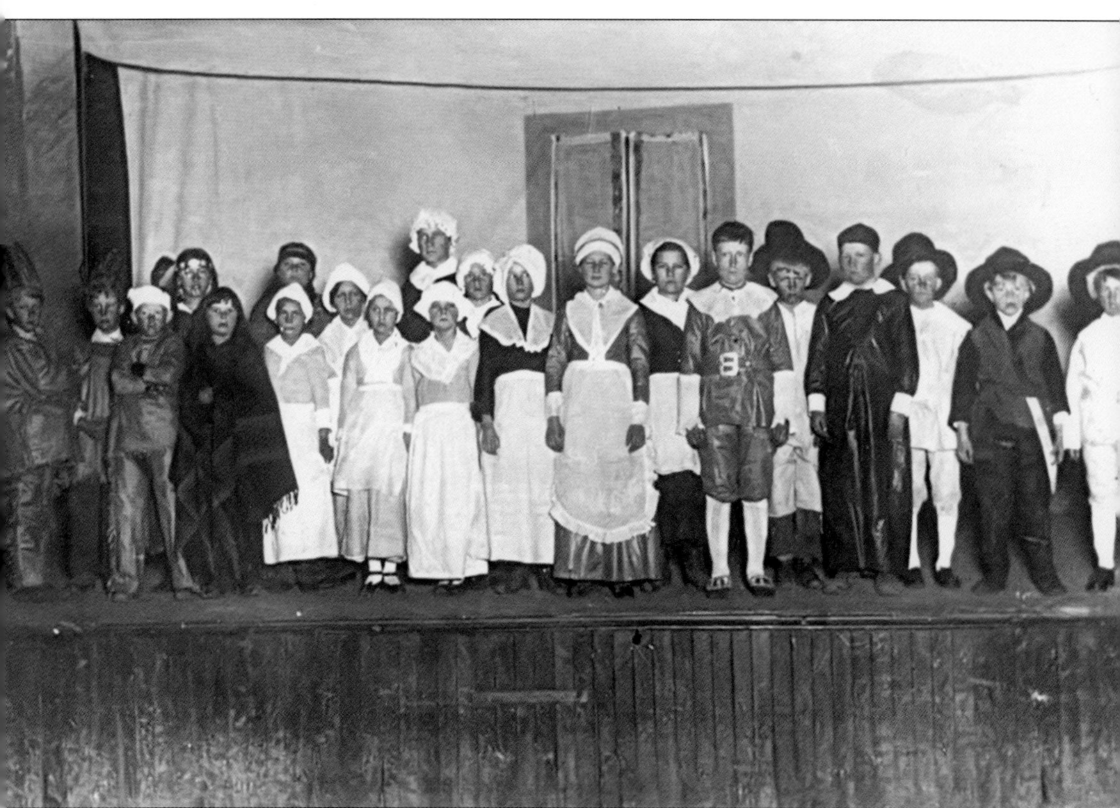

Thanksgiving Program at the Auditorium. Much fun was had at the auditorium on Thanksgiving. Festivities included basketball games, skating, and films. Following the day's activities was generally a big dance. The *Plateau Voice* reported in 1912, "The usual big Thanksgiving Dance will be given at Collbran Auditorium Thursday evening. Best music obtainable, arrangements made for supper, and all possible plans taken to have this a night of Unalloyed Enjoyment. . . . There will be skating at the Auditorium all afternoon Thanksgiving Day." The following year, the organizers requested some restraint in the dance selections: "no tango, turkey-trot, bunny-hug, or other dances of like character will be permitted, and those who do not wish to comply with the regulations of the Management are requested to stay away." (Plateau Valley Historical Preservation Society.)

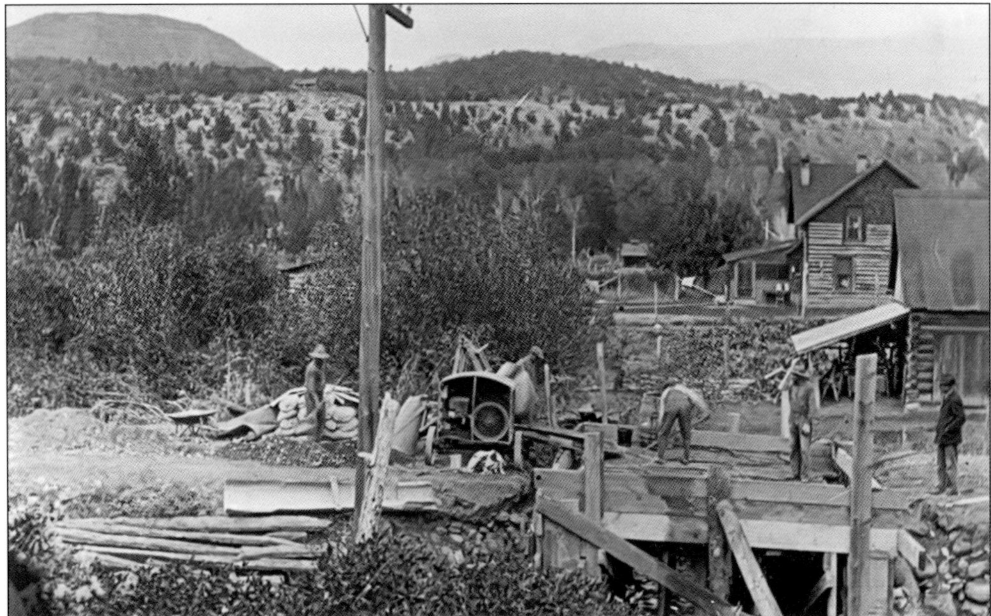

GROVE CREEK BRIDGE. The bridge was replaced in April 1914. The *Plateau Voice* reported: "It has come pretty straight from Grand Junction that if Plateau Valley wants much road work done this year our citizens will have to do it themselves. So the sooner Plateau Valley gets wise to this truth, and organizes local clubs to promote road work the better." (Rudy and Arita Charlesworth.)

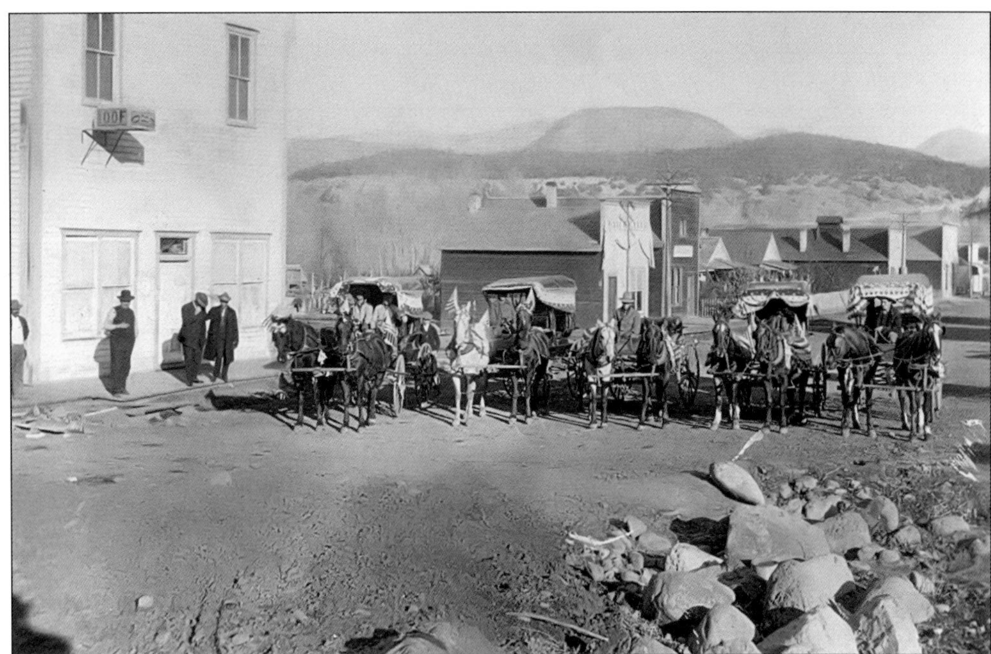

IOOF HALL. The IOOF hall on Main Street was originally a wooden structure, as seen here. The building was destroyed by fire and replaced by a brick building in 1954. (Plateau Valley Historical Preservation Society.)

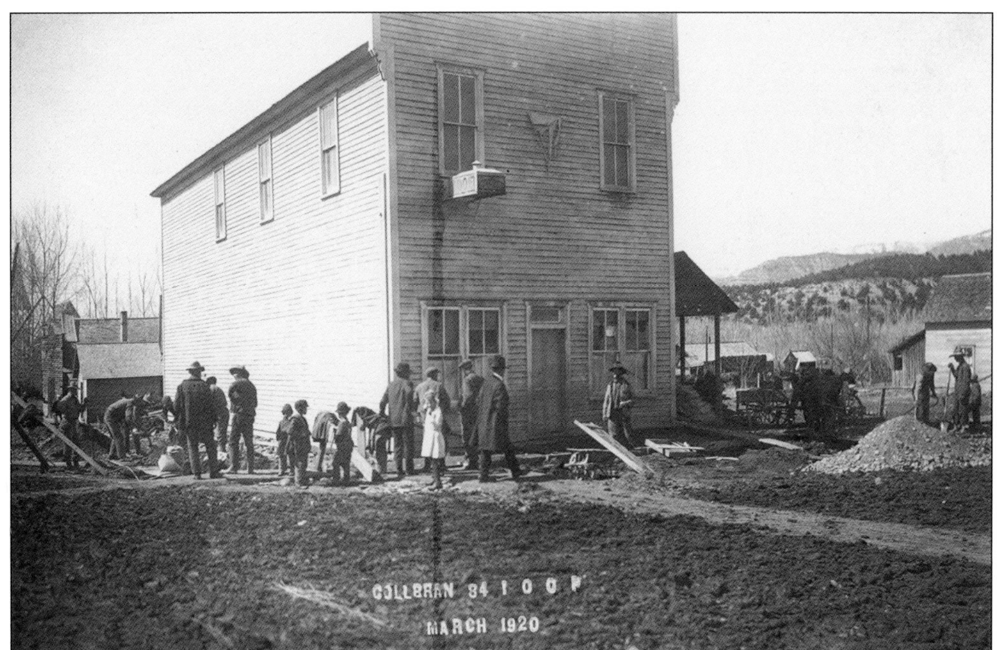

NEW SIDEWALK AT IOOF HALL, 1920. The IOOF hall was one of the first buildings to get a cement sidewalk. According to a March 26, 1920, report in the *Plateau Voice*, the push for sidewalk improvements was headed by William Wallace and others. Men of the lodge and their teams of horses supplied the sand, gravel, and labor. The walk was 50 feet long and seven feet wide along Main Street and 125 feet long and six feet wide on High Street. It required 100 loads of sand and gravel and 150 sacks of cement to complete. The ladies supplied a noonday meal of chicken, beef, pork, mutton, pickles, jellies, jams, pie, cake, and coffee. (Above, Plateau Valley Historical Preservation Society; below, Rudy and Arita Charlesworth.)

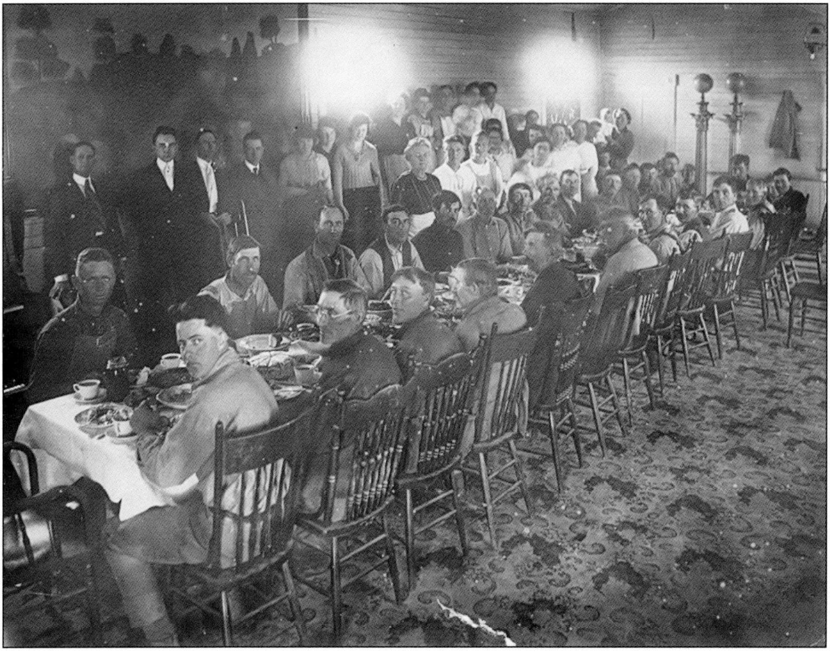

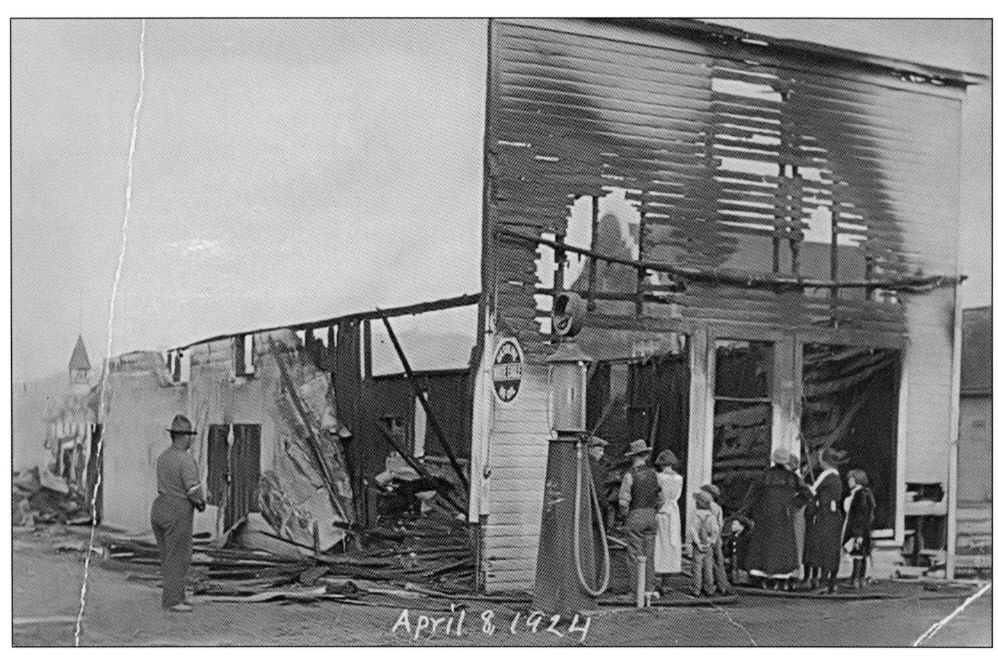

DISASTROUS FIRE AT E.F. COLLINS GENERAL STORE. The building and stock of E.F. Collins's store, the town hall, and the jail burned in a fire on April 8, 1924. Presumably, combustible oils in the warehouse were the cause; however, faulty wiring was also suspected. The Stockmen's Bank building across the alley to the south caught fire as well but was saved. The fire might have been much worse if not for little or no wind blowing at the time and the fact that tin covered the frame store building and wareroom. (Both, Rudy and Arita Charlesworth.)

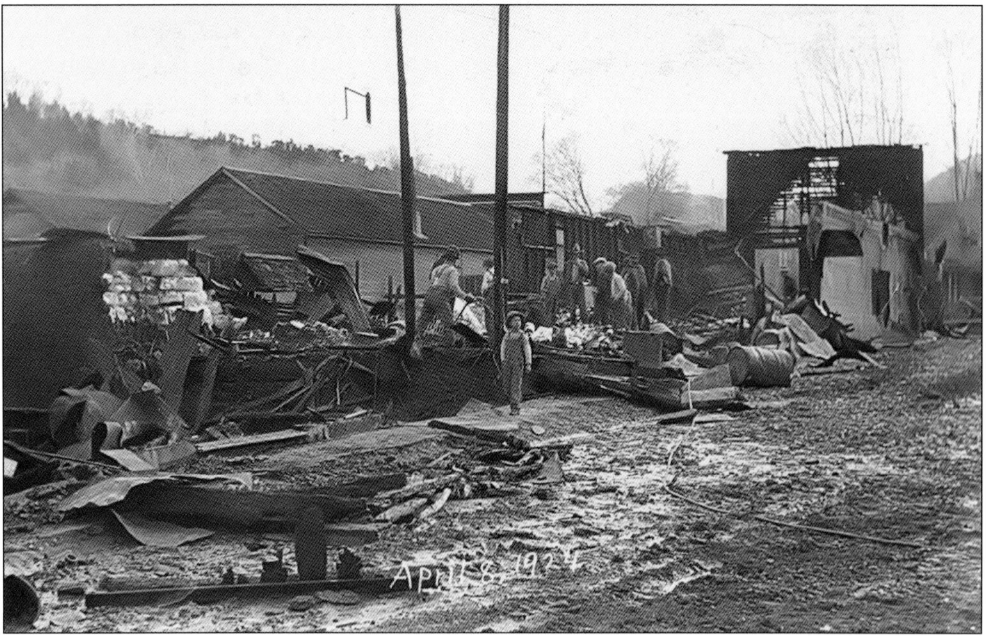

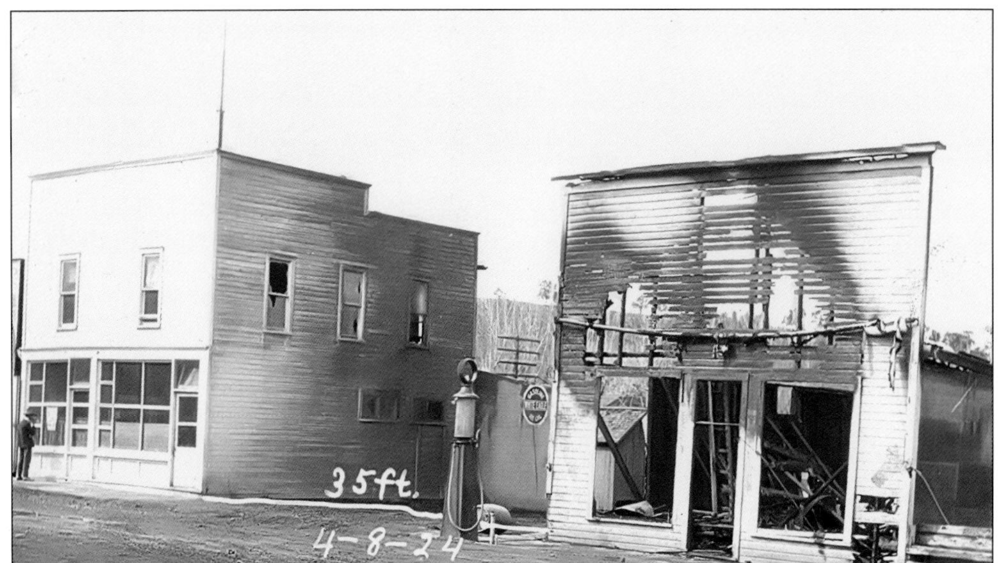

E.F. Collins General Store. This photograph shows the distance separating the E.F. Collins store from the Stockmen's Bank building. The bank building, as seen here, suffered damage to its windows from heat and water, as well as scorching to the sides of the building, but luckily, the fire was overcome by the quick action of the firemen on the scene. (Rudy and Arita Charlesworth.)

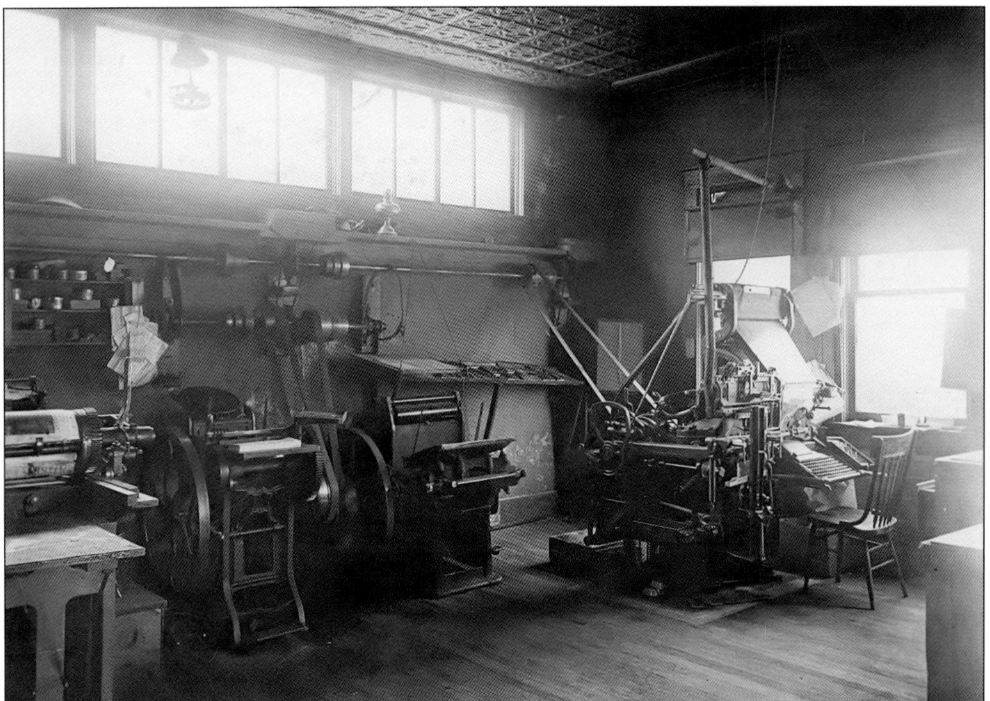

Printing Press. The first newspaper in Collbran was the *Plateau Valley Herald*. C.M. Danford was editor. The first issue was published on August 9, 1895. Other newspapers were the *Collbran Oracle* and the *Plateau Valley Voice*, which was also known as the *Plateau Valley Stockman*. The Old Star Printing Press was constructed shortly after the Civil War and spent its retirement years in Collbran, printing its last issue in 1926. (Rudy and Arita Charlesworth.)

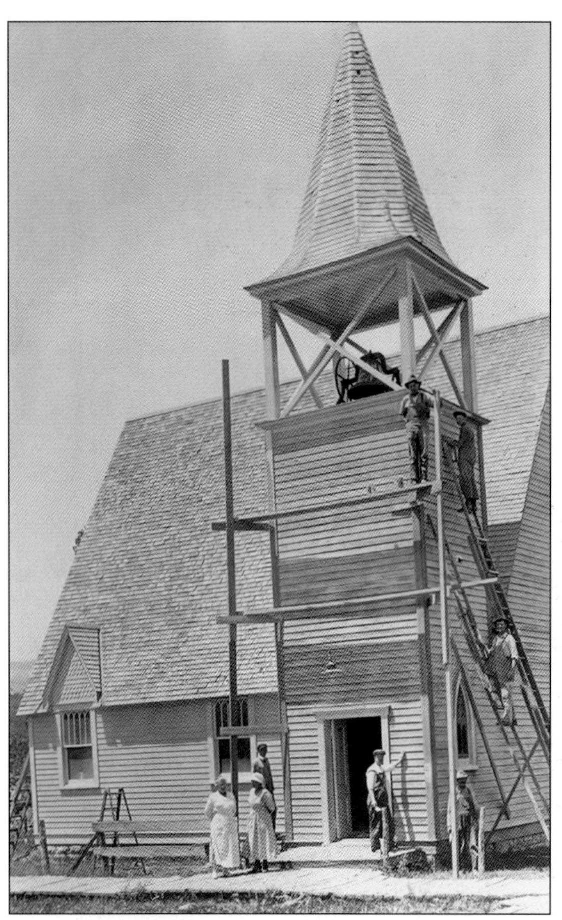

Congregational Church Construction, c. 1903. The first Congressional Church Board was organized for the purposes of building a church in 1901. George Noble, a Methodist circuit rider, donated the land for the church building. Reverend Brooks is credited with the church's construction. Early newspaper editorials indicate a certain amount of animosity surrounding the Gothic style of architecture, which at the time was considered a waste of lumber. (Plateau Valley Historical Preservation Society.)

Congregational Church Addition, c. 1921. According to an account written for the church's 100-year anniversary, this addition to the church was the last significant change in the outward appearance of the church building. The addition included classrooms and office space, a family room for privacy during memorial services and overflow on special occasions, and a gymnasium and dining hall for community dinners. (Plateau Valley Historical Preservation Society.)

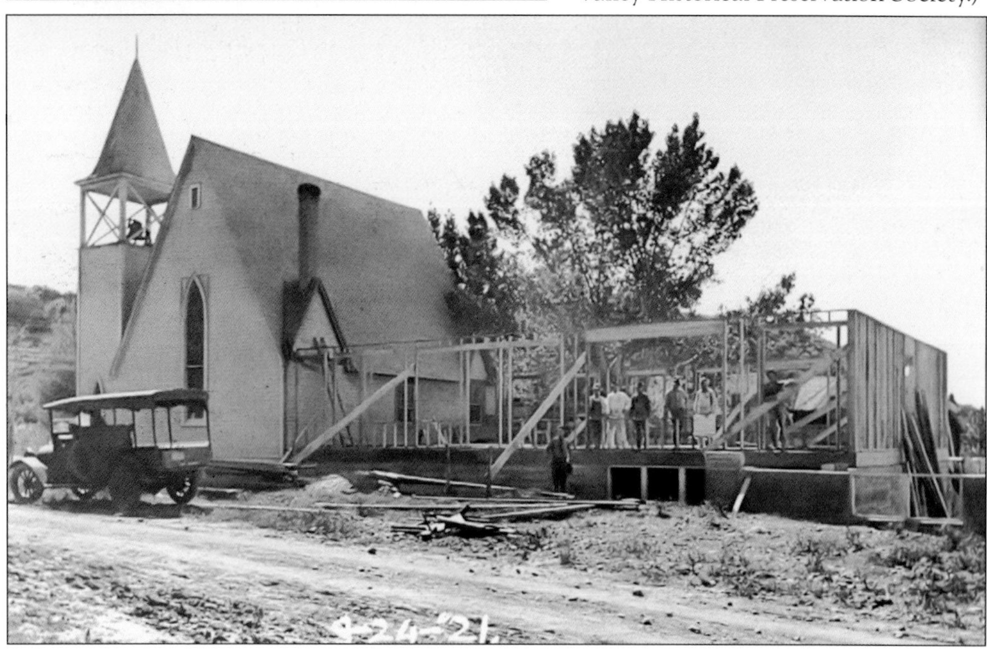

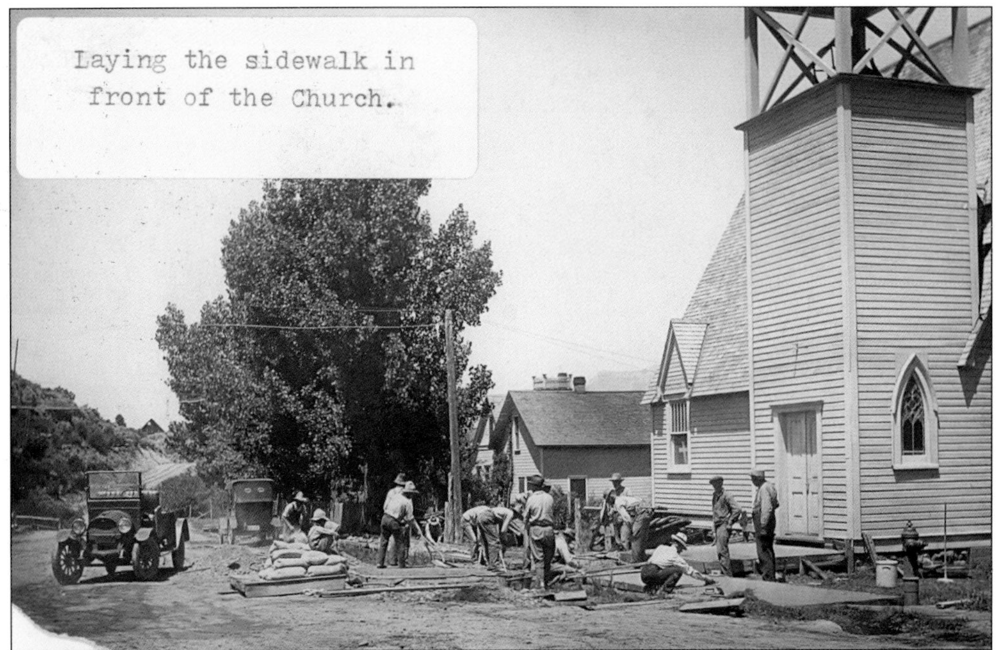

Congregational Church Sidewalk. In 1924, the *Plateau Voice* reported many improvements that had been made to the church. These included the new shell and heating system for the gymnasium, the installation of an electric generator, improvements to the auditorium, and a new sidewalk. (Rudy and Arita Charlesworth.)

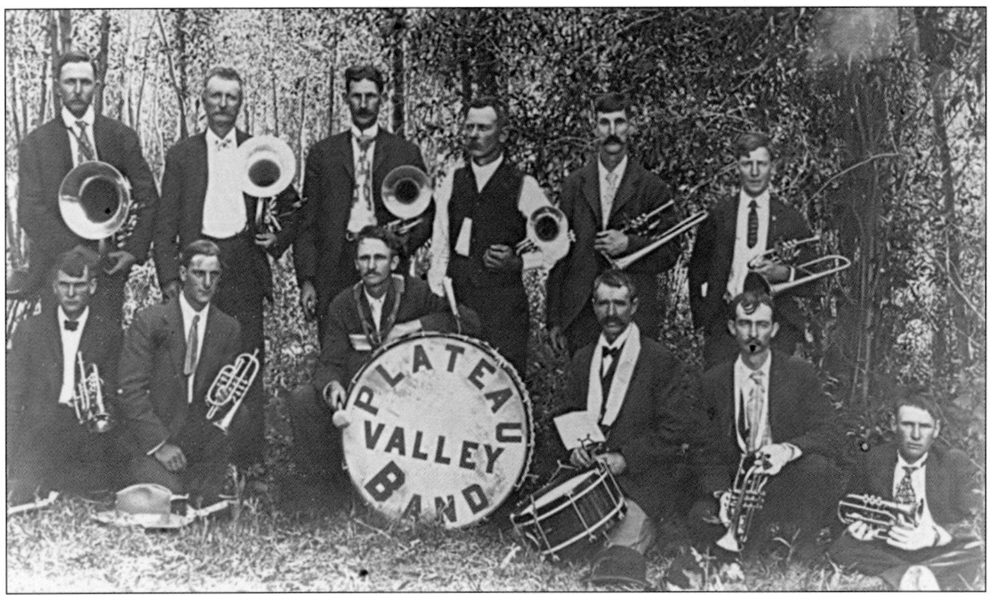

Plateau Valley Band. A program detailing Independence Day events was published in the *Plateau Voice* on July 4, 1913. Morning events included a 13-gun sunrise salute, music by the Plateau Valley Band, men's and women's quartets, and speeches. Dinner was held at noon, followed by a relay horse race, a baseball game featuring Palisade v. Collbran, and street sports for cash prizes. The evening events consisted of a street band concert, again featuring Plateau Valley Band, and a grand ball at the auditorium. (Plateau Valley Historical Preservation Society.)

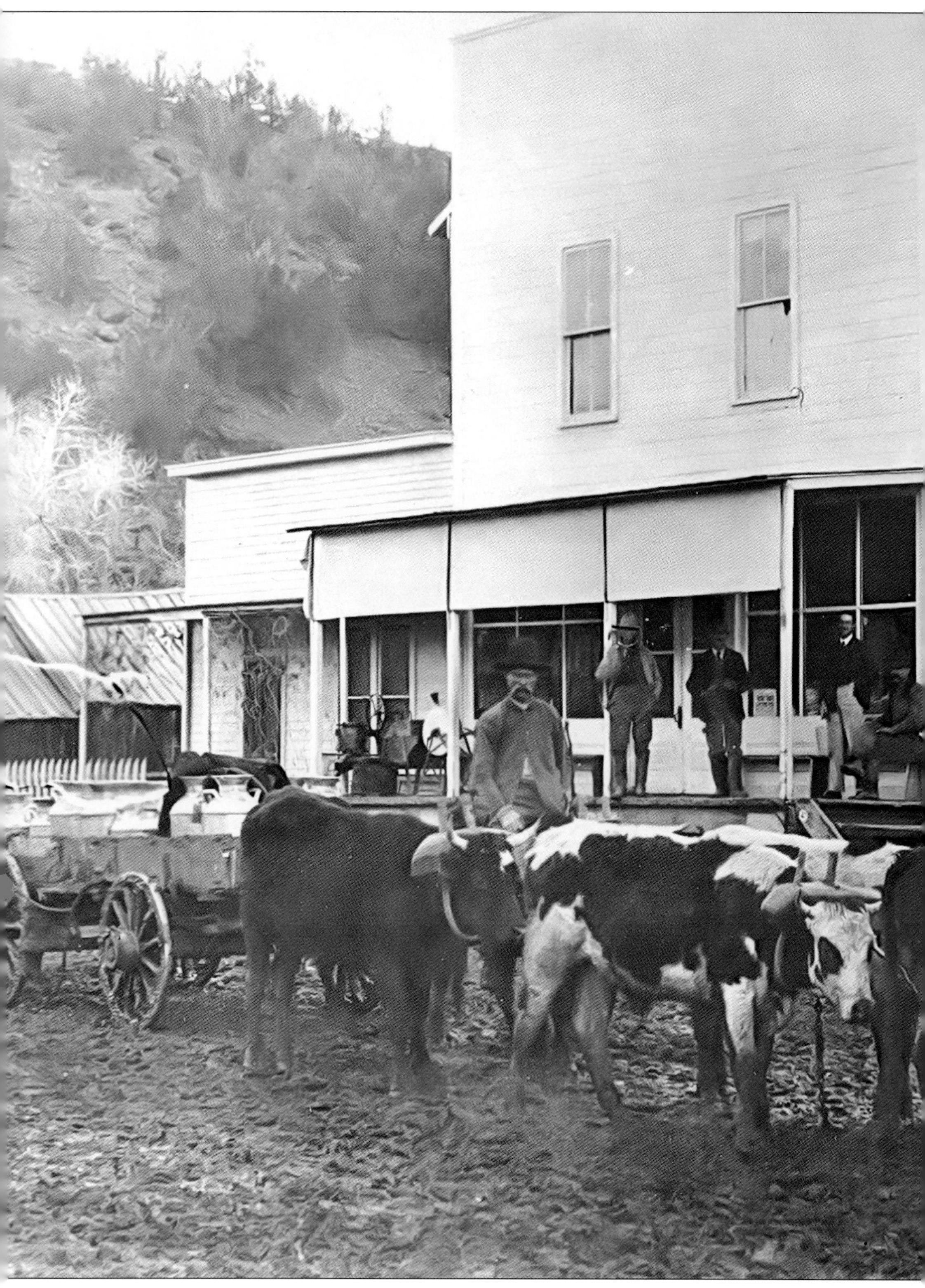

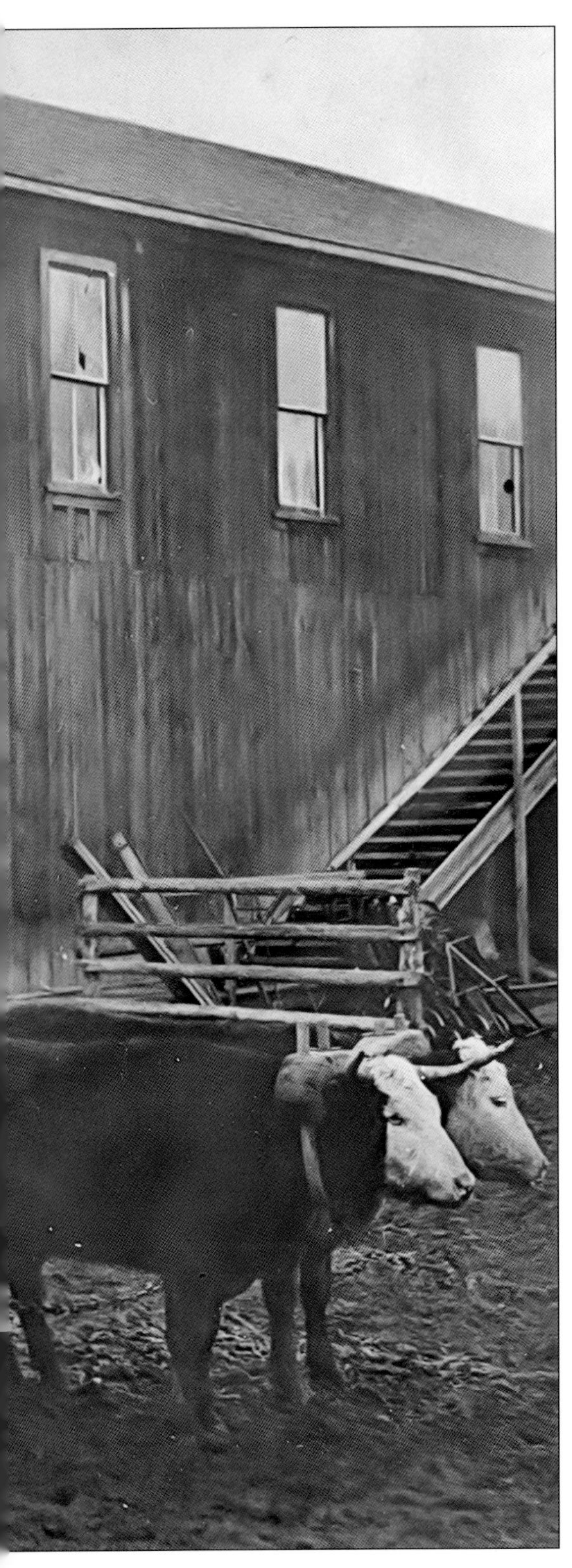

UNDERHILL'S STORE. T.G. Underhill, owner of Underhill's Store (also known as the Ziegel Building), was killed by a bucking horse in 1903. According to the local newspaper, he was headed to the home of E.S. Coakley to sit with little Sophia Coakley, who had died that day. He suffered a head injury when he was bucked from the horse he was riding and was taken home; Drs. Larson and Hanson were called and helped Dr. Zinke trepan the skull, but there was a large amount of clotted blood, and Underhill never regained consciousness. After the death of T.G. Underhill, B.C. Underhill took over the store's business operations. This photograph shows Charles Samworth and his ox team in front of the store. Samworth ran a milk route on East Kansas Mesa after the creamery was started. (Museum of Western Colorado, Lloyd Files Research Library.)

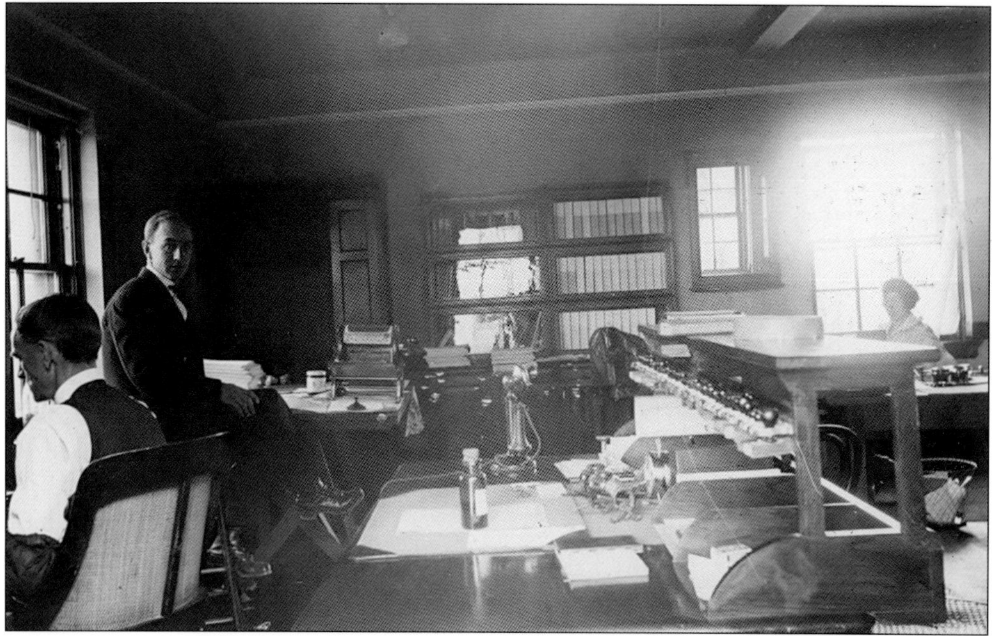

Early Day Ranger Station, Collbran. Pictured here is J.W. Spencer, the supervisor for the Battlement Mesa National Forest. Spencer was anxious to make the forestlands an ideal summer resort but also wanted to maintain sustainability. In 1921, he requisitioned 300,000 native trout to stock Mesa Lakes and the various creeks throughout the forest area. (Plateau Valley Historical Preservation Society.)

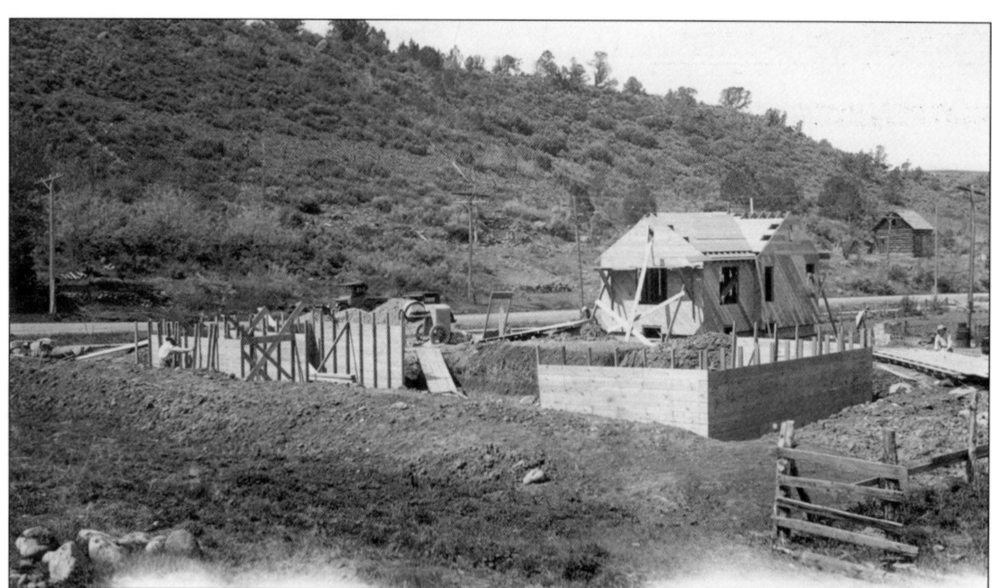

Collbran Office. The US Forest Service began construction on this office building in 1937. W.S. Brown, a former forest ranger, was engaged during the summer in ranger station construction supervision in both Carbondale and Collbran. (Plateau Valley Historical Preservation Society.)

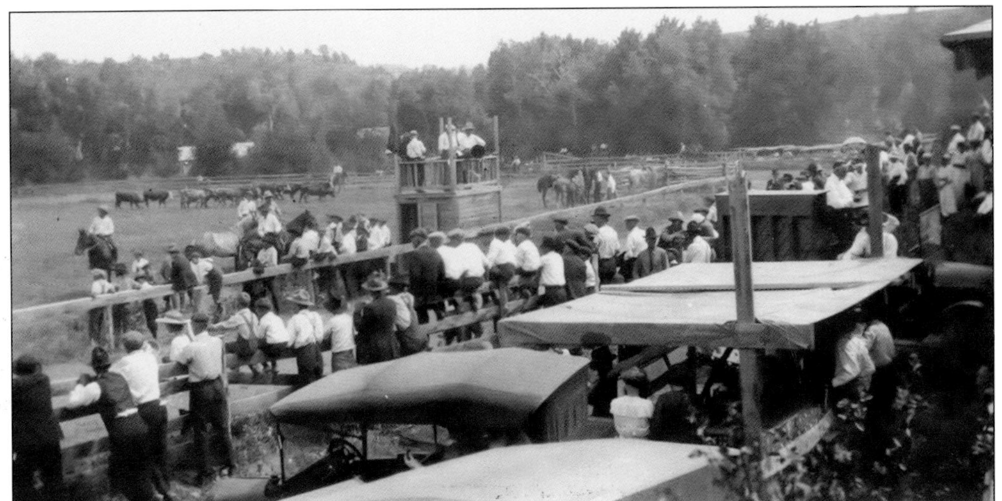

Collbran Rodeo Ground. The following was stated about the fairgrounds facility in a small booster publication: "Collbran has the beginning and the making of one of the most attractive athletic parks in the west, and plans are gradually being worked out to properly improve the same. Here is held the annual Fourth of July celebration and rodeo, and the regular baseball games in season." (Plateau Valley Historical Preservation Society.)

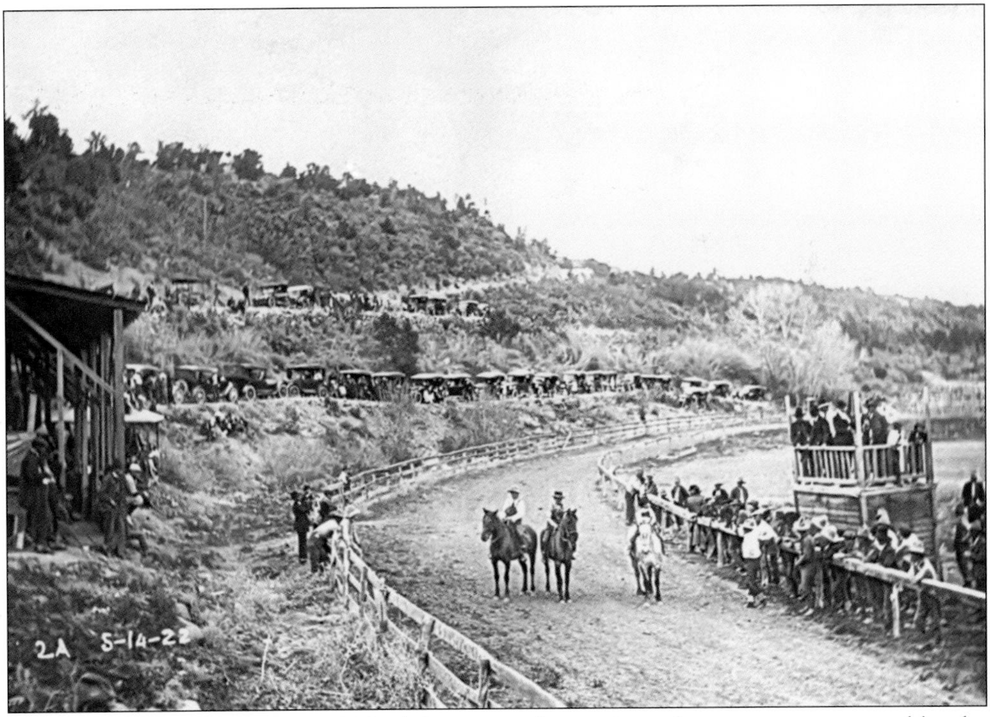

Collbran Rodeo Grounds, 1922. A large crowd turned out for an event sponsored by the Plateau Valley Fair Association on May 14, 1922. Events included music by the Cowboy Orchestra of Grand Junction, a Roman race, a baseball game, bucking broncs, and a pony race. There was also a "wonderful feat of a rider jumping from the back of his race horse, going full speed, and lighting on a fence rail," according to the *Plateau Voice* of May 19, 1922. (Plateau Valley Historical Preservation Society.)

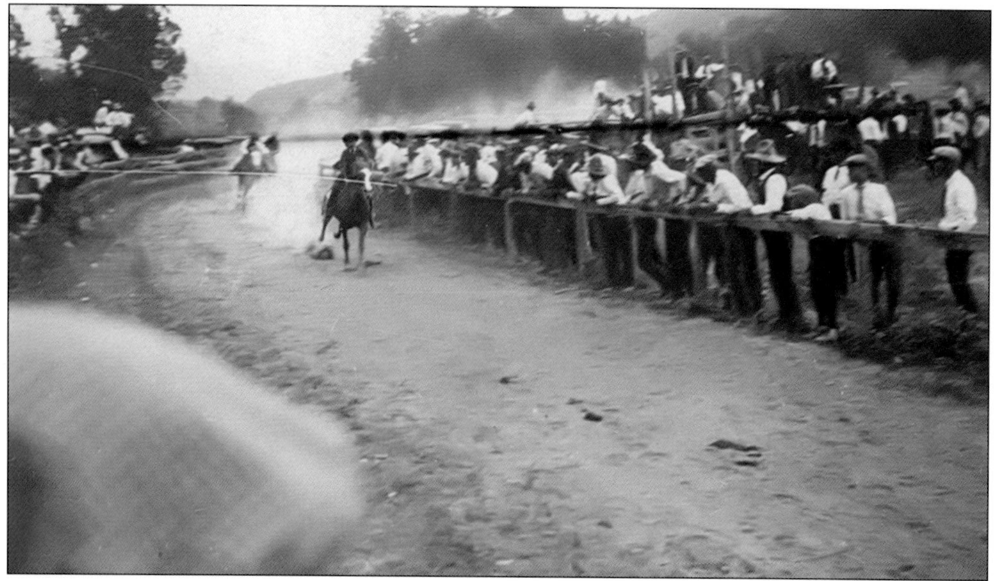

Fourth of July, 1923. Pictured here in a pony race are Dale Click, who came in first, and Dick Silliman, second. More than 3,000 people made this event the biggest the town had seen to date. This holiday was big entertainment to the people of Plateau Valley, with a rodeo and horse races, and it ended with a big dance in the auditorium. According to the *Plateau Voice*, "There were bucking horses and bucking steers; and oh boy! those cowboys, how they did their stunts to the enjoyment of the big crowd supplemented with exciting races, etc. A three-ring circus was nowhere in comparison to this program." (Above, author's collection; below, Plateau Valley Historical Preservation Society.)

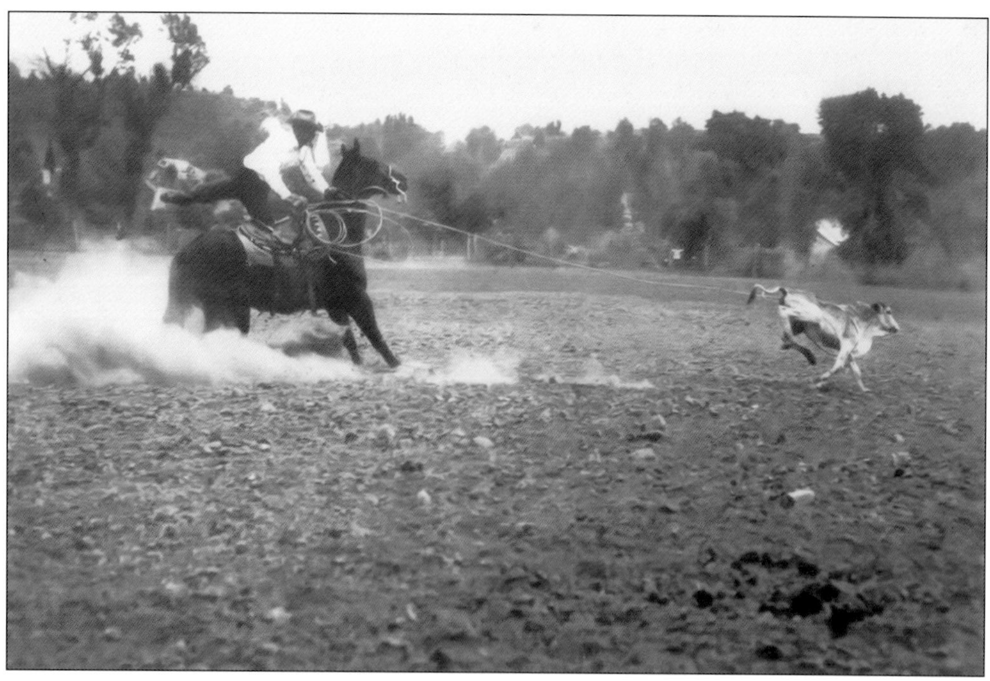

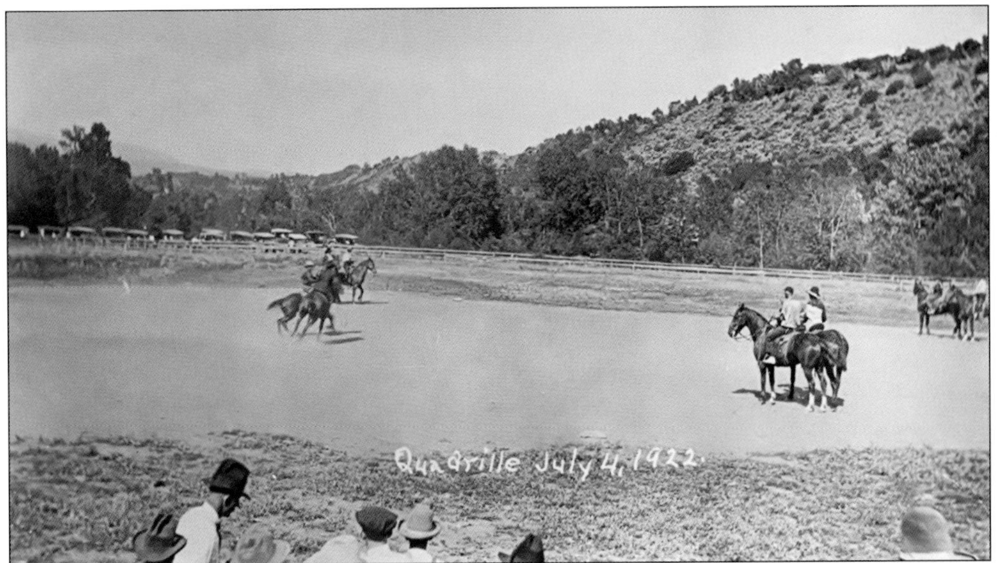

Collbran Rodeo Ground, 1922. At the Fourth of July celebration, there were 10 races, 2 bulldogging exhibitions, 11 bucking broncs, 10 steer-riding events, 2 solos, and 2 quadrilles. The quadrille event, pictured here, featured eight horses galloping to "Turkey in the Straw." A quadrille is performed with a minimum of four horses performing movements together. (Plateau Valley Historical Preservation Society.)

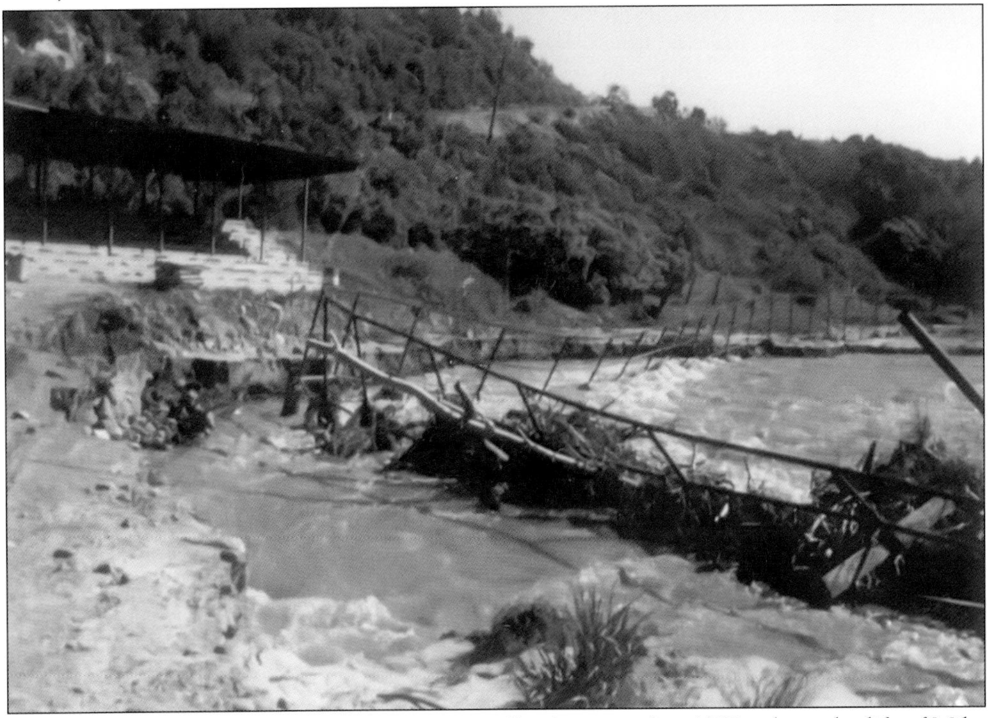

Collbran Rodeo Grounds, 1983. A 100-year flood occurred in 1983, taking the life of Mike Lane as he and Gene Click were checking bridges and the Gunderson Bridge washed out from under them. Buzzard Creek changed course and cut a new channel through the middle of the arena and in front of the grandstands. (Plateau Valley Historical Preservation Society.)

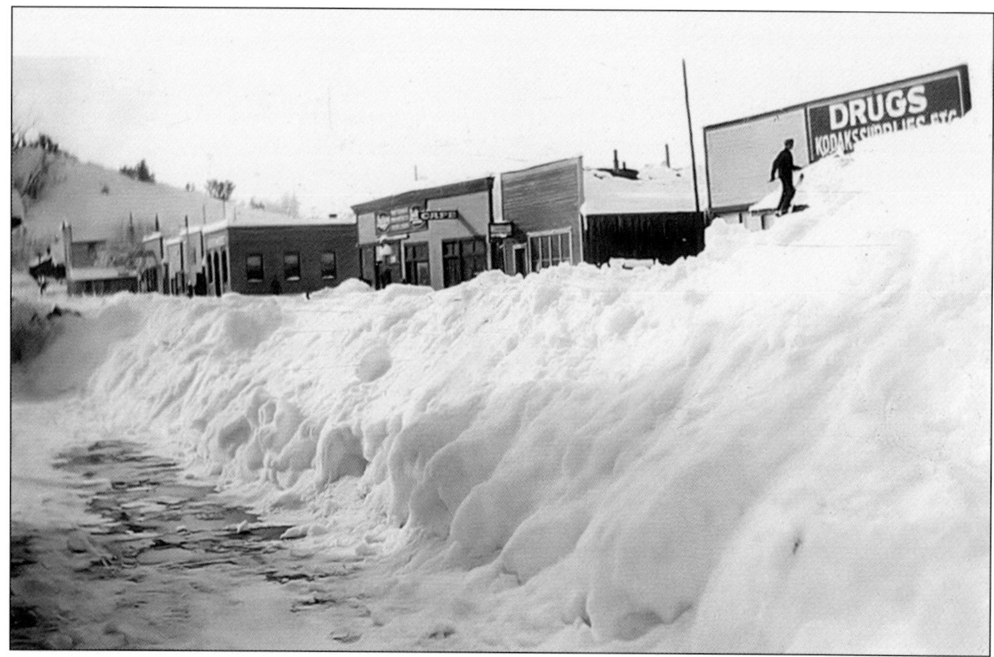

Main Street Snow. Many older residents claim that the snowfall was much greater in the past than it is today. Many man-hours were spent shoveling snow and chopping ice to maintain access to roads, doorways, and trails. Haystacks were shoveled off and water holes were kept open to water livestock. Ice was cut and stored for summer use. Not everyone owned a smaller icebox or ice pond, but most farms had an icehouse. The ice was packed in sawdust, with a layer on the bottom, around the outside walls, and in between each block. Residents living in town could take their perishable foods to a commercial icehouse for storage if they did not own an icebox. (Above, Plateau Valley Historical Preservation Society; below, Rudy and Arita Charlesworth.)

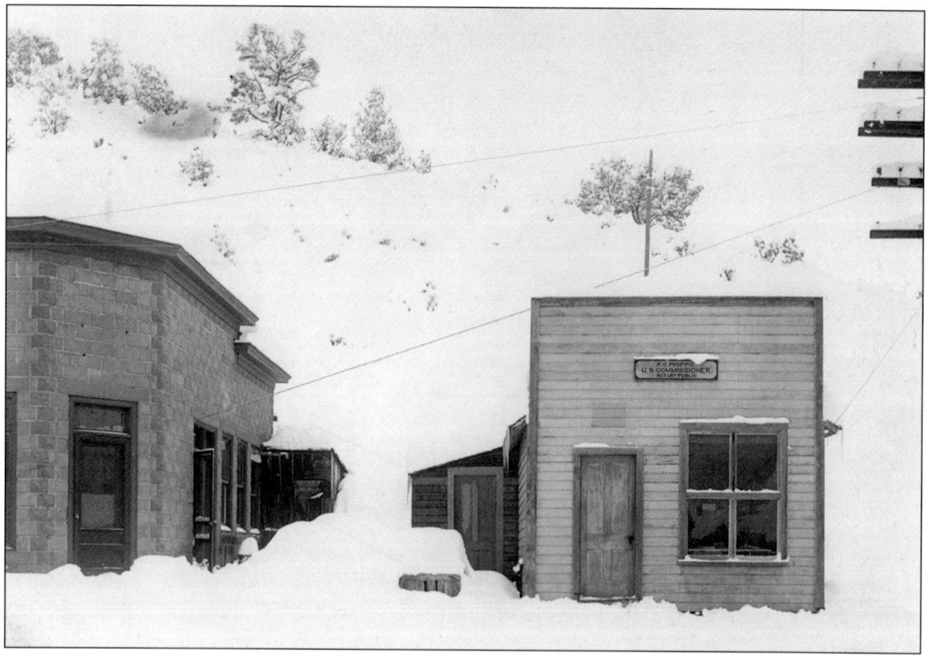

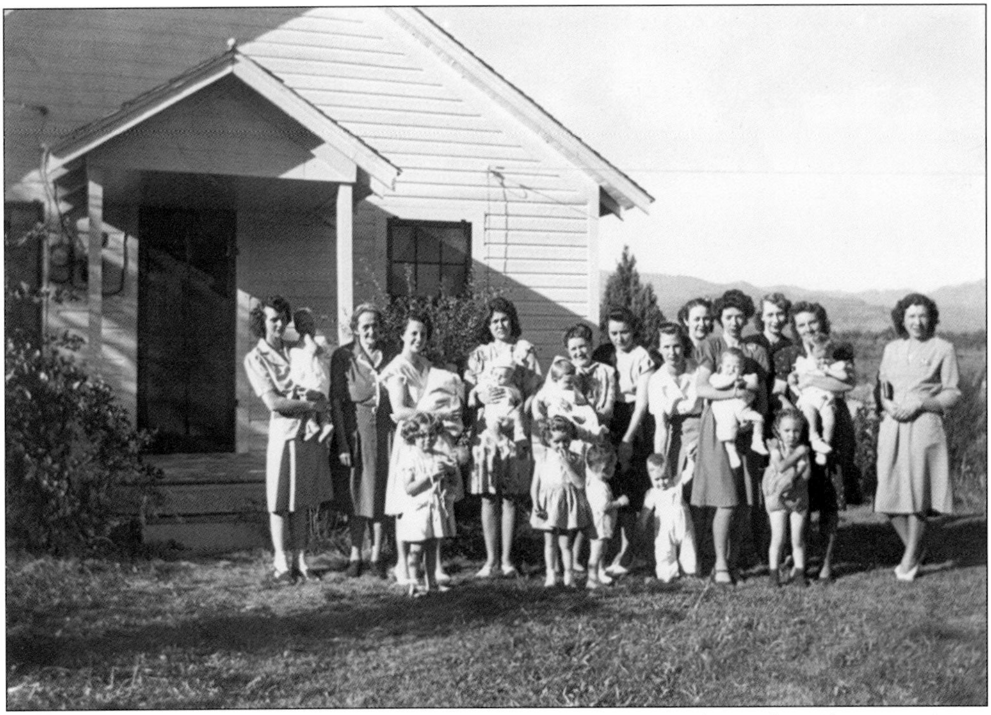

Baby Boomers, Late 1940s. Pictured here are, from left to right, Helen Chapman, Nina Milholland, Eleanor Nichols, Roylee Walck, unidentified, Mickie Charlesworth, unidentified, Helen Hittle, Billie Reed, Betty Arney, Ilda Phillips, and Louemma Milholland. (Plateau Valley Historical Preservation Society.)

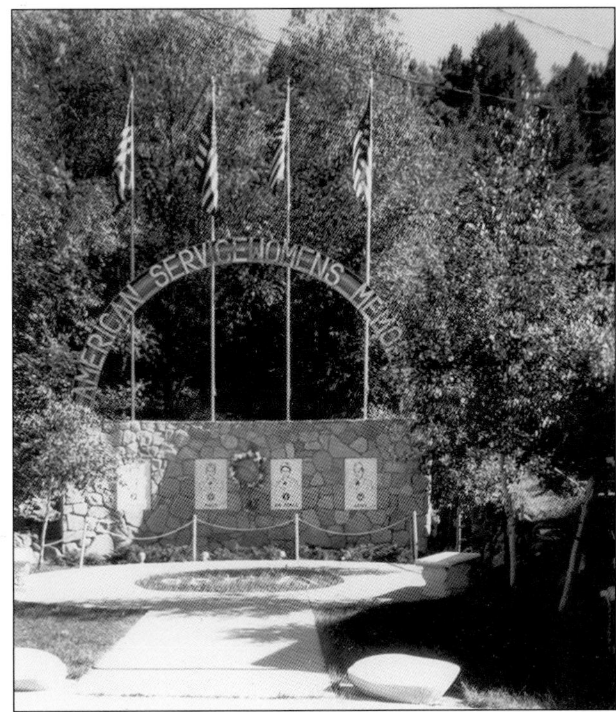

American Servicewomen's Memorial. Dedicated on July 4, 1991, Collbran's monument to the American servicewomen was the first of its kind in the United States. A true community effort, the creation of the monument took 11 years and was headed by the efforts of Dick Cummins. (Plateau Valley Historical Preservation Society.)

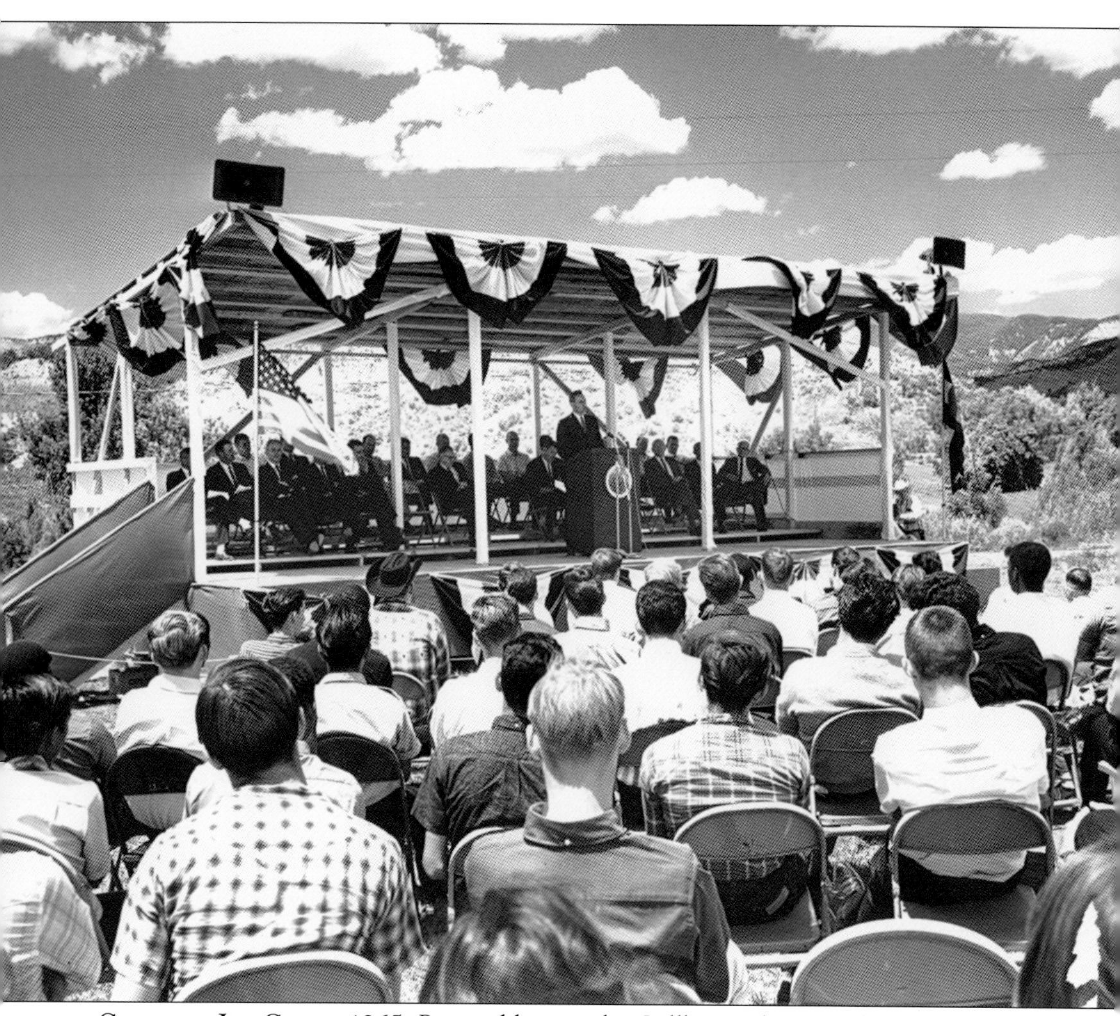

COLLBRAN JOB CORPS, 1965. Pictured here is the Collbran Job Corps dedication ceremony. US representative Wayne Aspinall is speaking. This center was one of the first opened by the US Department of Labor. Job Corps was part of the Johnson administration's War on Poverty under his domestic agenda known as the Great Society. It was modeled after the Depression-era Civilian Conservation Corps (CCC). Job Corps combines classroom, practical, and work-based learning experiences to prepare youth for stable, long-term, high-paying jobs. (Chuck Zobel and Joyce Hawkins, Collbran Job Corps.)

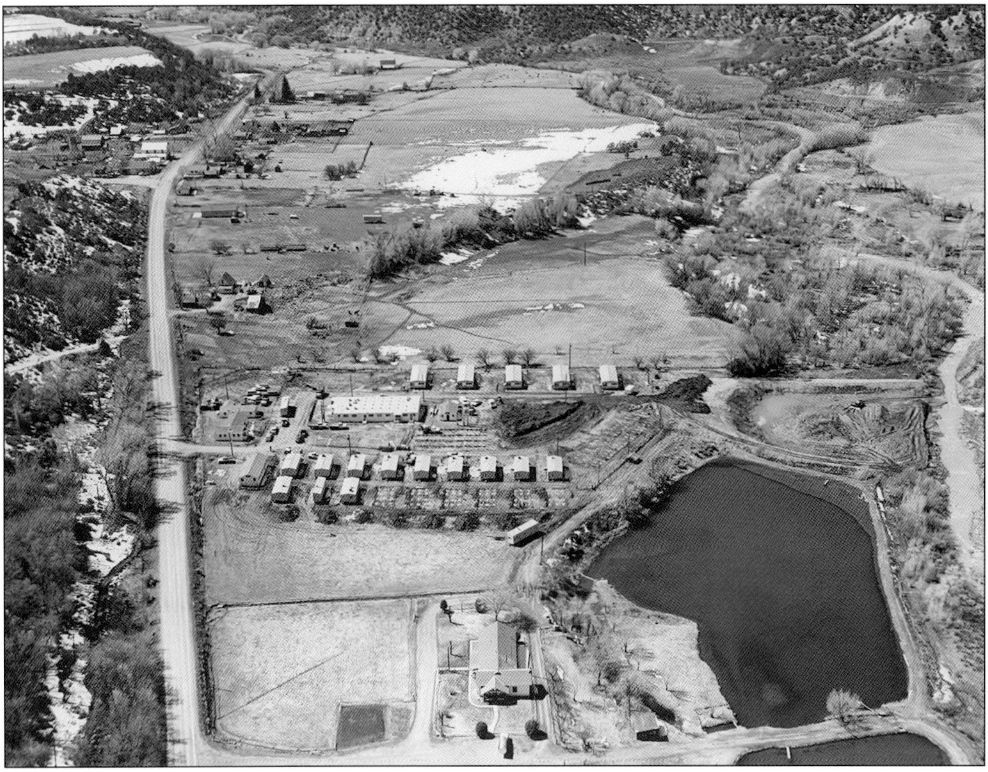

Job Corps Expansion, c. 1970s. Job Corps was piloted as a five-year program. The US Bureau of Reclamation made use of the housing in place during the Vega Reservoir building project, but by 1968, it became clear that new facilities were needed. Students did most of the construction of dormitories and renovations. They not only built and made enhancements to the center but were also involved in projects and improvements in Collbran and other areas. Some of the projects included the construction of several of the campgrounds on the Grand Mesa, the rifle range in Collbran, installation of culverts, dam building, building projects at Lincoln Park in Grand Junction, and road improvements, including the road at Rifle Gap Reservoir, to name a few. (Both, Chuck Zobel and Joyce Hawkins.)

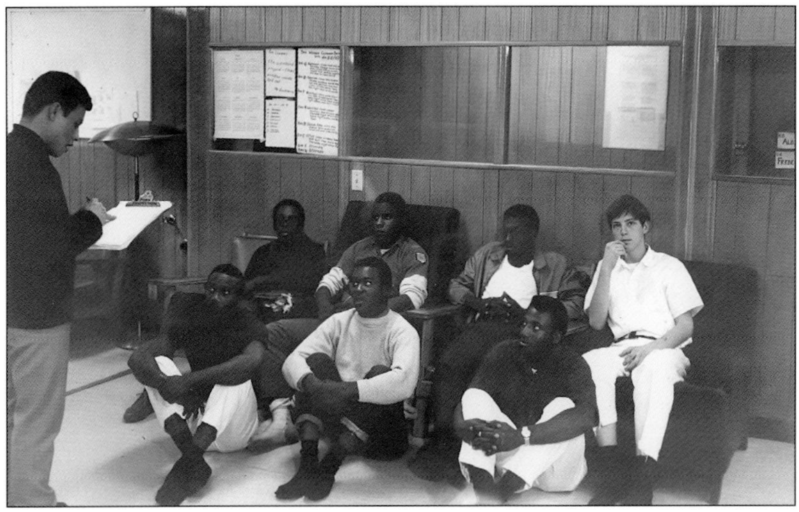

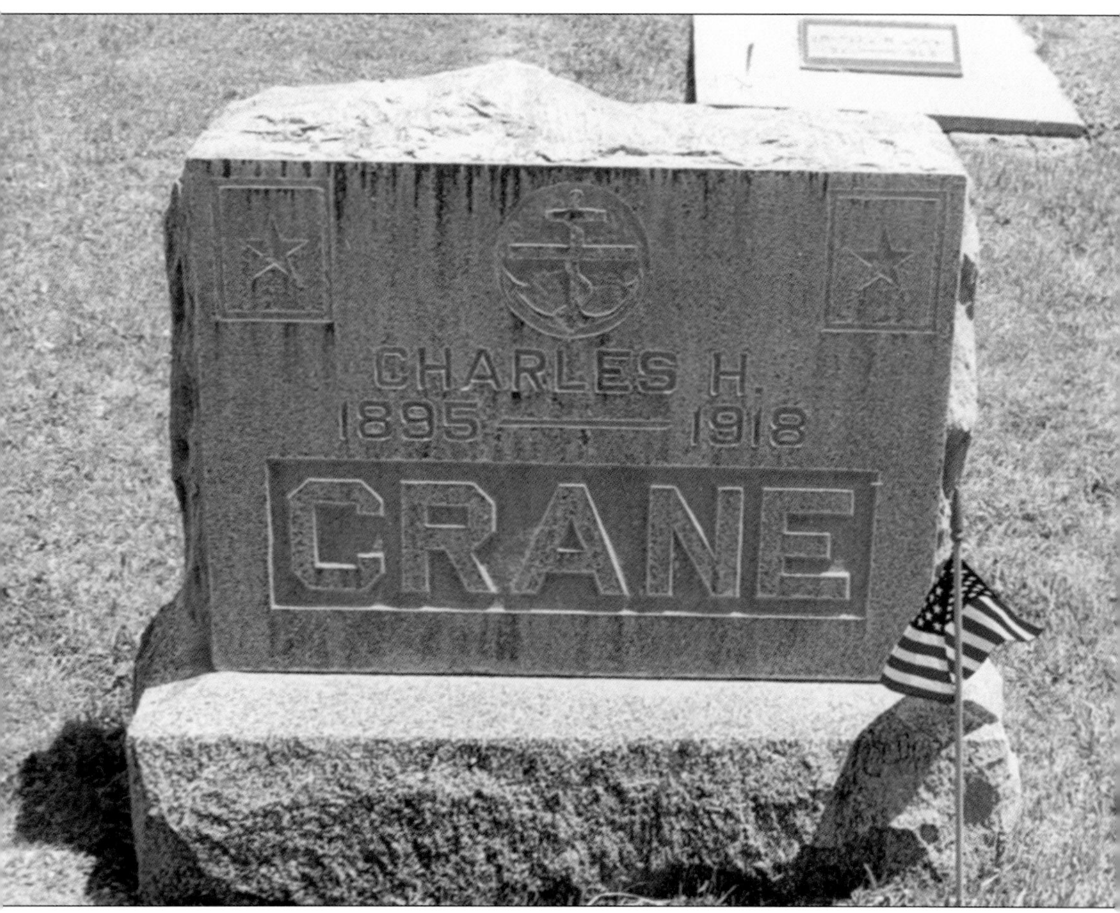

Headstone. Shortly after the end of World War I, schools, public gatherings, and businesses where people congregated such as pool halls were closed in an attempt to staunch the spread of Spanish influenza. Charles Herbert Crane died from complications of Spanish influenza after returning from naval service. His obituary stated, "He had sterling qualities, and gave promise of a life of great usefulness as a mechanic and a citizen of his country. But he heard his country's call, and with millions of others of our best youth, nobly responded." (Griffith family collection.)

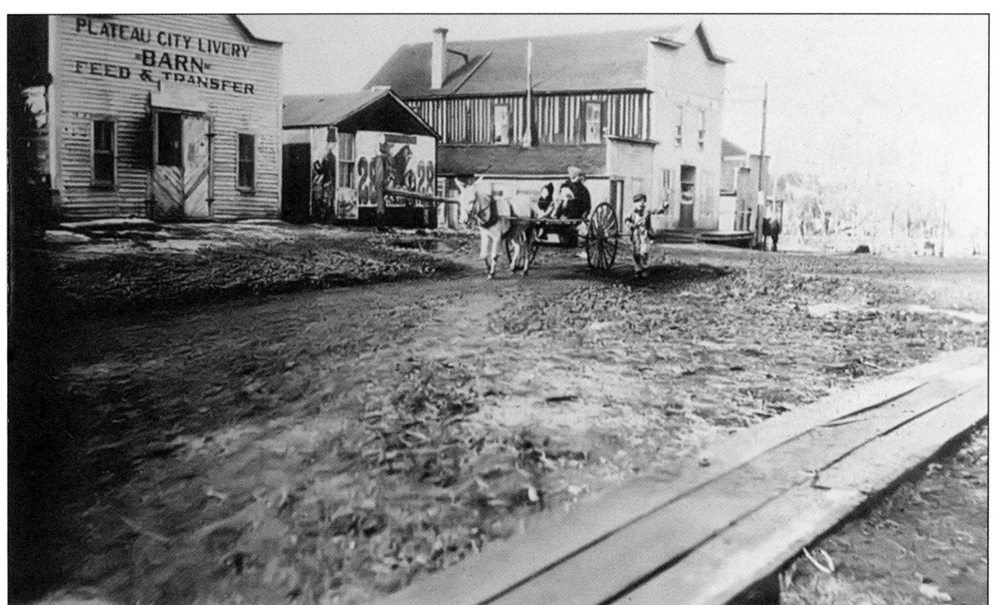

Plateau City Livery. John Carlos Charlesworth ran the livery stable in Plateau City. Charlesworth came to Colorado and located an excellent ranch on Mormon Mesa. On this property, which he had greatly improved, he conducted a prosperous and profitable business as a general farmer and stockman. (Plateau Valley Historical Preservation Society.)

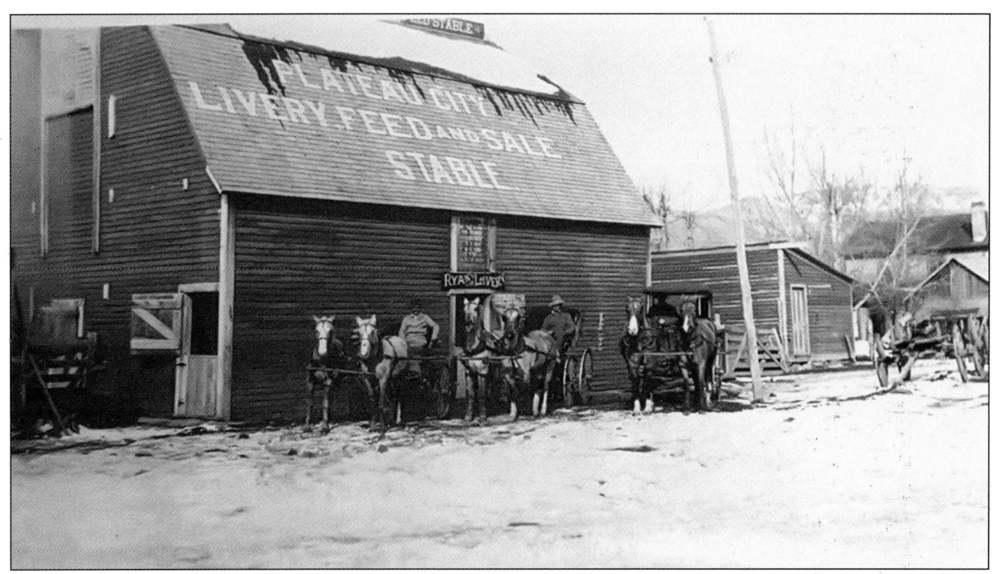

Plateau City Livery, Feed, and Sale Stable. The Plateau City Livery advertised first-class rigs and teams available at all times. At this time, Leo I. Ryan was proprietor. In 1911, Ryan was accused of inhumane treatment of his teams. Witnesses for the defense included F.A. Bloss, Willis Hodgson, W.J. Wallace, and Mr. Bann. The jury promptly decided that there were no grounds for prosecution. (Plateau Valley Historical Preservation Society.)

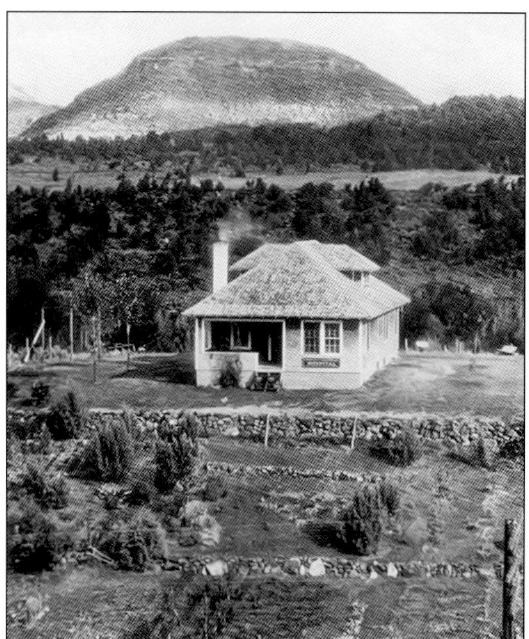

PLATEAU VALLEY CONGREGATIONAL HOSPITAL. In 1903, the Collbran Congregational Church purchased the grounds and building to meet the maternity needs of women in Plateau Valley. The Kansas Mesa Club furnished one room, and the Masons furnished another; the other rooms were furnished by donations, mostly local but partly from many other states. (Author's collection.)

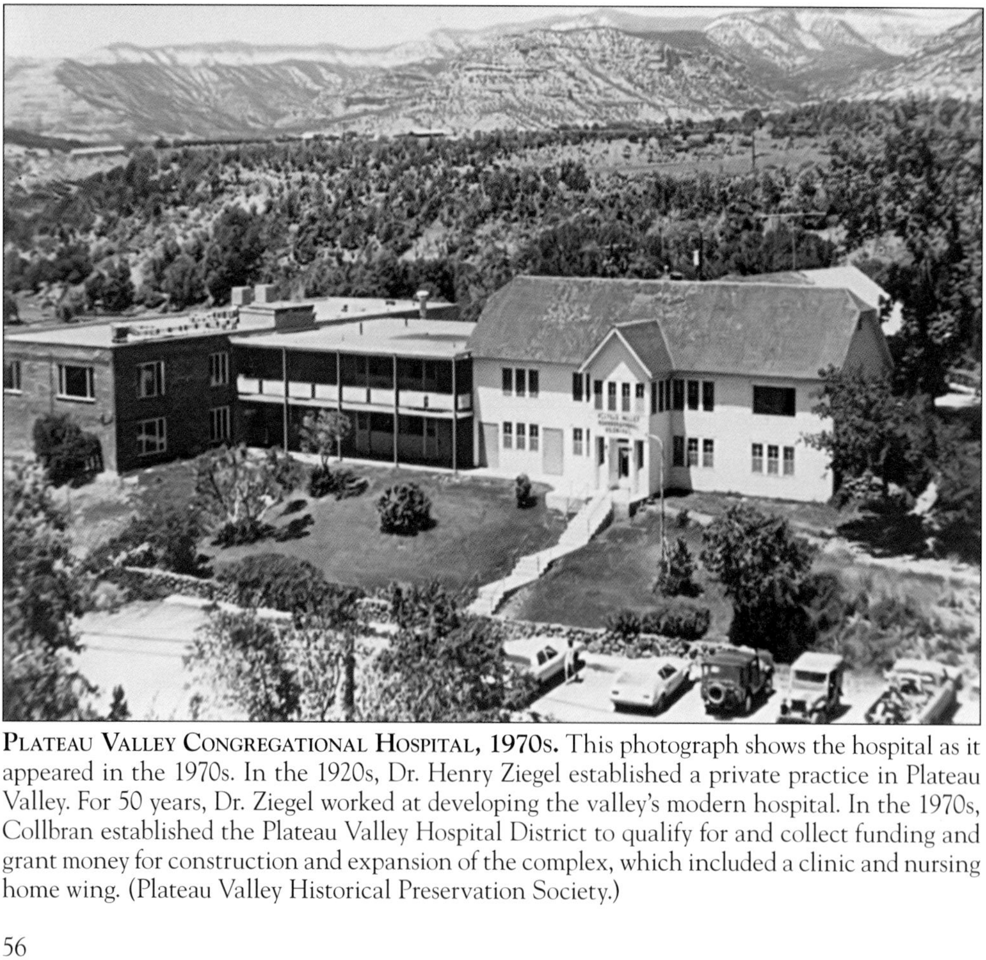

PLATEAU VALLEY CONGREGATIONAL HOSPITAL, 1970S. This photograph shows the hospital as it appeared in the 1970s. In the 1920s, Dr. Henry Ziegel established a private practice in Plateau Valley. For 50 years, Dr. Ziegel worked at developing the valley's modern hospital. In the 1970s, Collbran established the Plateau Valley Hospital District to qualify for and collect funding and grant money for construction and expansion of the complex, which included a clinic and nursing home wing. (Plateau Valley Historical Preservation Society.)

Plateau Valley Congregational Hospital, 1929. Pictured here are Rennie Silliman and Iva Bergrum. James Renwick "Rennie" Silliman and his wife, Myra, brought their family from Winterset, Iowa, to Plateau Valley in 1907. They and their belongings traveled on an immigrant train to Towner, Colorado, and from there by wagon to Plateau Valley, where they bought a ranch on Kansas Mesa. (Author's collection.)

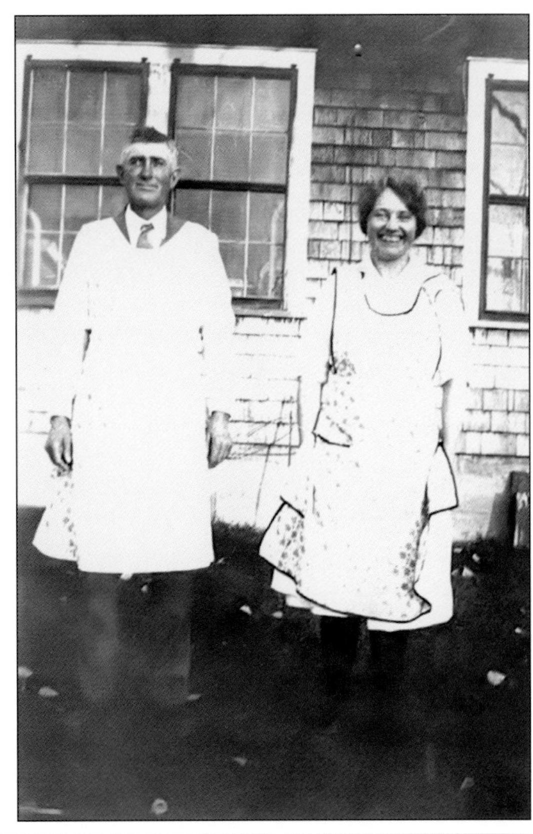

Molina, Colorado. The word *molina* refers to one who lives near a mill. Seen here on the right side of the road are several businesses: S.C. Skinner's blacksmith shop, Skinner's store, and Old Henry Davis's Store. The Skinner family and the Davis family were some of the area's early pioneers. Skinner's store was used as a trading center. (Stites Collection, Courtesy of Museum of Western Colorado, Lloyd Files Research Library.)

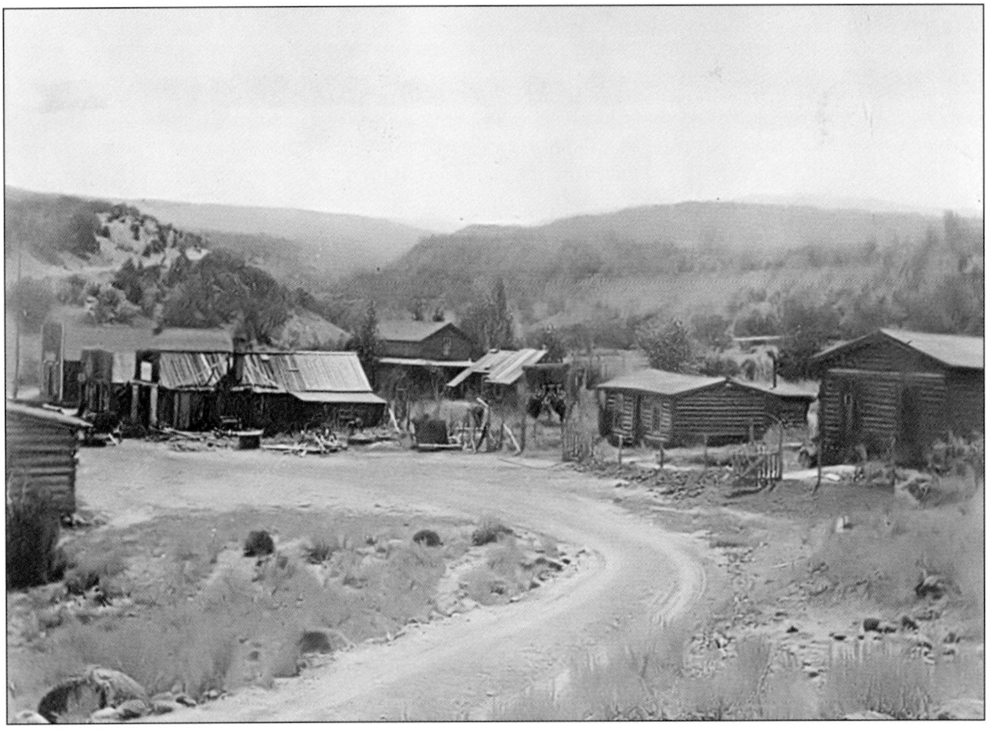

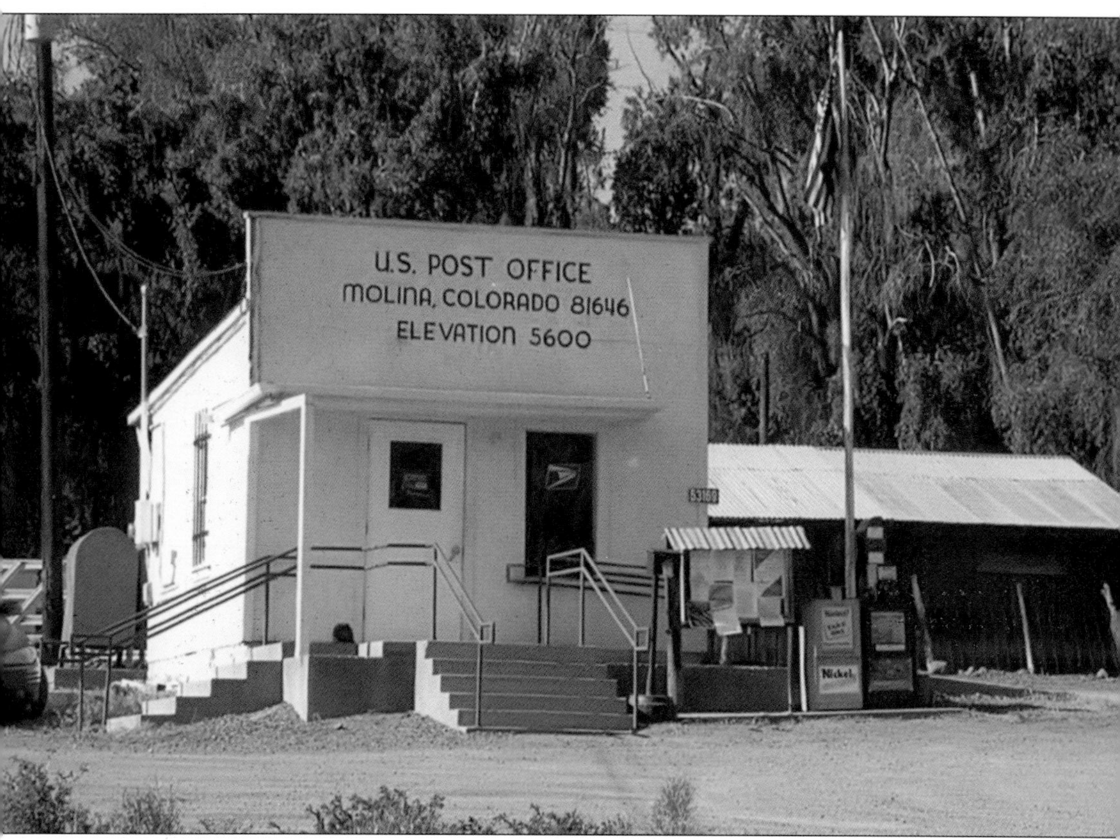

Molina Post Office. The Molina Post Office moved a number of times before settling at its current location. In *Skin and Bones*, Julia Hall summarized the little post office's history. It was first opened in Orson, at the home of Frank Reed, then moved to Molina across Cottonwood Creek at the old Ford place, operated by Frank Jamison. The Jamison family moved away, and for a time, the community was without a post office. John Snipes circulated a petition, and the post office was operated at the Snipes place, and was called Snipes. This name caused much comment, and was eventually changed back to Molina, with S.C. Skinner serving as postmaster. (Plateau Valley Historical Preservation Society.)

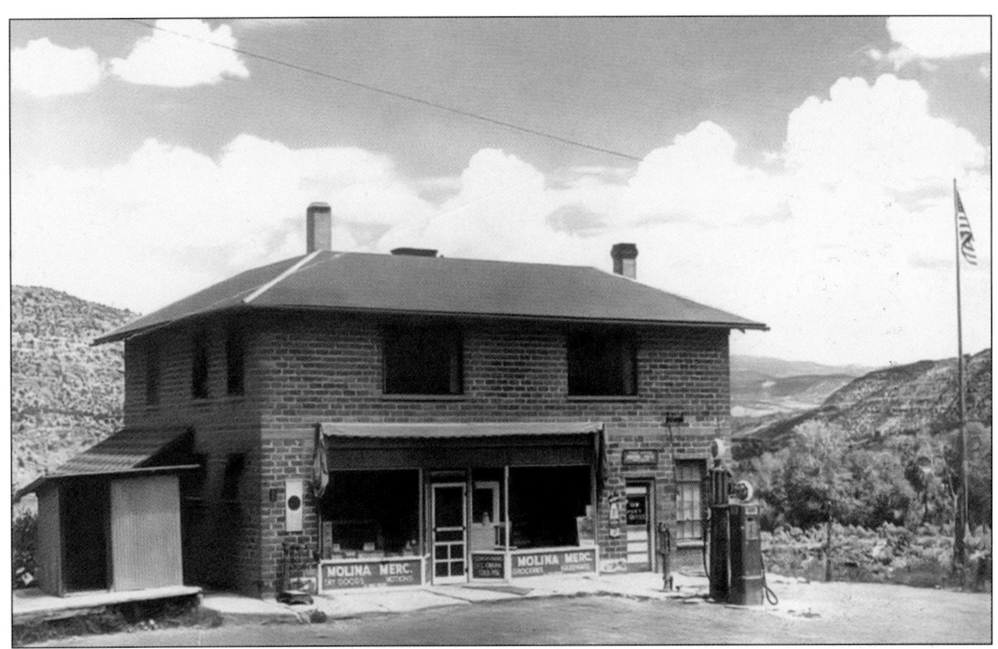

MOLINA MERCANTILE. The name of this store changed to Sunnyside Cash Grocery in 1932. It was home to the Molina Post Office, and the DeCamp family lived upstairs. (Plateau Valley Historical Preservation Society.)

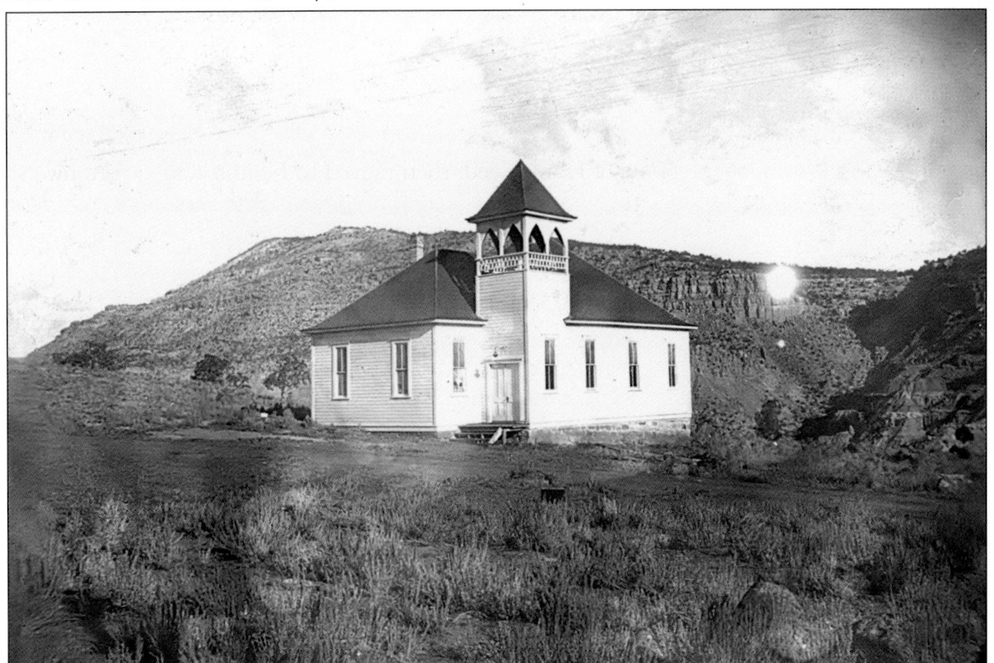

MOLINA CONGREGATIONAL CHURCH. The Molina Congressional Church was organized by members from Georgia Mesa and Molina. According to *Skin and Bones*, members included Nettie Kirkendall, Ella Moore, Nora Monroe, Julia Hall, Mr. and Mrs. Barnett Colclasure, Faye Colclasure, Ellen Hart, Alice McCall, Mrs. Midwood, Mr. and Mrs. S.C. Skinner, and Mr. and Mrs. H.C. Hobert. (Stites Collection, Museum of Western Colorado, Lloyd Files Research Library.)

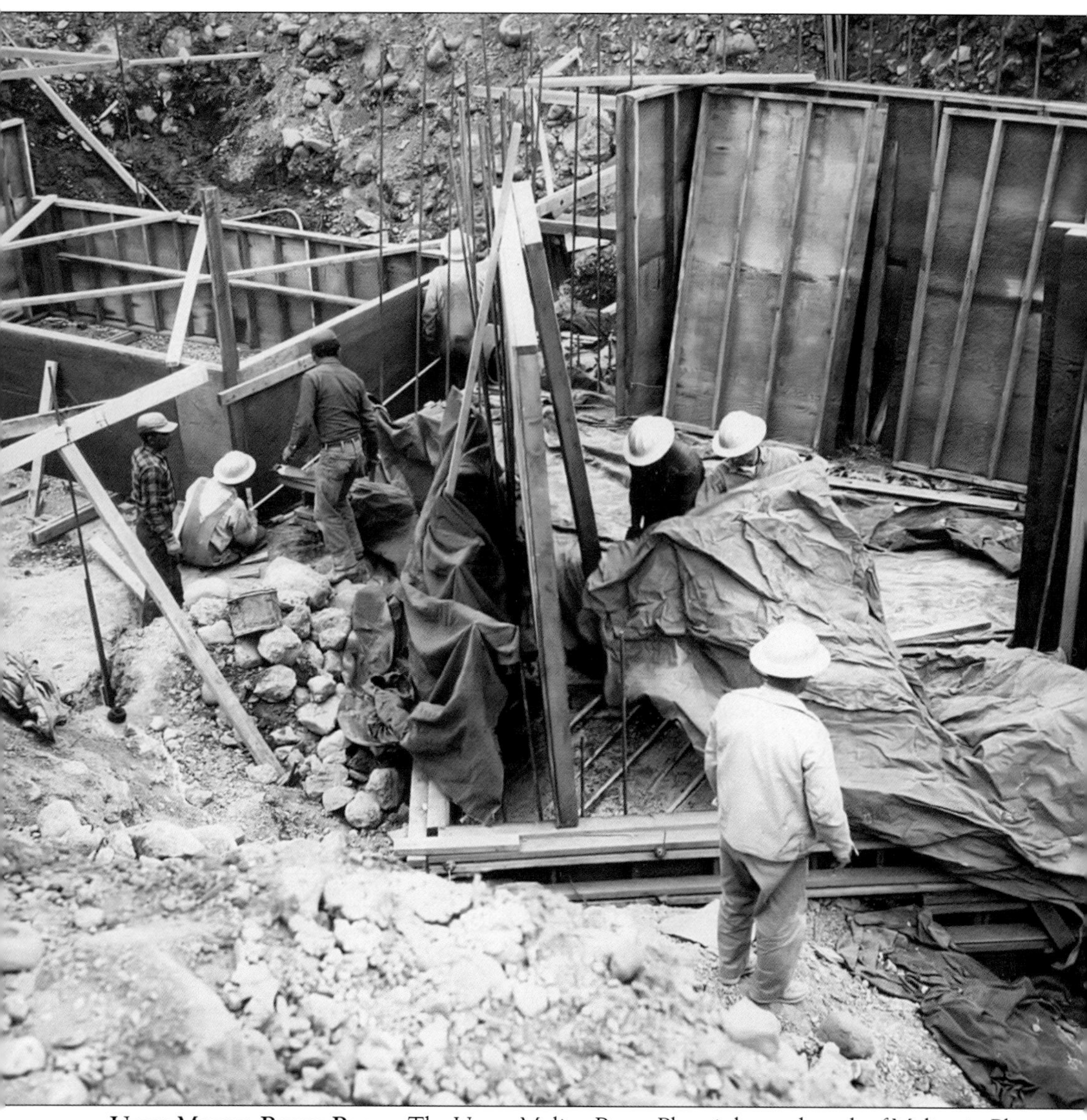

Upper Molina Power Plant. The Upper Molina Power Plant is located south of Molina in Plateau Valley. It was constructed as part of the Bureau of Reclamation's Collbran Project. Workers are seen here laying forms for the substructure. According to the Bureau of Reclamation, the Upper Molina penstock extends from the Bonham and Cottonwoods pipeline and continues approximately 2.4 miles down the north slope of Grand Mesa to the Upper Molina Power Plant. The penstock consists of welded steel pipe with a capacity of 50 cubic feet per second ranging in diameter from 36 inches at the junction of the Bonham Cottonwood collection system to 33 inches at the lower section. (William H. Nelson Collection, Colorado Mesa University Special Collections.)

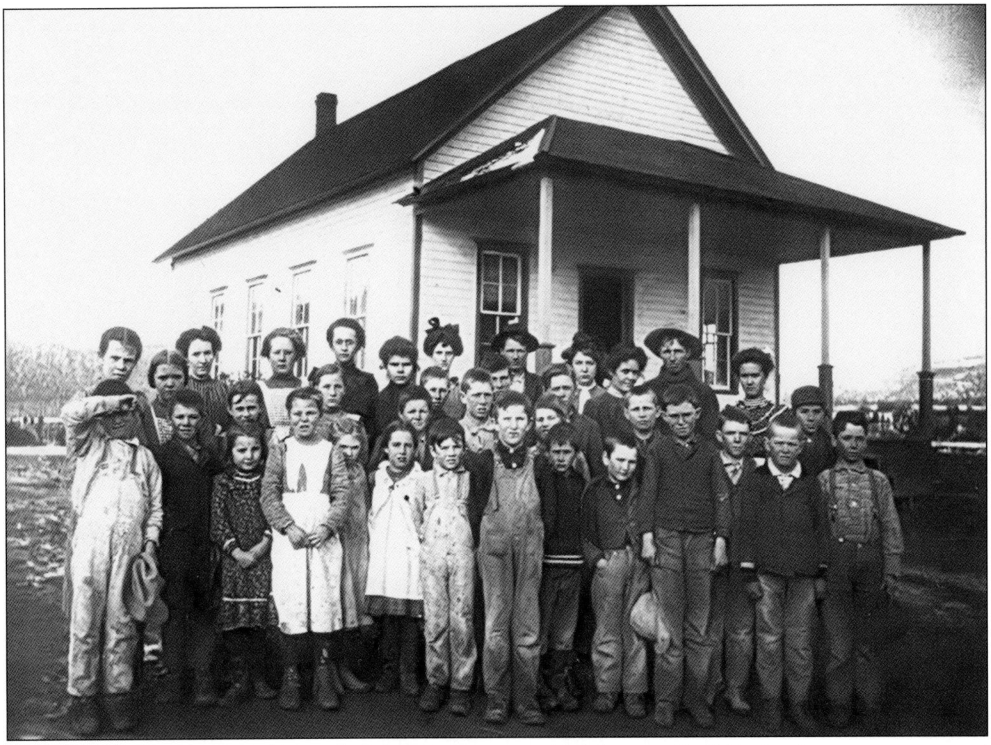

Bull Creek School. Bull Creek School was west of Molina in Bull Basin. It was constructed in the early 1890s, and the building is still standing. Sara Kruh taught her first term of school at Bull Creek. Later she taught in Collbran, Loma, Fowler, and Grand Junction for a total of 47 years. Vena Woodward taught at Bull Creek the last year that school was held there. (Plateau Valley Historical Preservation Society.)

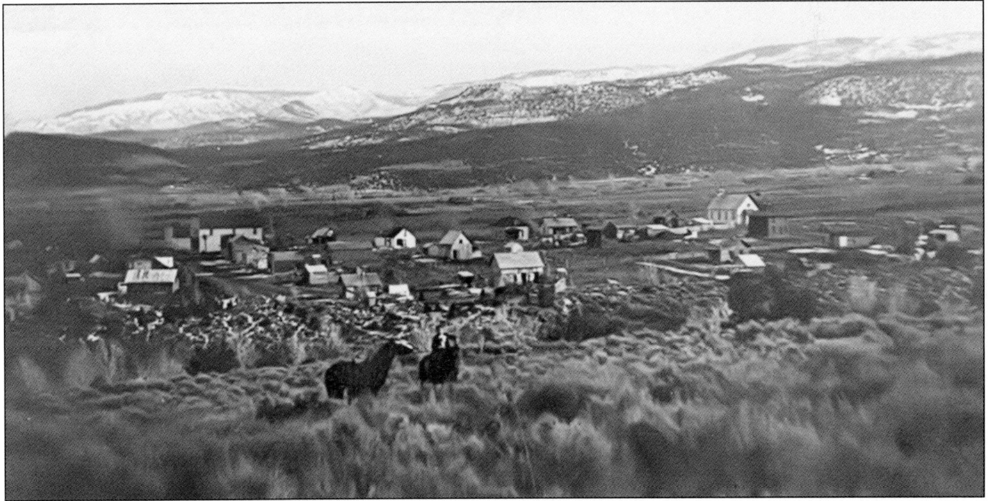

Town of Mesa. Mesa was the first stop on the southern trip over Grand Mesa. John Brown was the first settler. According to *Skin and Bones*, he came over the old Government Road into the Meadows in 1882. He was a Civil War veteran who punched cattle and freighted in Montana before coming to Colorado. He is credited with bringing the first cattle to Plateau Valley. (Plateau Valley Historical Preservation Society.)

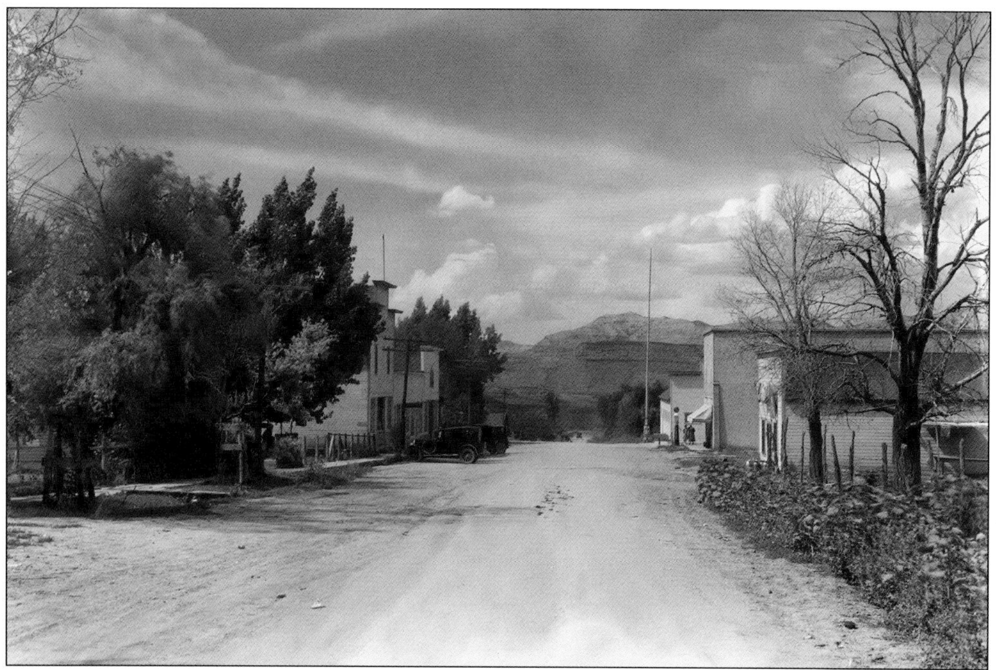

MAIN STREET OF MESA, C. 1910S. This view of the town's main street shows frame commercial buildings flanking a dirt street, cars, women by a glass tank gas pump, canvas awning, a flagpole, cream cans, and a false-front building with a sign reading "Post Office." (Denver Public Library, Western History Collection [Call X-12319].)

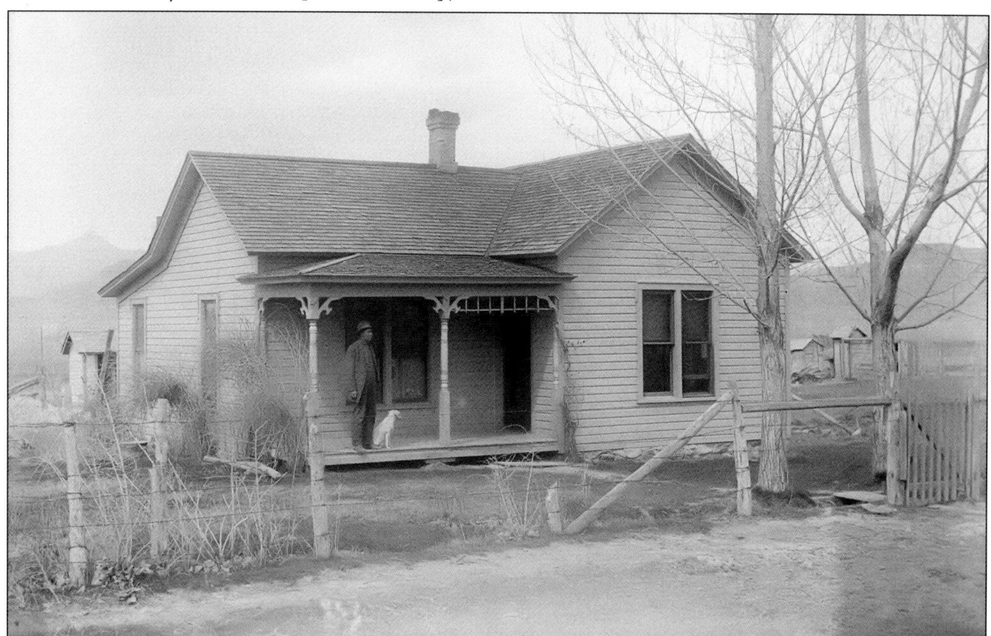

MESA, COLORADO. A man and a dog stand on the porch of a house that served as the Mountain States Telephone and Telegraph Company exchange building in Mesa. The building is a one-story clapboard structure with a single roof. A wire fence surrounds the yard. (Mountain State Telephone Company Photograph Collection, PH. 00287 [Scan 20007353], History Colorado.)

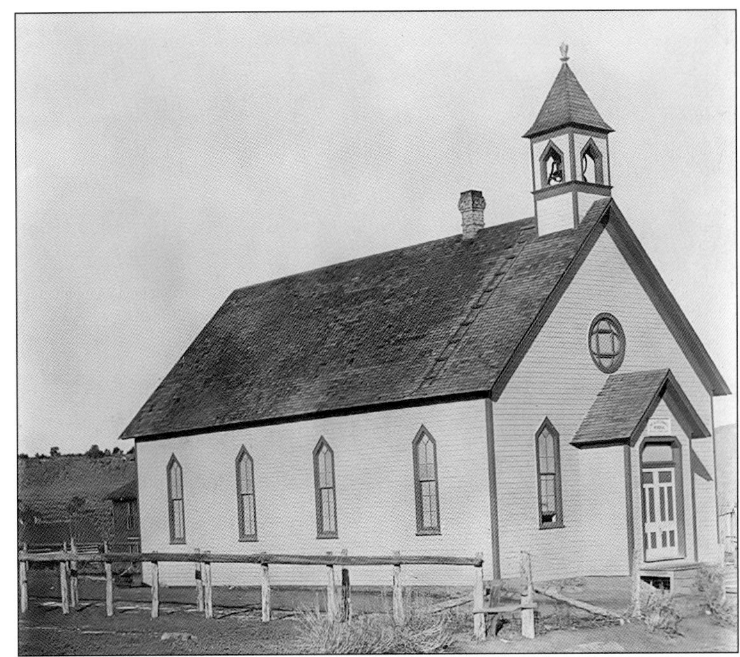

Methodist Episcopal Church, Mesa. In 1900, land for a Methodist Episcopal church was donated, and a building was soon erected. It was in continuous use until 1975. A parsonage was built in 1904. In 1941, electricity came to the valley, and in 1952, gas heat was installed in the building. (Stites Collection, Museum of Western Colorado, Lloyd Files Research Library.)

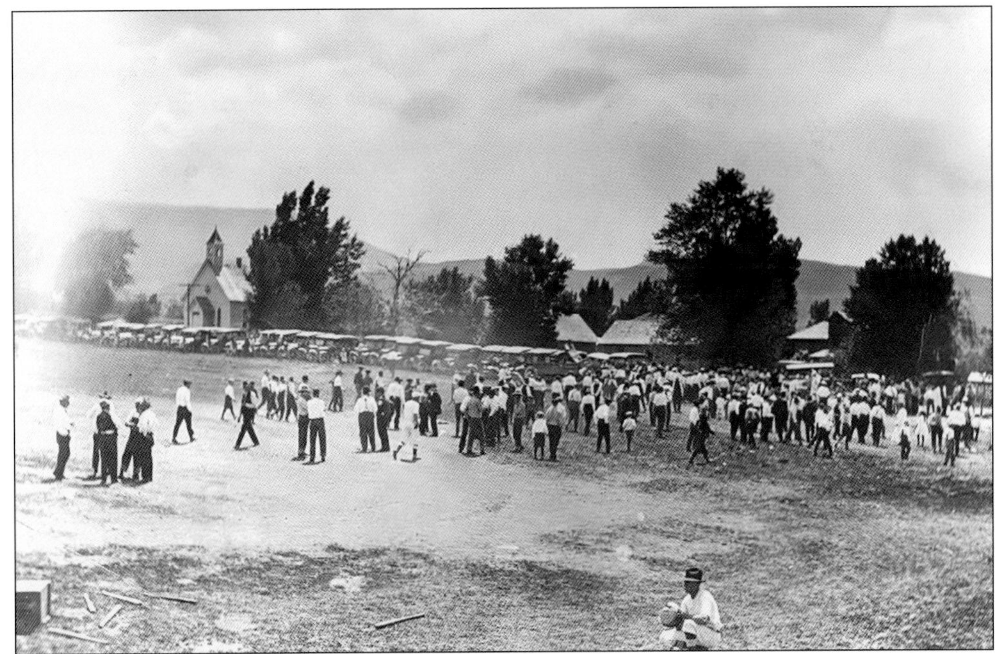

Baseball Game, Mesa. Many of the local communities had their own baseball teams, which met regularly for the fun of the sport. Collbran, Mesa, Molina, Palisade, and DeBeque held regular games. (Plateau Valley Historical Preservation Society.)

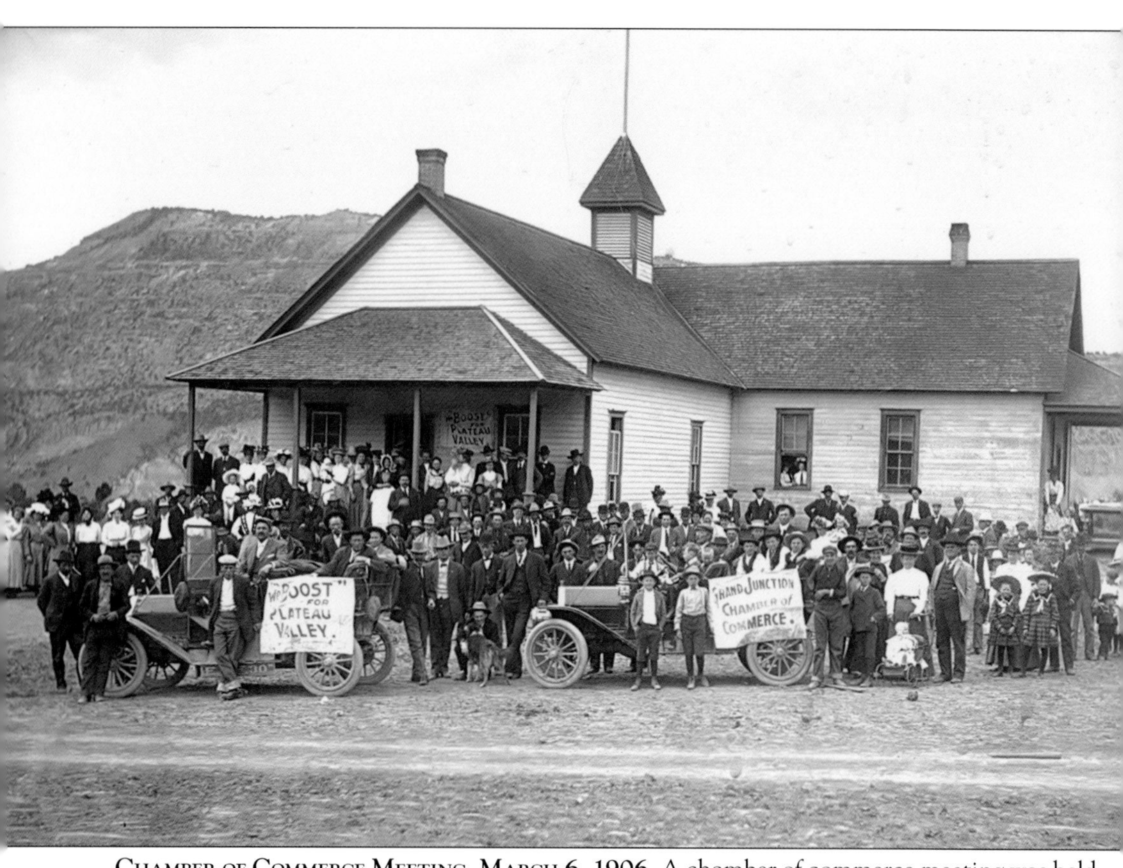

CHAMBER OF COMMERCE MEETING, MARCH 6, 1906. A chamber of commerce meeting was held at the Bull Creek School. More than 300 citizens attended, despite bad weather. People came from all over the valley, and there was an emphasis on unity in order to advertise the valley, stimulate home-seekers, and secure a railroad route. As a result, 200 people enrolled in the chamber. The first humanitarian project sponsored by the chamber was a donation dance to pay to ship 30,000 pounds of potatoes to San Francisco after the earthquake of 1906. (Stites Collection, Museum of Western Colorado, Lloyd Files Research Library.)

Three

Plateau Creek and Valley Ranch Life

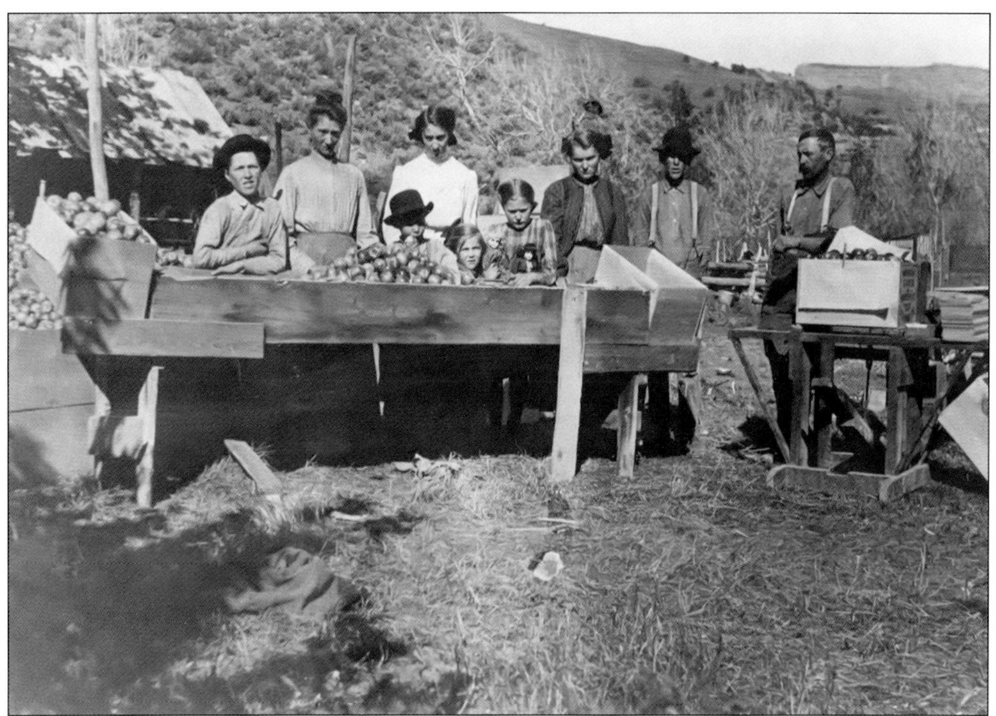

Harvest Time. This image features a family showing off their harvest. It may have been taken at Harris Ranch. Many orchards were planted in anticipation of the Colorado Midland Railway being constructed through the valley. Although the railroad did not materialize, apple orchards flourished. Varieties grown in the valley included Ganno and Ben Davis, Jonathan, Strawberry, and Wolf River. (Julia Harris Collection, Museum of Western Colorado, Lloyd Files Research Library.)

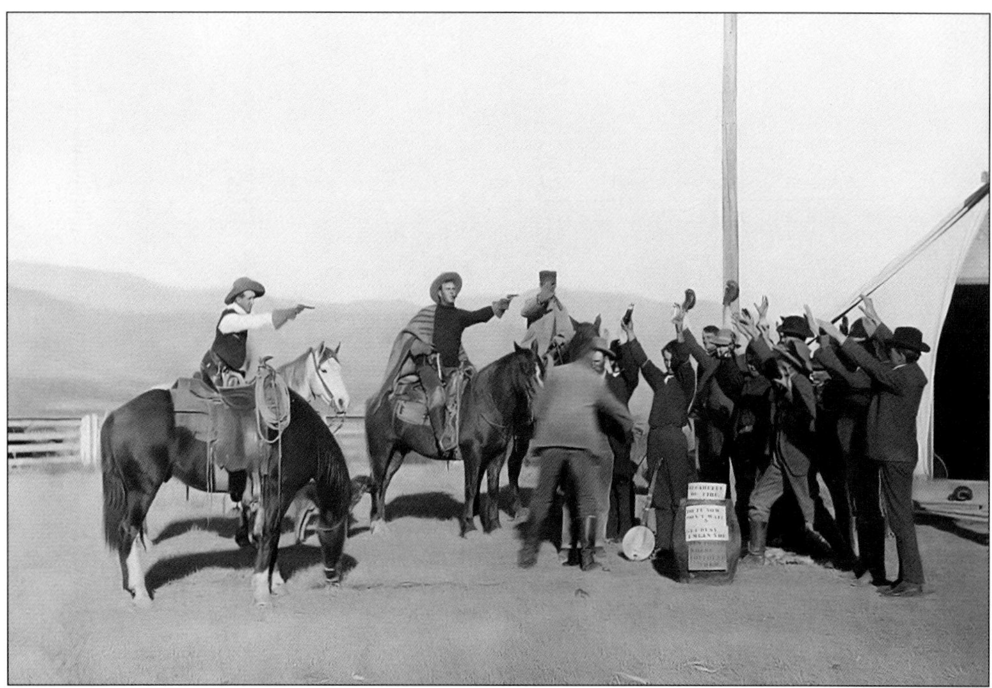

Stiles Ranch. Apparently, these photographs were taken during a Fourth of July celebration. Vernon Stiles hosted all-male parties with good food and barrels of beer. Markings on the photographs indicate that the mounted gentleman holding the gun at far left is C. Washington, the man in the derby hat holding the bottle is B.F. Pitts, the hatted and mustached boxer is Joe Long, his opponent is Willis Hodges, and the reclining man with the tennis racquet is C.B. Pitts. (Both, the Scott Walck collection.)

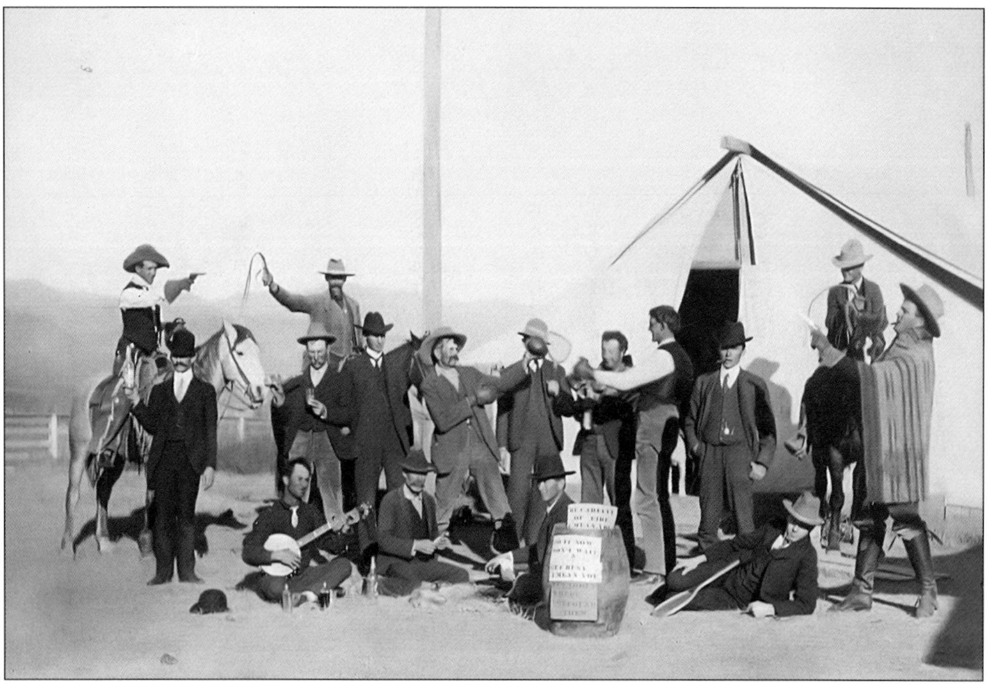

Vernon M. Stiles. Vernon Mase Stiles was an internationally renowned opera singer. His brother, Ed Stiles, was a dentist who set up a tent house in the front yard and worked at his profession while vacationing there. The Stiles family purchased their ranch from Willis Hodgson in 1899 and sold it to J.J. Long in 1912. While the property was in the Stiles family, they spent summers there. (Plateau Valley Historical Preservation Society.)

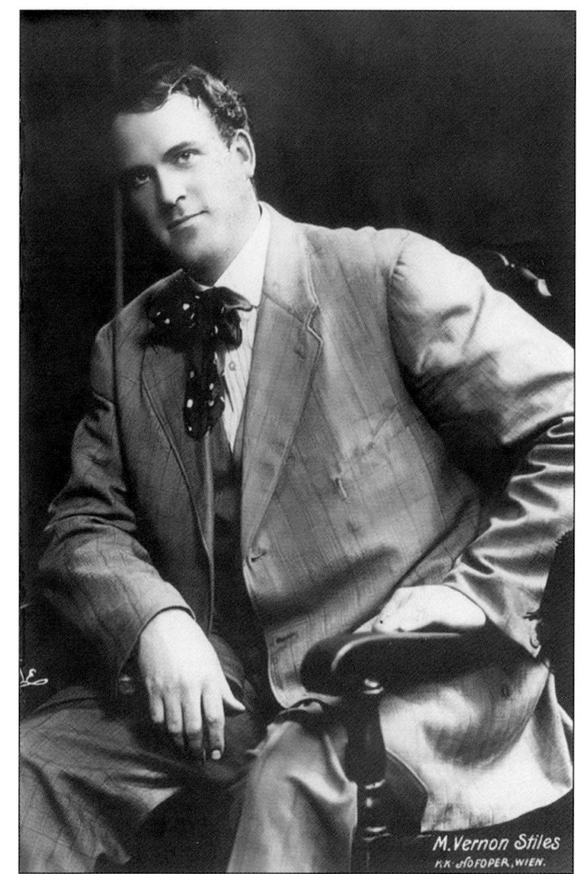

Swim Season. Neal B. Johnson is pictured here with his wife, Adelaide Rhea, to his right. The boy and the other woman to his right may be Bess Wheeler and son Danford. They are pictured in 1917 or 1918 by the new pond built for swimming and ice. Johnson was secretary of the Bull Creek Reservoir, Canal and Power Company. (Plateau Valley Historical Preservation Society.)

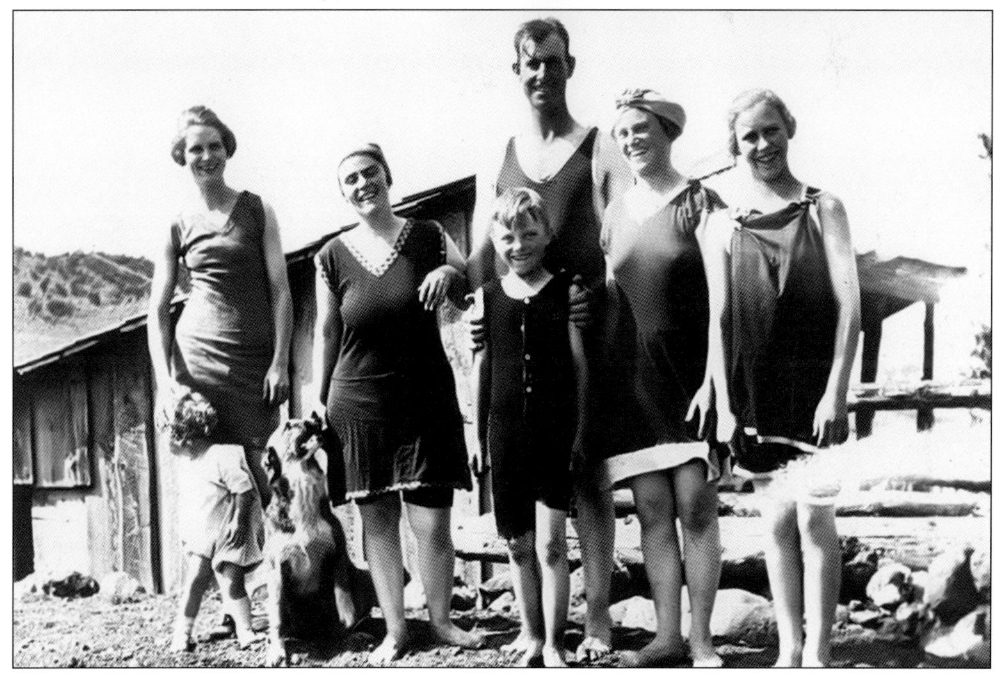

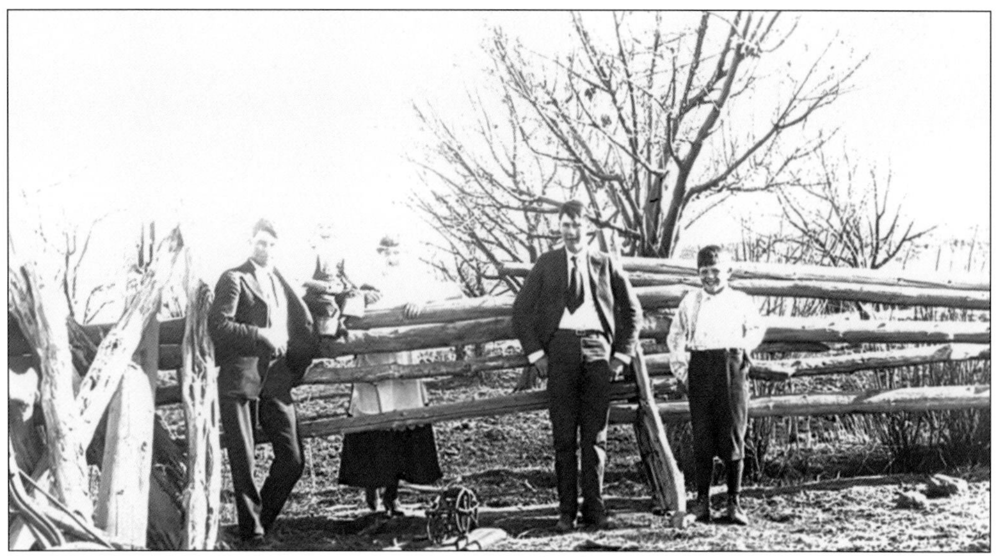

RAYMOND RANCH ON KANSAS MESA, C. 1917. A family poses in front of a rail fence at their ranch in Collbran. From left to right are Ashby Richardson, Lynn Raymond (on fence), Naomi Raymond Richardson, Rupert Raymond, and Wilbur Raymond. (Author's collection.)

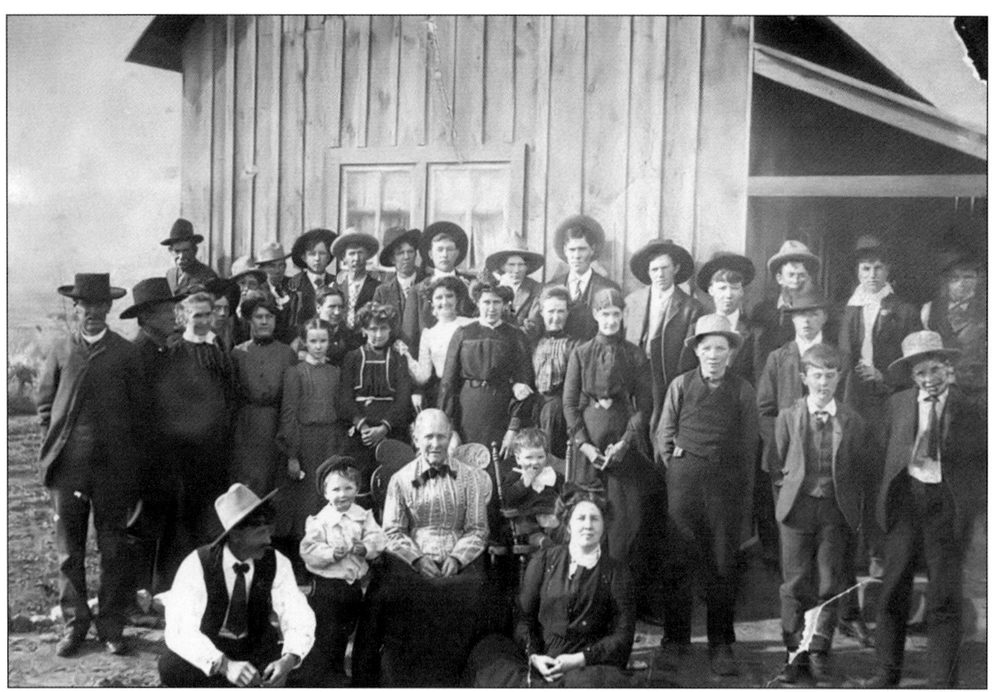

KANSAS MESA, 1903. Kansas Mesa was so named due to the large number of settlers who hailed from Linn County, Kansas. A few of the notable families include the Acas and son Tem Palmer, Edwin Hopes, the Towners, the Stites, and the Shattucks. (Plateau Valley Historical Preservation Society.)

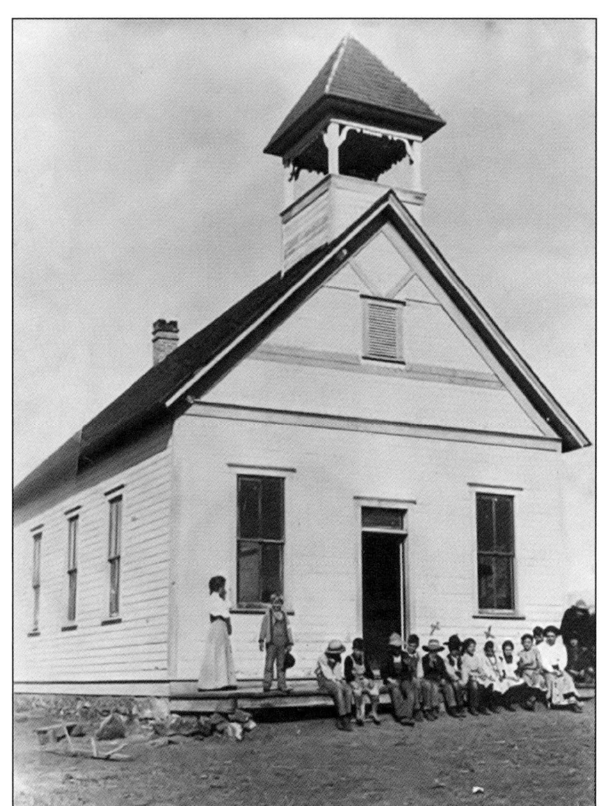

EAGALITE SCHOOL, SPRING 1895. Eagalite School was located on Kansas Mesa near Big Creek. In 1893, it was a temporary tent structure that went by the name Palmer School. It was replaced in 1894 by a log building and renamed Eagalite. It was last used as a school in 1960. Teachers included Miss Rundle (the first teacher), Eudora Stites, Johnny Conitant, Harriet Long, Mable Lee Corey, Mrs. Curtis, Miss Baldridge, Tillie Michaelson, Laura Wampler, Miss Crawford, and Dora Michaelson. One student wrote of their time there: "We had programs for parents at Christmas with a tree, treats, gift exchange and Santa. Then the last day of school we would have another program for the parents. There would also be a box-supper sometime during the winter. The school was part of the social life of people living in the district." (Both, Plateau Valley Historical Preservation Society.)

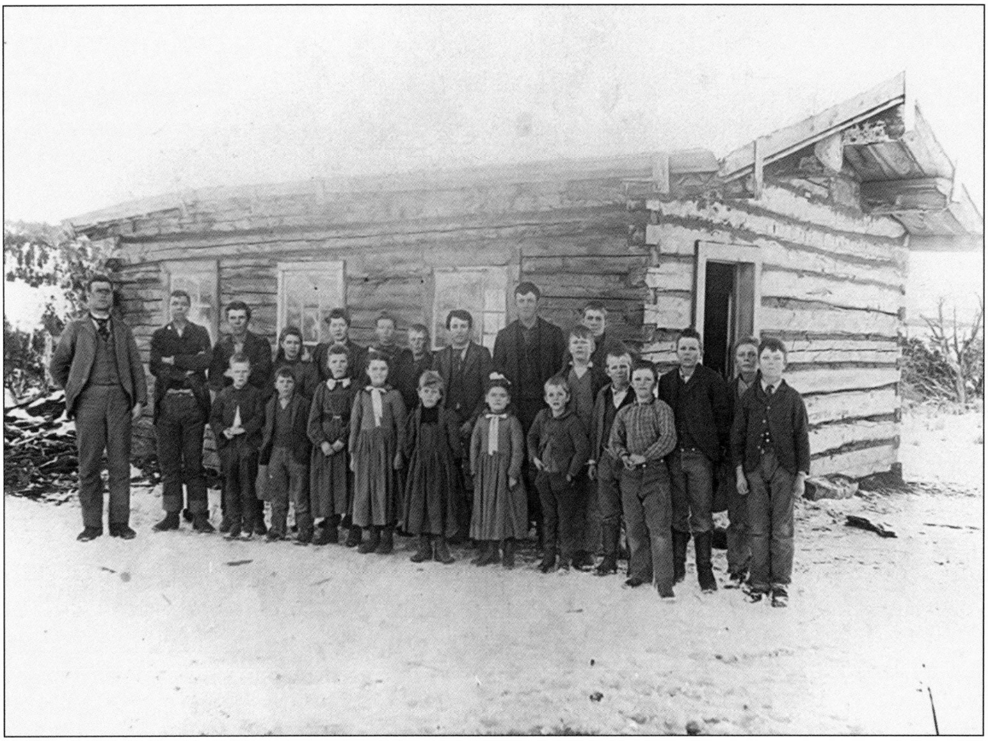

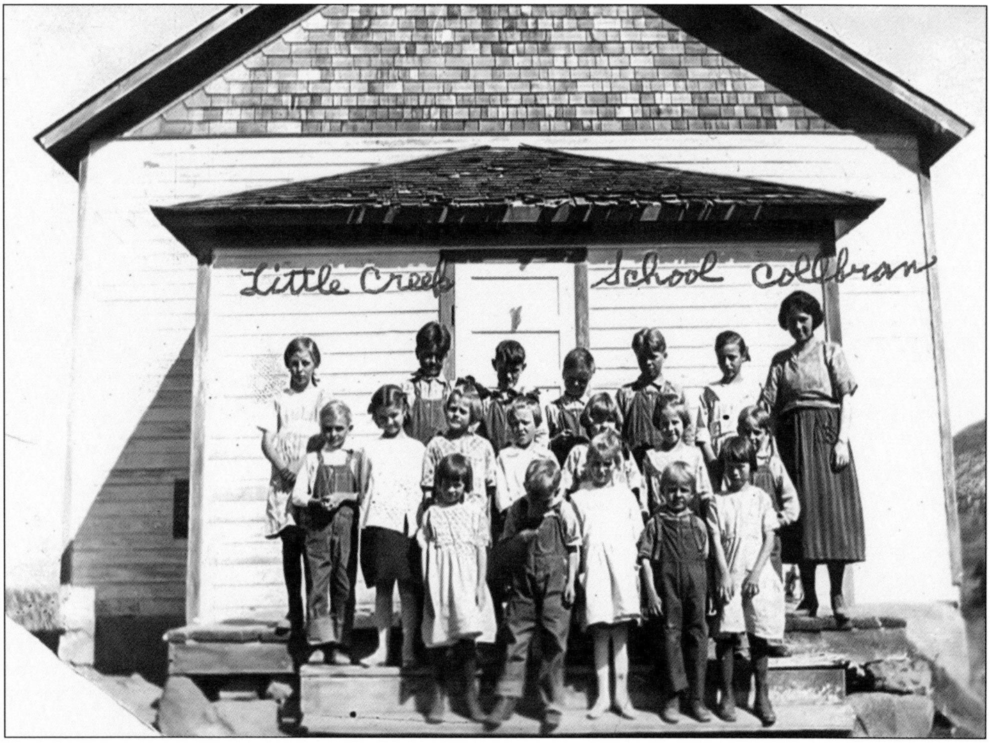

LITTLE CREEK SCHOOL, C. 1920. Above, students pose for a class photograph. Dick Silliman is third from left in the back row. The teacher and other students are not identified. The photograph below shows students at play. Little Creek School was located on Kansas Mesa. It was a one-room school until the mid-1920s. Hazel Hurd, Ruby Harris Tupper, and daughters Janet and Joan Tupper were some of the teachers. Ruby Tupper taught there the longest, giving generously of her time and talent. (Both, author's collection.)

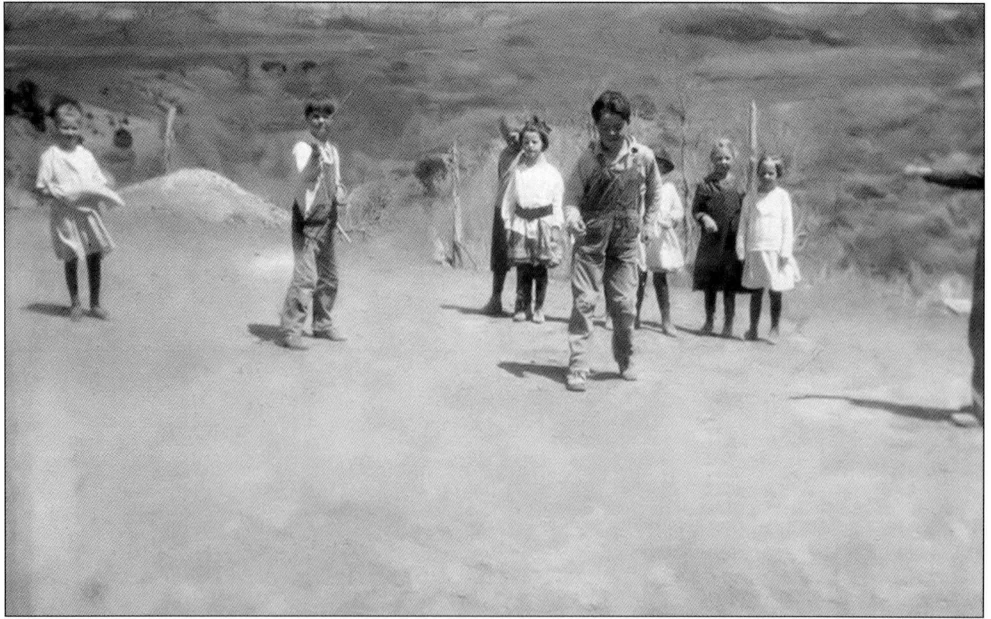

DEBEQUE CUTOFF. The DeBeque Cutoff Road was petitioned for by citizens of Plateau Valley in 1891. The petitioners were John Carmichael, A.T. Jones, S.J. Kiggins, L.B. Kirkendall, A.C. Henderson, and J.H. Jamison. According to Mesa County Courthouse records, they proposed a route from Durant Gulch to the ferry at DeBeque "following as near as possible the Old Ute Trail." The petition was accepted in 1892 and a survey of the route ordered so that bids for construction could be taken. The woman in the wagon is not identified. Below, Clyde Kelley is in the truck and Ben Nichols is in the grader. (Both, Plateau Valley Historical Preservation Society.)

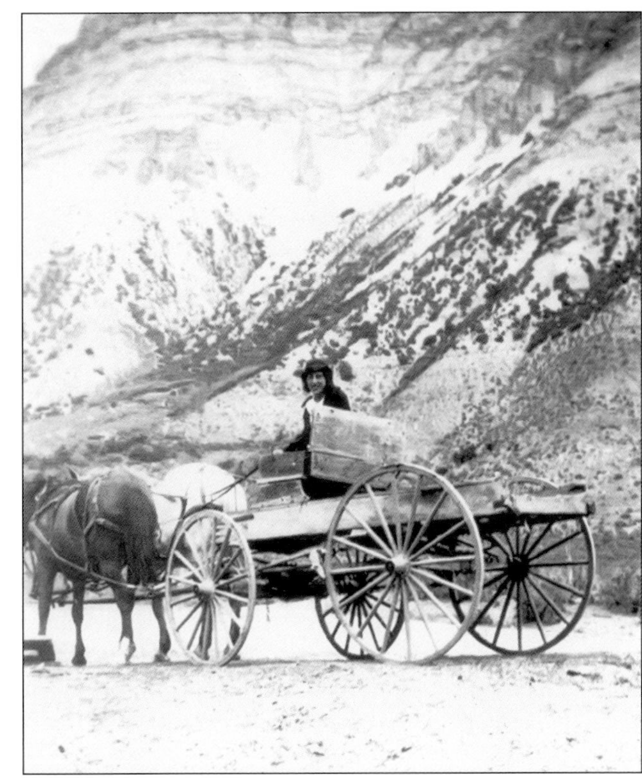

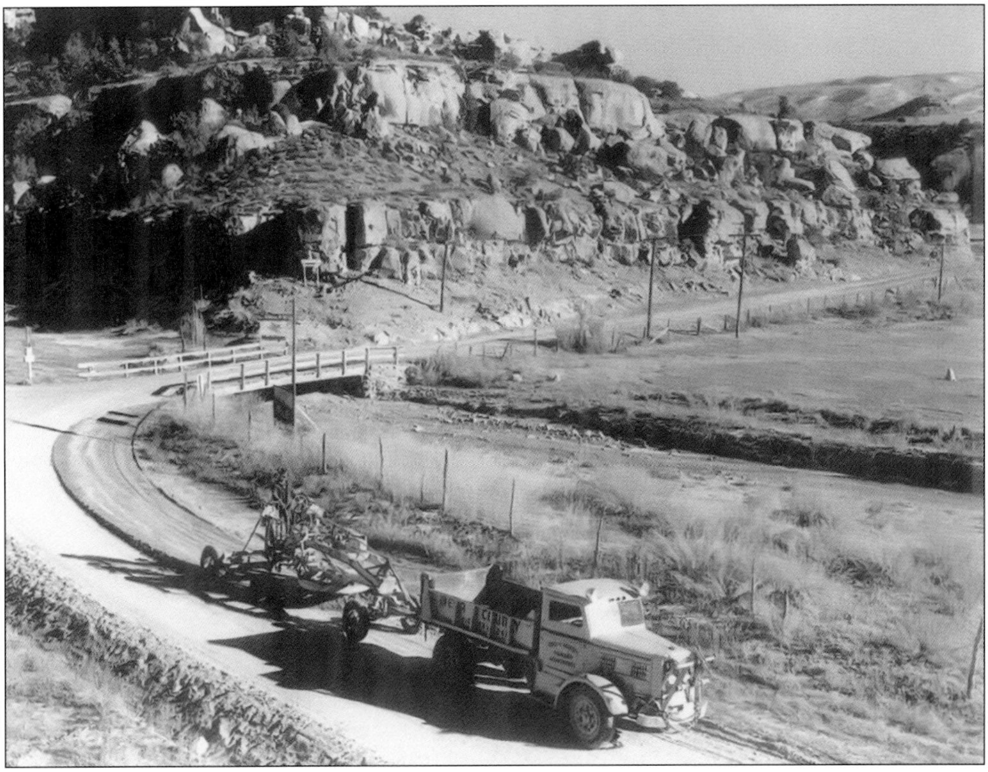

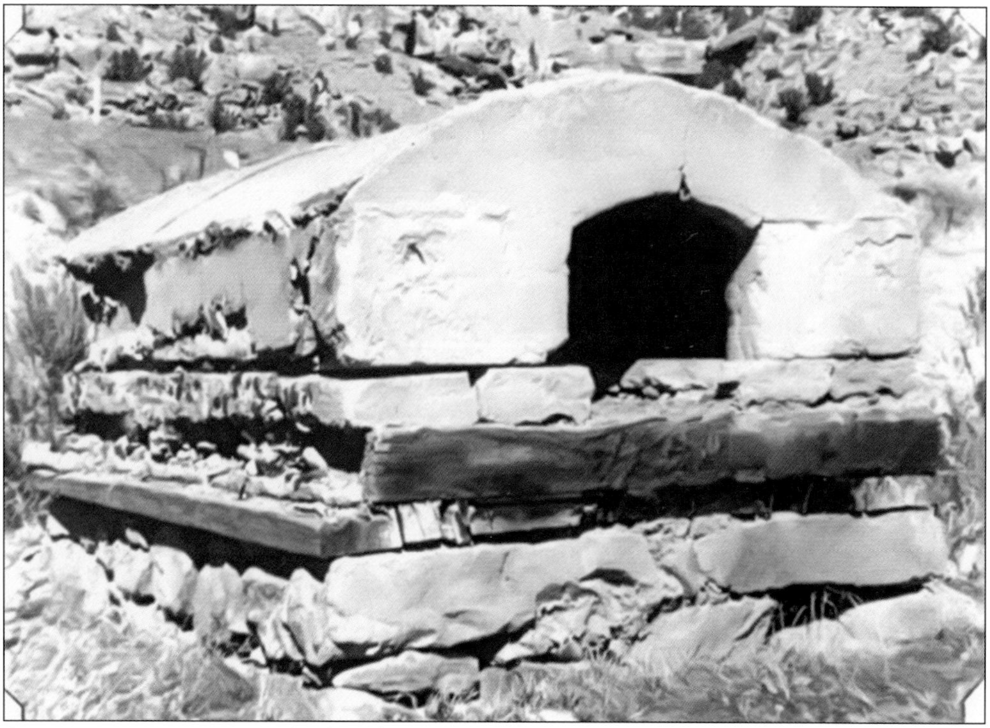

CONVICTS' BREAD OVEN. This bread oven was built in 1911 to service a road camp of convicts. It is a Mexican adobe-type oven. When the interior was heated sufficiently, the coals were raked out and the bread inserted to bake in the declining heat. Bread was baked daily from April 1911 through July 1912 to feed an encampment of 30 prisoners and their guards who built roads throughout this area. (Plateau Valley Historical Preservation Society.)

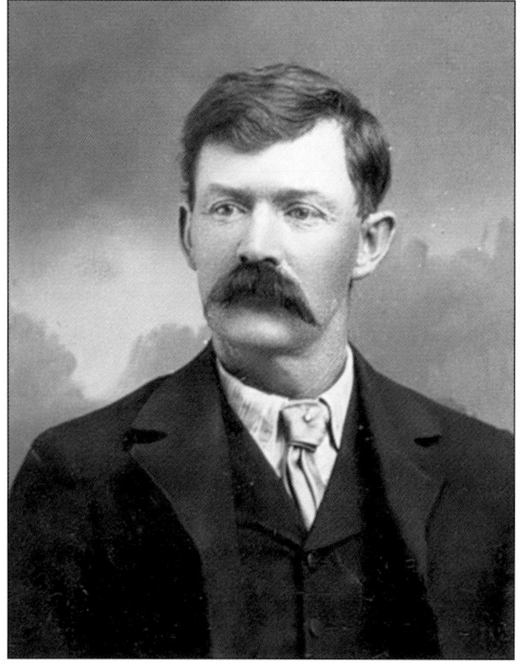

DICK MARTIN. Dick Martin owned a ranch in Plateau Valley. He was one of the earlier settlers, coming to the valley before 1890. (Plateau Valley Historical Preservation Society.)

Camprock Store. Camprock Store was located in Plateau Canyon. It was a popular rest stop for people traveling from Grand Junction to Plateau Valley. Prices at the store were said to be better than those in the bigger towns. (Plateau Valley Historical Preservation Society.)

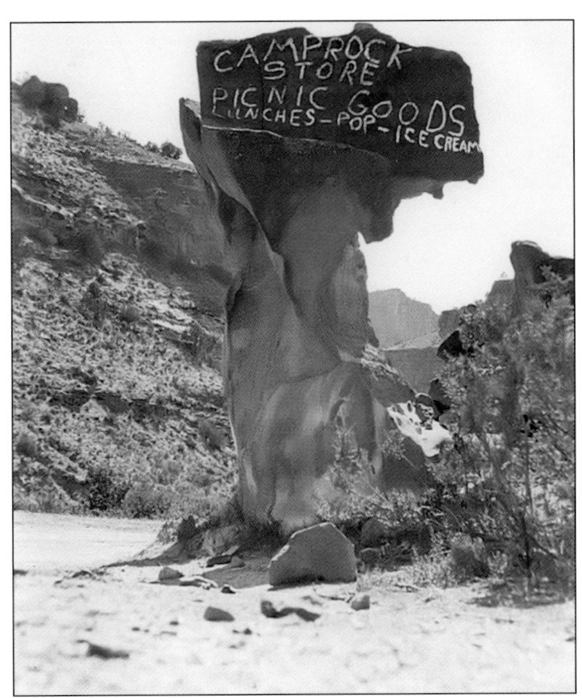

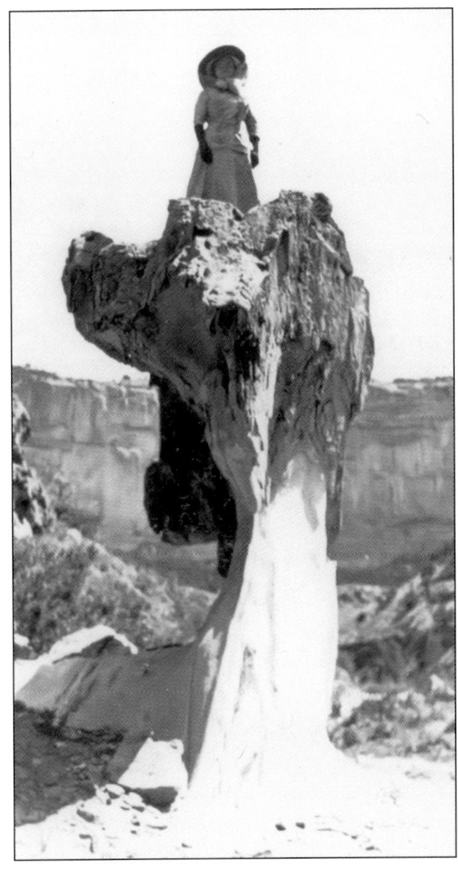

Pearl Barker at the Camprock Store. Perched on the Camprock Store sign is Pearl Barker, sister of Anna Foster. The rock sign was demolished for construction of the Plateau Creek Road. (Plateau Valley Historical Preservation Society.)

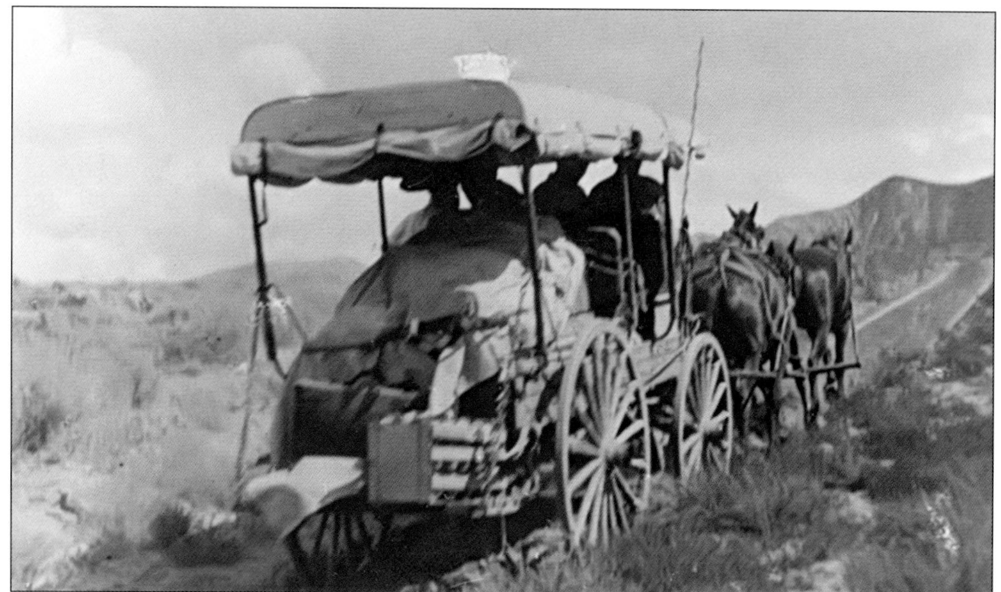

DeBeque Stage. Stage lines were a means of getting supplies and people into and out of the valley. There was daily service from the valley to DeBeque. From there, one could catch the train west to Grand Junction or east to Glenwood Springs. (Plateau Valley Historical Preservation Society.)

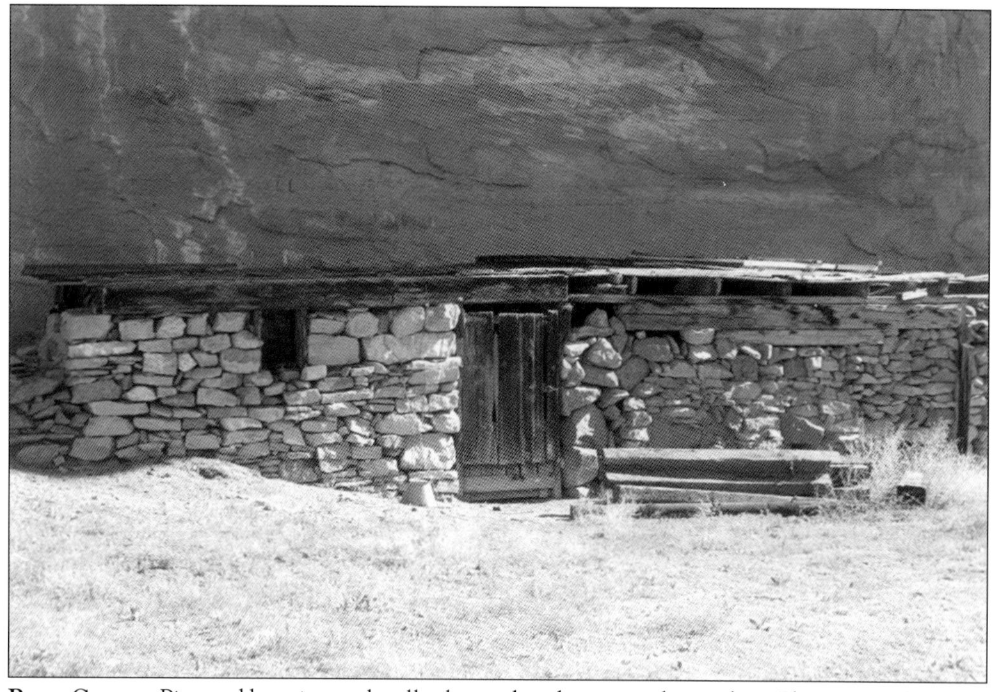

Rock Cellar. Pictured here is a rock cellar located under an overhang along Plateau Creek. Frank and Beckie Lewis, along with children Elizabeth and Richie, lived in a two-room cottonwood cabin. They had barns, sheds, and corrals, along with the notable rock cellar. It had iron bars on the window and door, giving the appearance of a jail. (Plateau Valley Historical Preservation Society.)

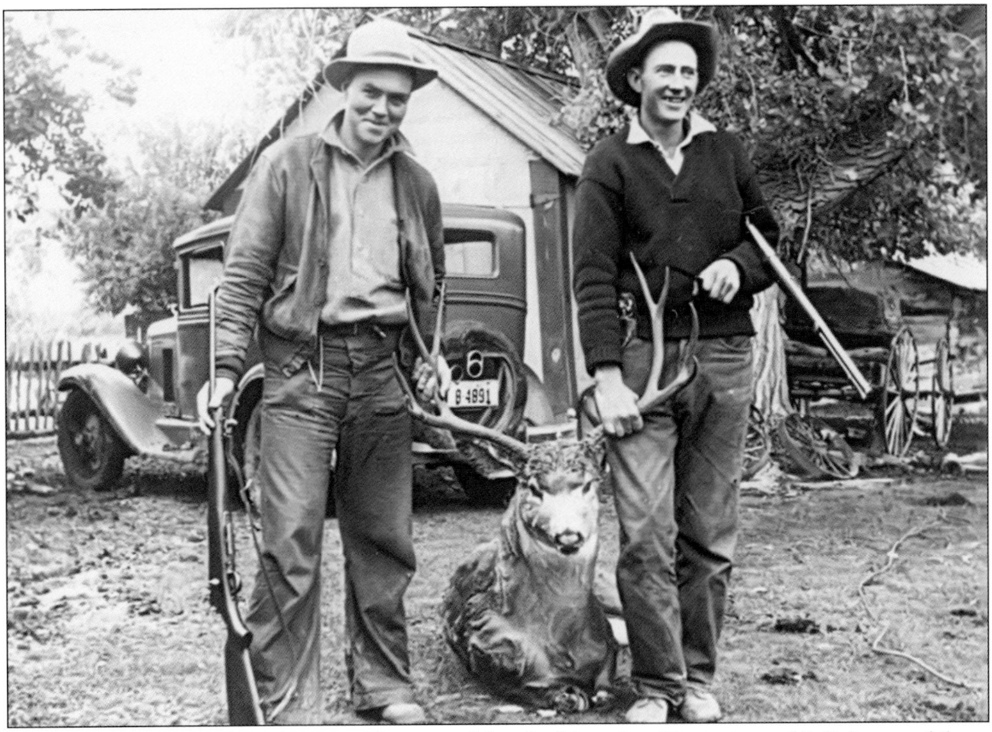

Harris Place. Joseph and Jennie Harris and family (Douglas, Virginia, and Julia) moved from DeBeque to their ranch on Plateau Creek in 1904. They purchased the ranch from Charles and Susan Jackson, parents of Jennie Harris. The ranch consisted of two log cabins and a cottonwood barn. In 1907, a large barn was built for freight teams. In 1912, a cement house was constructed. (Plateau Valley Historical Preservation Society.)

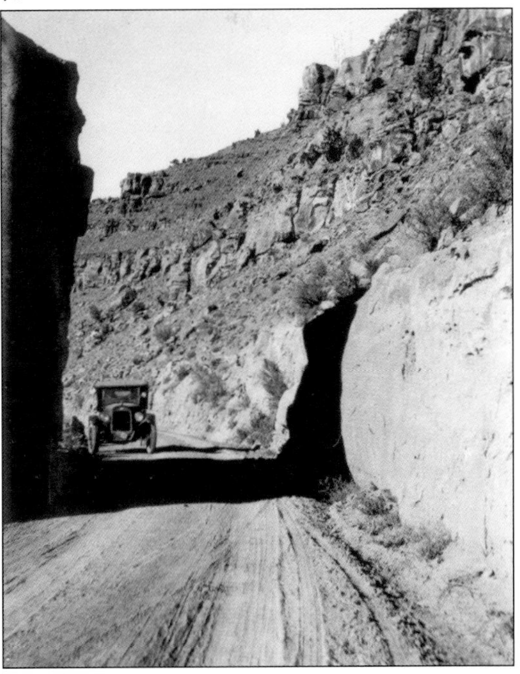

Large Rocks on Plateau Canyon Road. Even after the road was moved to the north side of the creek, it was still poor. It was narrow in places, steep at times, and had several blind curves. Falling rocks were also a problem. Many travelers had to roll rocks off in order to get through. With a large rock, it was common courtesy for the first man with a team to throw a chain around it and drag it from the road. (Plateau Valley Historical Preservation Society.)

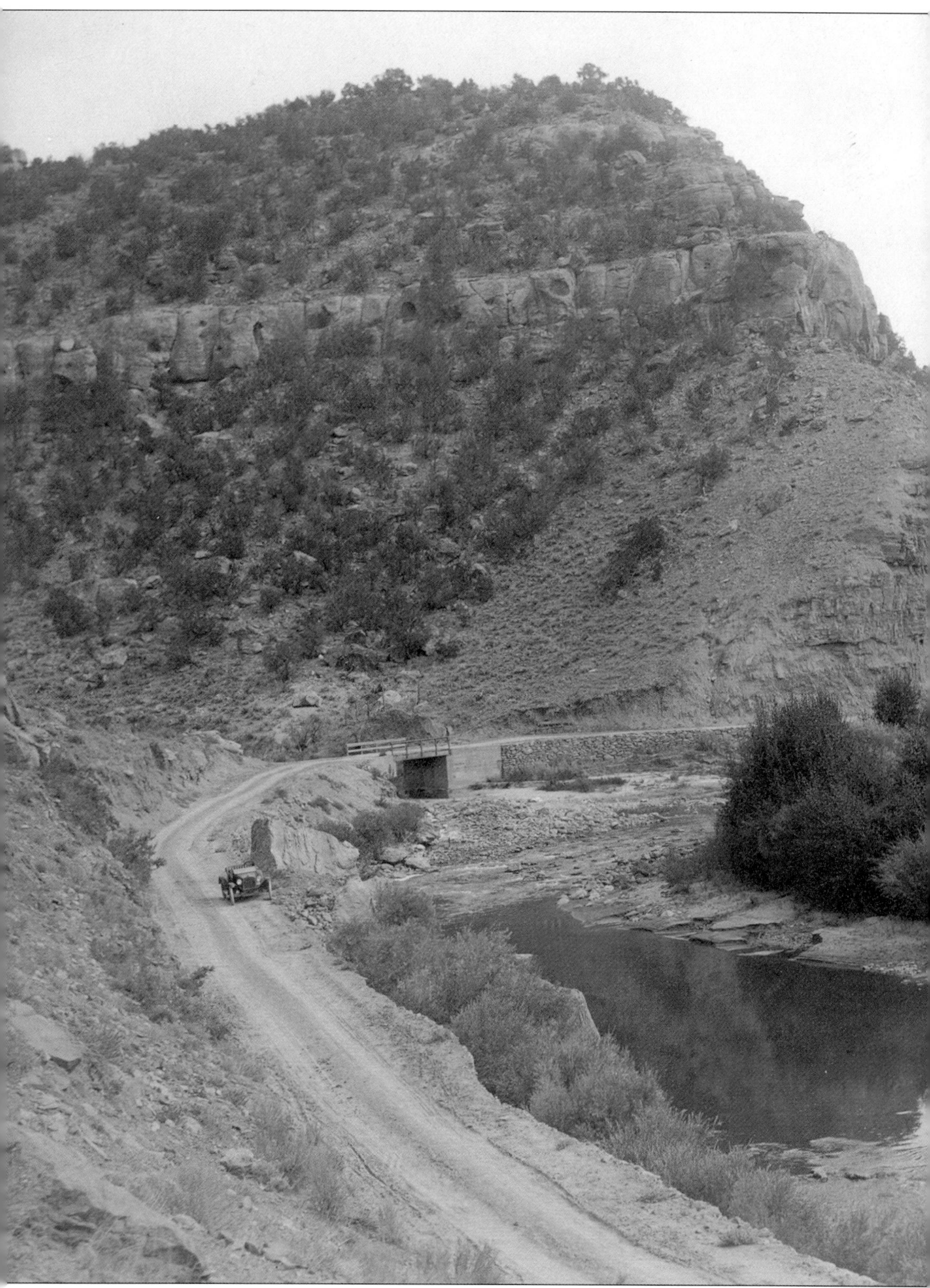

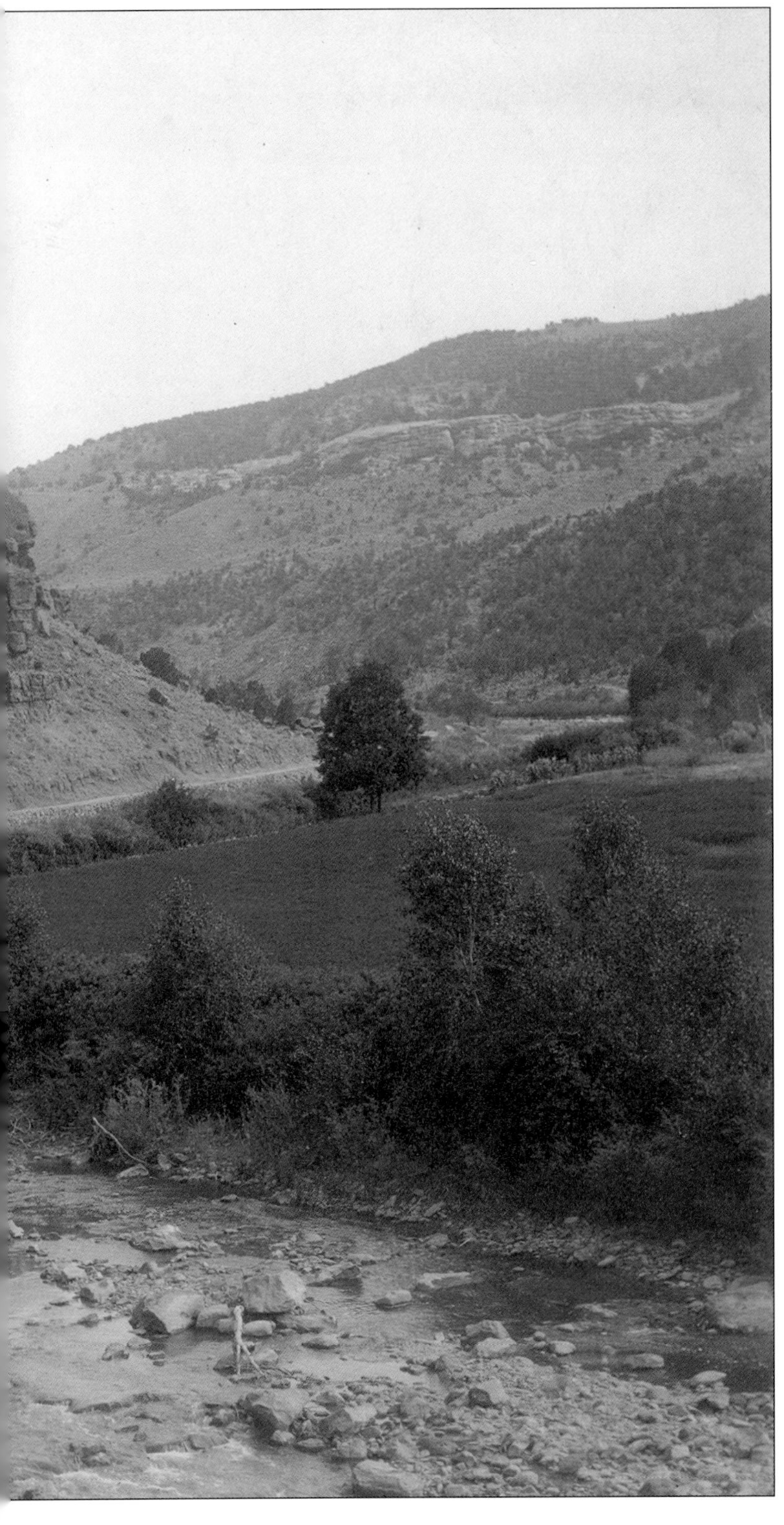

Plateau Canyon Road. Tom Kitson claimed to have been the first person through Plateau Canyon with a team and wagon; afterwards, he insisted that a road could be built from the Harris Ranch to Cameo. In 1894, a contract was given to the Baldridge brothers to build a road on the south side of Plateau Creek. Four bridges were placed along the route, none of which were sturdy enough to withstand floods and spring runoff. In 1910, prison convicts were used to construct a road on the north side of the creek. Hand tools were used during the construction. It was open for travel by 1912. This photograph, taken in 1913, features a Saxon Roadster driven by Jim Bertholf. Henry Nichols was his passenger. (Museum of Western Colorado, Lloyd Files Research Library.)

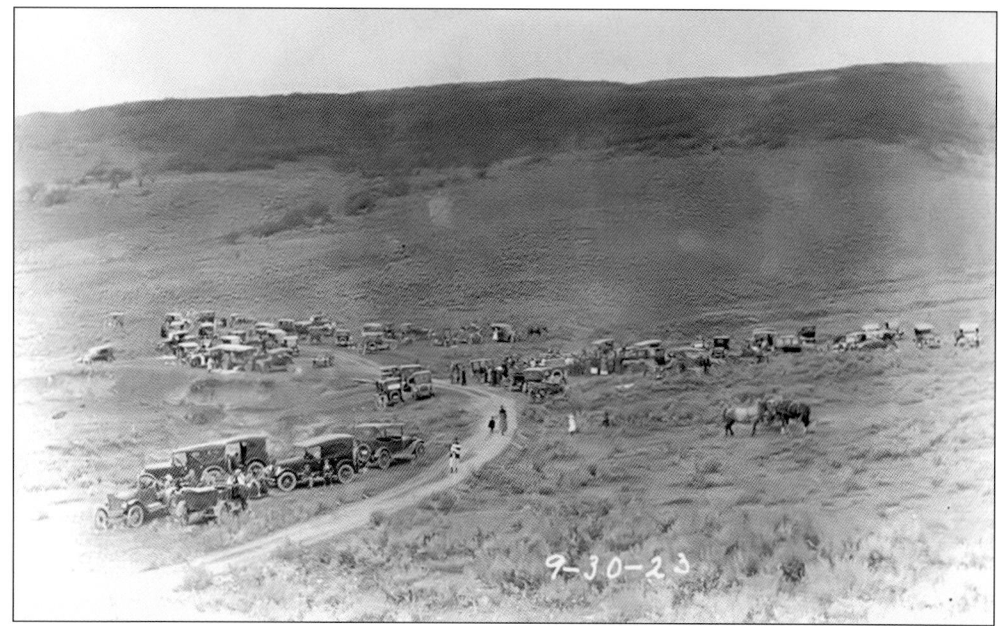

Silt Cutoff. The grand opening of the Silt Cutoff was celebrated on September 30, 1923. The Collbran-to-Silt road was touted as a commercial benefit to both Plateau Valley and Silt. Residents from both sides of the divide that separates Silt from Plateau Valley gathered to celebrate the great accomplishment that connected Garfield and Mesa Counties. (Plateau Valley Historical Preservation Society.)

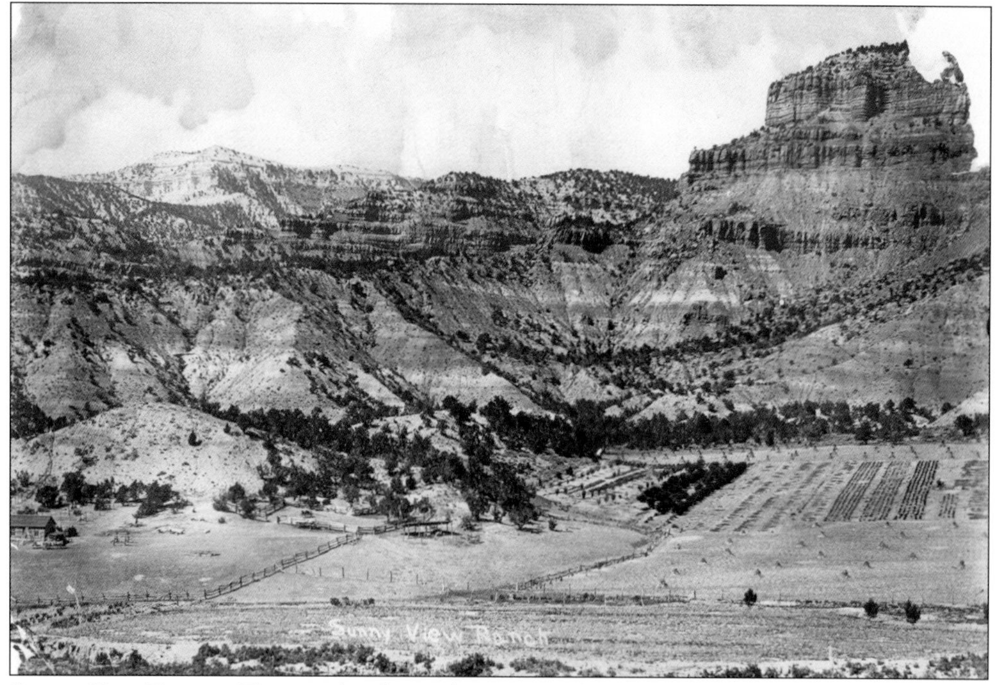

Sunny View Ranch. This ranch is located in Sunnyside, near Durant Gulch. It was reportedly a truck farm. Truck farms provide a steady supply of a wide range of fresh fruits and vegetables throughout the local growing season. (Plateau Valley Historical Preservation Society.)

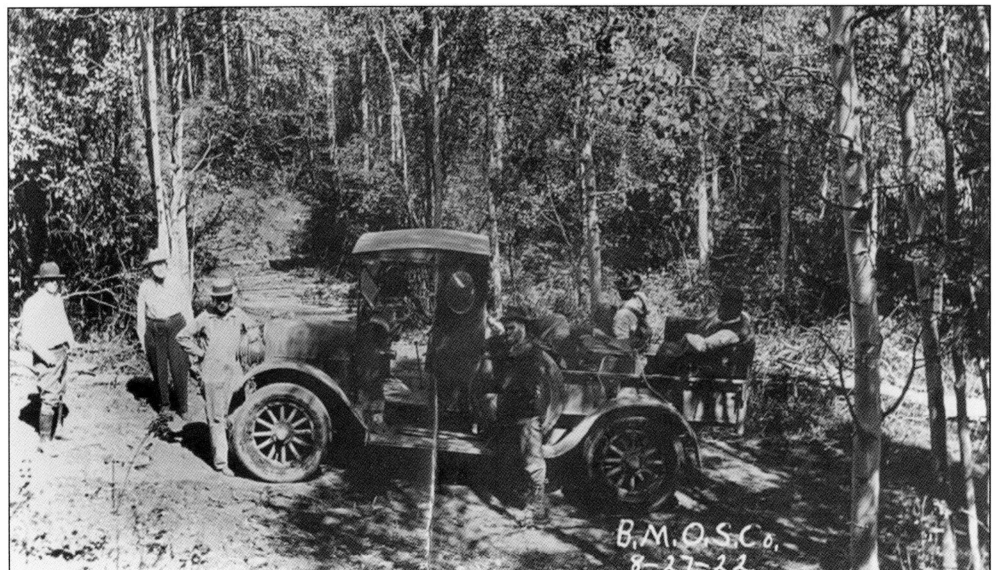

Battlement Mesa Oil Shale Company. This photograph shows a truck on Brush Creek. The initials on the picture, B.M.O.S.C., stand for Battlement Mesa Oil Shale Company. Charles Mattingly worked on Brush Creek conducting shale claim work. In 1917, the *Plateau Voice* was agitating for immediate attention—systematic, intelligent attention—towards securing capital to sink a well somewhere in the Plateau Valley area. (Plateau Valley Historical Preservation Society.)

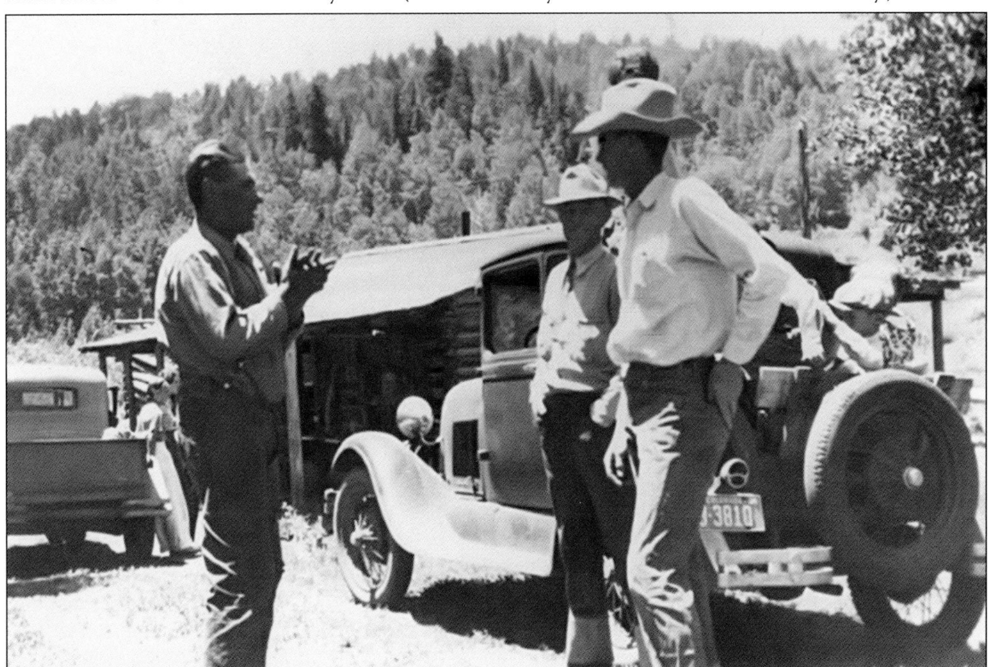

Oil Well Camp. Pictured here are Walt Carmichael and Lee Armour at an oil well camp on Buzzard and Crooked Creeks. In 1920, the *Plateau Voice* reported that operations at the oil field were expected to continue as fast as possible, according to Frank Smith, who was expected to take charge of the work. The well was operated by the Mesa Oil and Gas Co. (Plateau Valley Historical Preservation Society.)

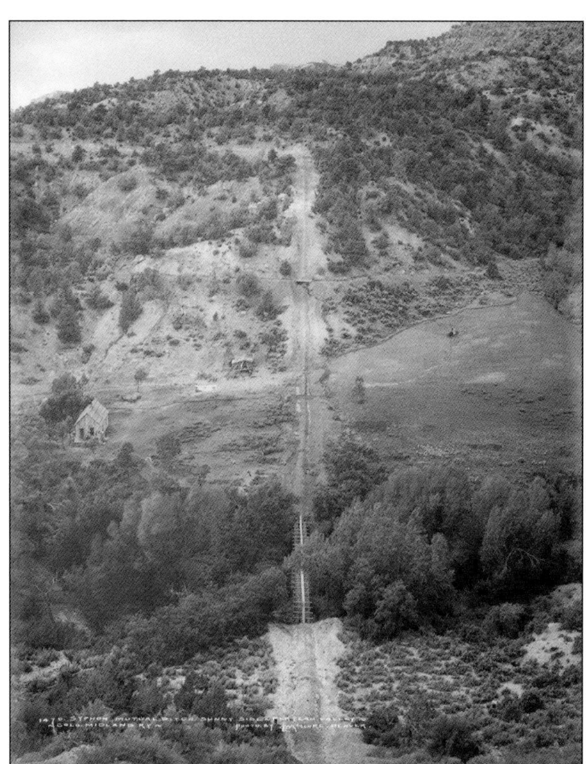

Mutual Ditch Siphon, c. 1910s. The Siphon Mutual Ditch was in Sunnyside, in Plateau Valley, and reached via Colorado Midland Railway. The dirt-covered and uncovered wooden flume extended down the hillside and across a small ravine. The image shows a small wood-frame residence, with a sod-roof cellar or shed in the hillside, and a man on horseback talking to people in a small, cultivated field. (Denver Public Library, Western History Collection [Call MCC-1470].)

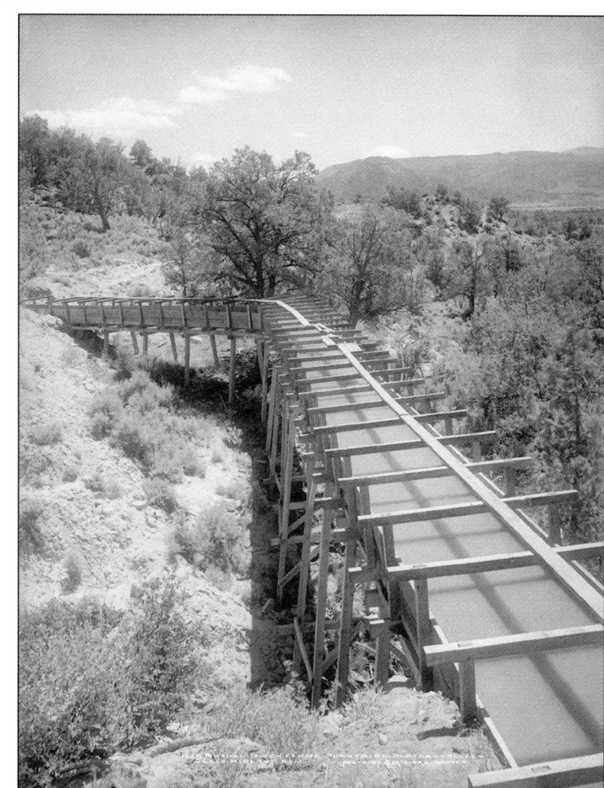

Mutual Ditch Flume, c. 1910s. The elevated wooden Mutual Ditch irrigation flume in Sunnyside is seen here with the mesa in the background. (Denver Public Library, Western History Collection [Call MCC-1468].)

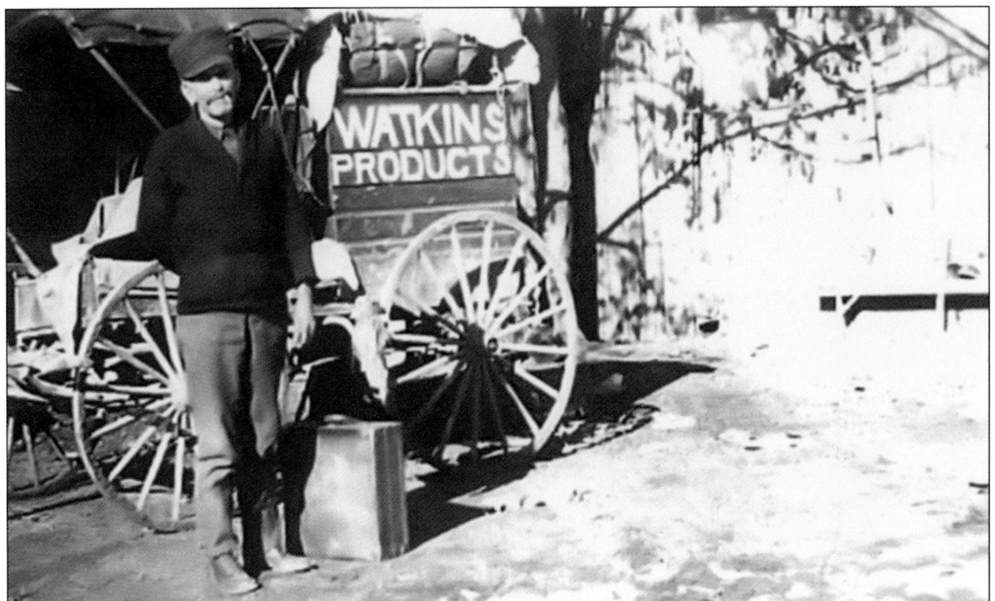

Lee Armour, c. 1940s. Lee Armour was a team boss on the Shoshone Dam project in Glenwood Canyon. After returning to Plateau Valley in 1909, he ran a freight service from DeBeque and Grand Junction. He also sold Watkins Products door to door from his wagon. When automobiles gained popularity, he purchased a wood saw and sawed wood for people, eventually catching his hand in the saw and injuring it badly. (Plateau Valley Historical Preservation Society.)

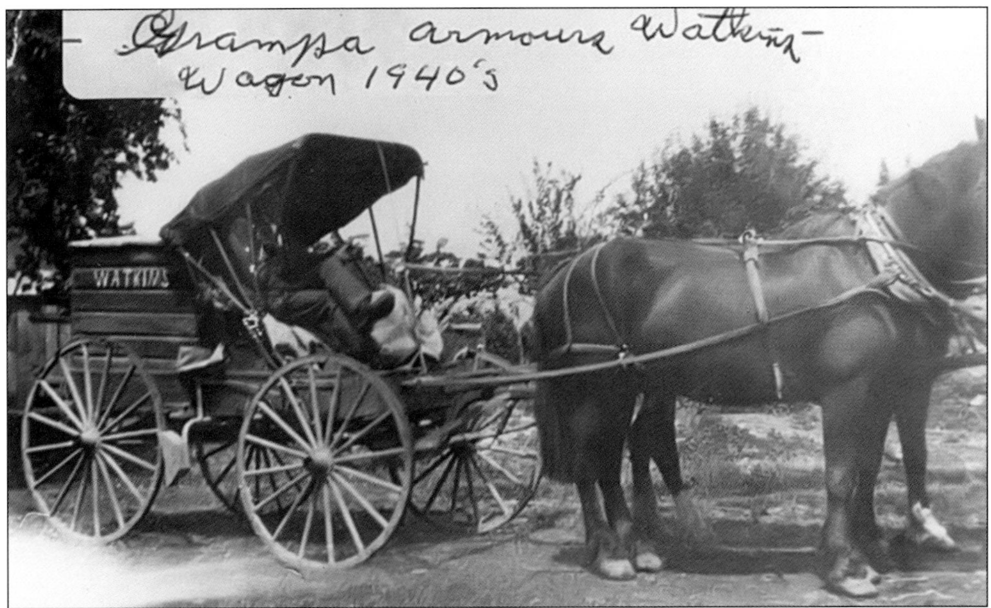

Lee Armour's Watkins Wagon. Armour covered Kansas Mesa, Parker Basin, Mormon Mesa, Georgia Mesa, Bull Creek, and Mesa. Then he would go across DeBeque Cutoff to Blue Stone and up Roan Creek, then on to Grand Valley (Parachute), up the river to Silt, across to Divide Creek, and over Silt Cutoff before working his way back home. He made the trip at least twice a year. In these photographs, he appears to be hiding his injured hand from the camera. (Plateau Valley Historical Preservation Society.)

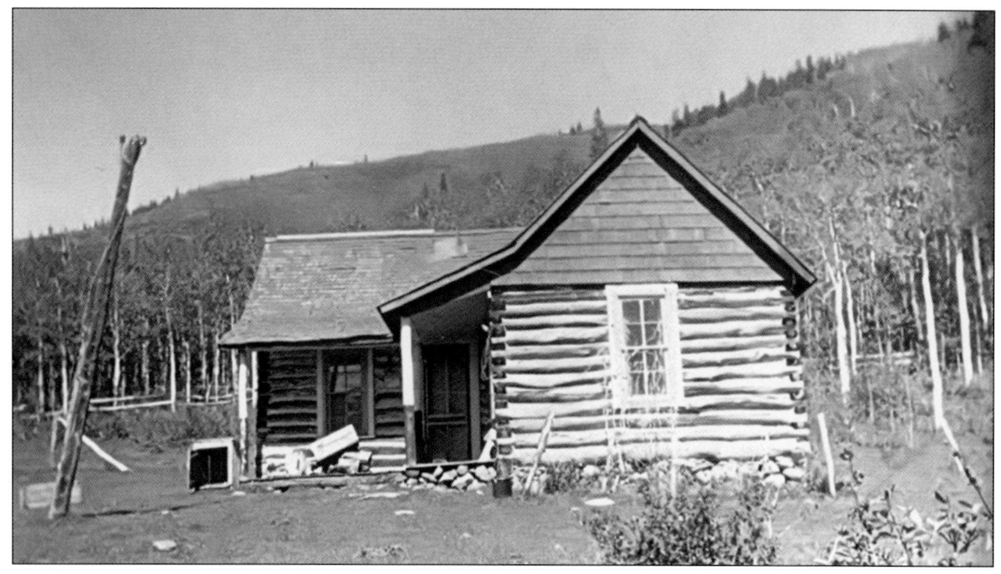

Cow Camp. Basic chores at a cow camp consisted of keeping the water bucket full, keeping the wood box full, washing the dishes, sweeping the floor, and jingling the horses in the morning and turning them out at night, in addition to anything else that needed tending. Breakfast consisted of steak, biscuits, and oatmeal. Everyone made his own lunch. Night meals included roast beef, boiled potatoes, a vegetable, coffee, and applesauce. The following night might consist of boiled beef and noodles or a stew. There was always jam or jelly for the biscuits. Big Creek Cow Camp is pictured above; Hawxhurst Cow Camp is pictured below. (Both, Plateau Valley Historical Preservation Society.)

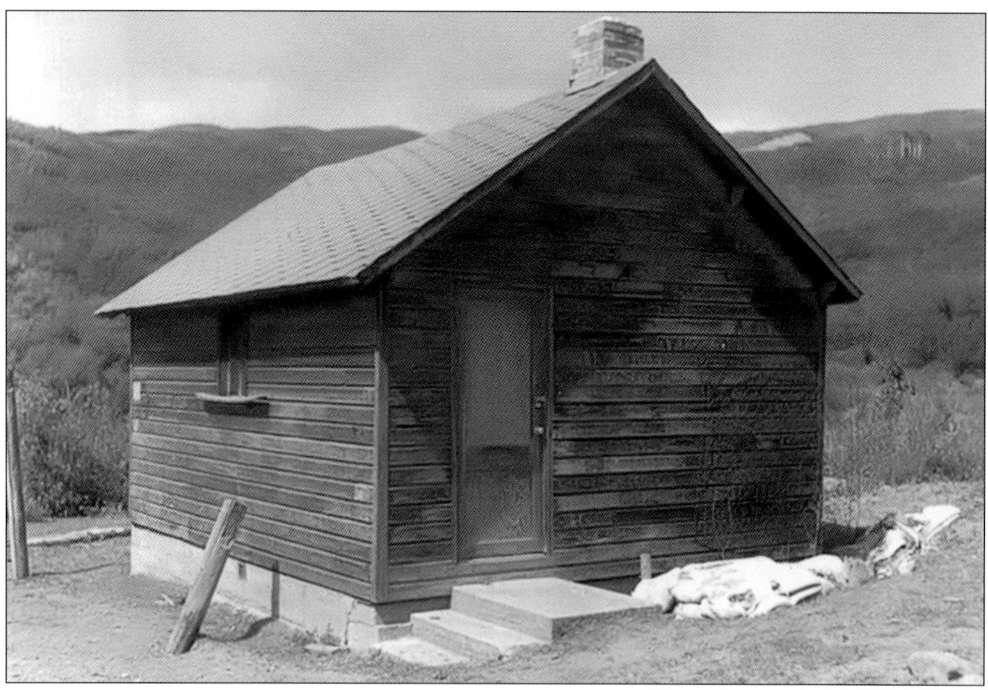

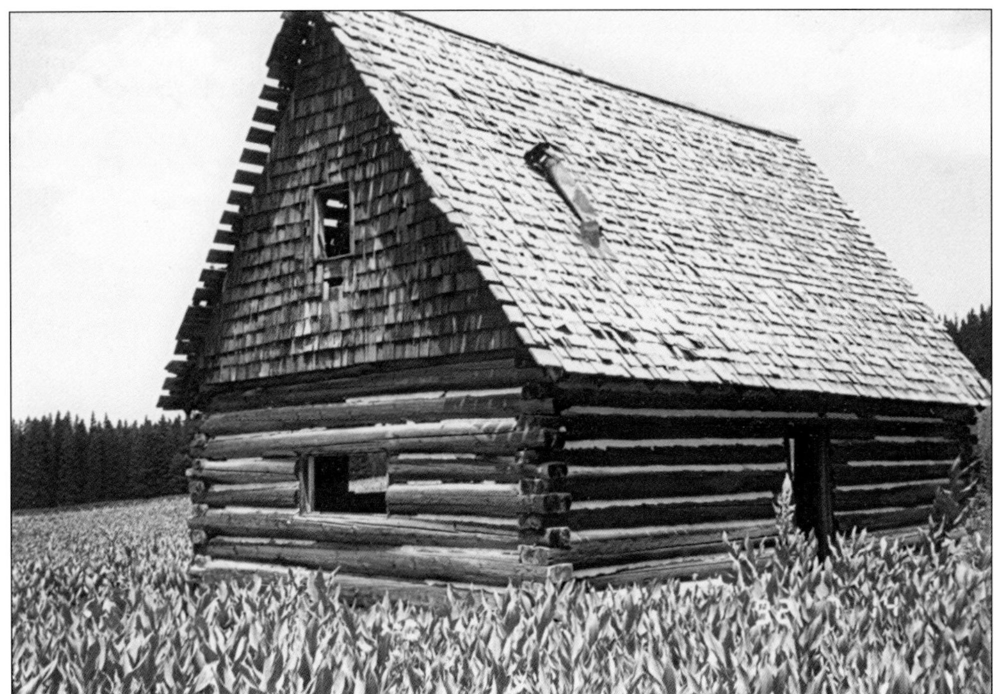

Raber Cow Camp. Raber Cow Camp was used by the Raber family from the 1930s until 1966. The cow camp was occupied during the summers, when the family moved cattle from the nearby lowlands to the well-watered grasslands on top of Grand Mesa. Winifred Raber stayed at the cow camp every summer. (Plateau Valley Historical Preservation Society.)

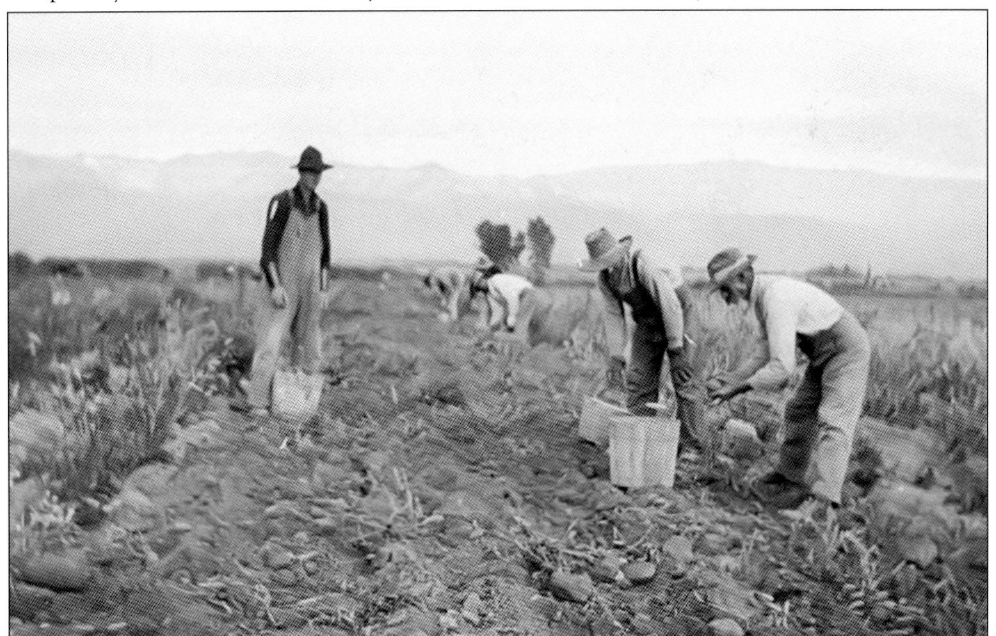

Potato Picking in Parker Basin. In the early years, potatoes were dug by hand or using a walking plow. In later years, implements were developed that aided in the harvest. Potatoes were stored in a dirt cellar, which was often the first structure built on a homestead. (Scott Walck collection.)

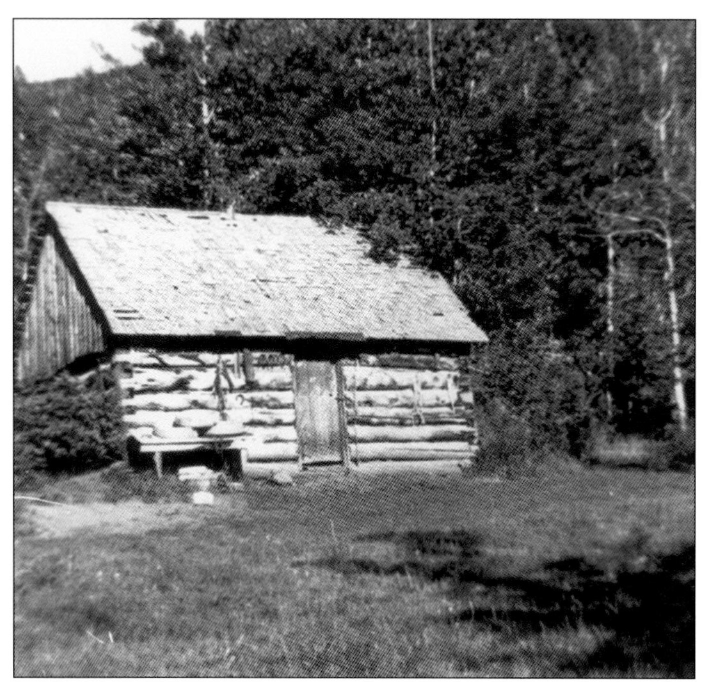

Leon Allotment. Dean Walck remembered going to the Park Creek Cow Camp in 1934: "We drove the old Model A to the Meadows, now known as Vega. We went to Charley Campbell's house to get horses. Probably some of the horses belonged to my dad because at that time, people would leave horses where they were going to use them next. . . . We stayed at the old Park Creek Ranger Station. It was used as a cow camp for many years after that." (Plateau Valley Historical Preservation Society.)

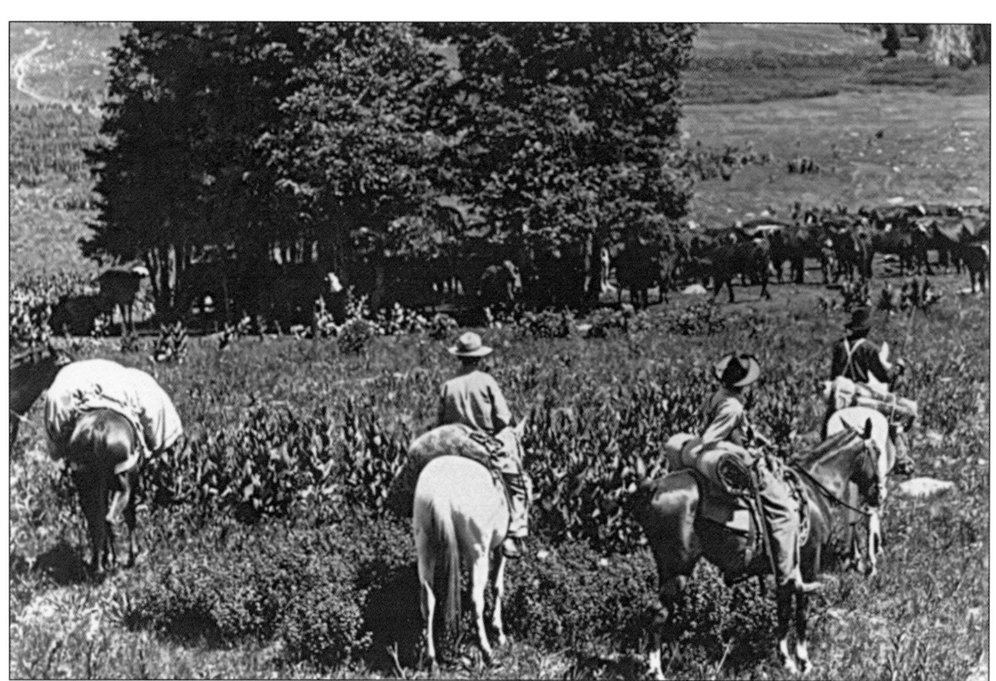

Riders on the Leon Allotment. Riders are pictured cutting off cattle on Rock Creek Bunch Ground at the head of Rock Creek. This area is part of the Leon allotment. (Plateau Valley Historical Preservation Society.)

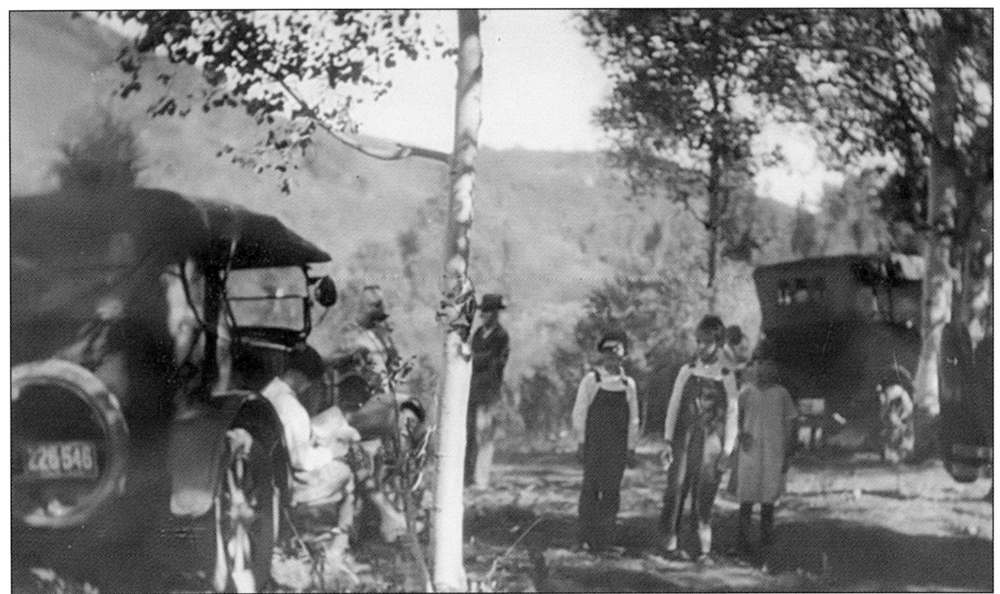

Griffith Ranch, Buzzard Creek. Pictured in the c. 1927 photograph above are, from left to right, Ray Hittle and Jack and Rose Griffith. Below, many from the Griffith and Hittle family pose for the camera at the farmhouse on Buzzard Creek. According to *History Colorado*, Jess Hittle, father of Ray Hittle, bought 289 acres of land near Collbran in 1914. Jess and his wife, Alice, formed a cow and calf operation, raising crops as well. Their son Ray and his wife, Helen, bought the ranch on December 25, 1951, and their son Less and his wife, Loi, bought the ranch on December 24, 1980. Several buildings from 1923 are still in place and in use, including the farmhouse, chicken coop, gas house, milk barn, and horse barn. (Both, Griffith family collection.)

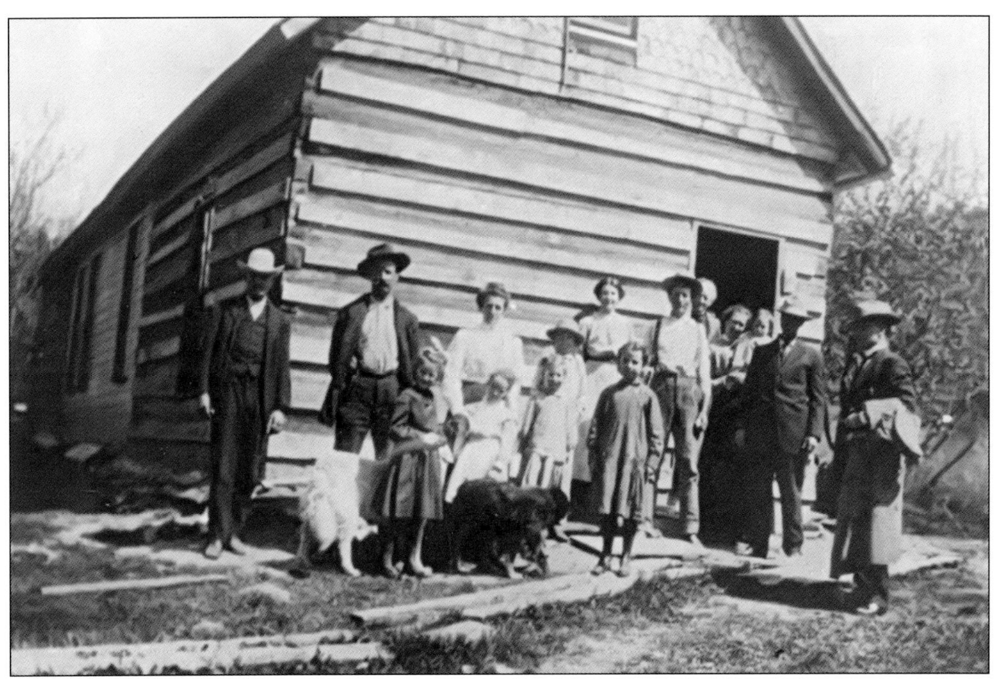

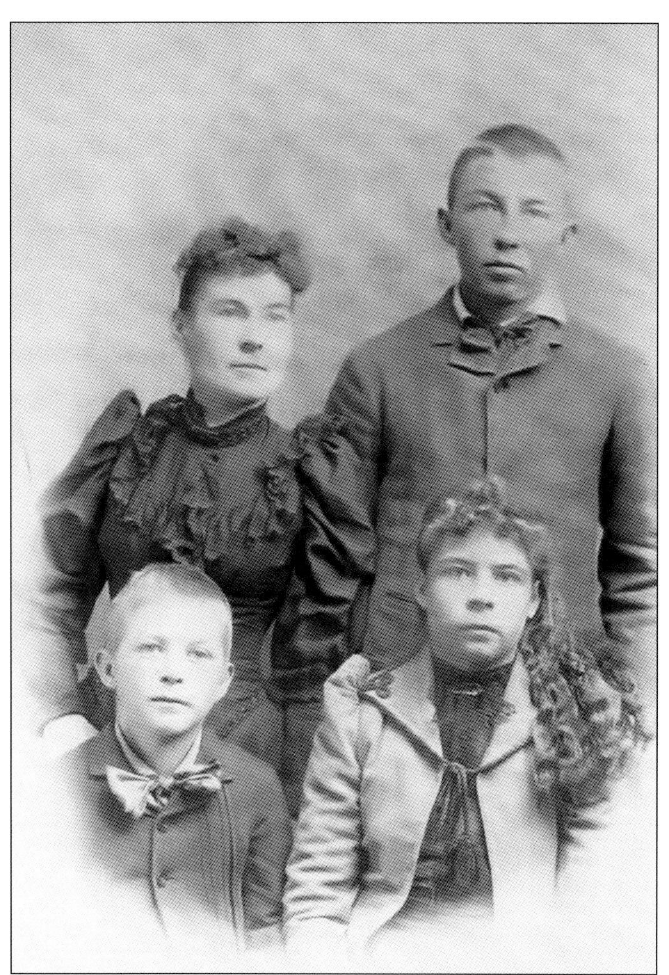

Cline Family. Mrs. E.M. Cline was often mentioned in the *Plateau Voice* for decorating community buildings and businesses. She papered and decorated the storeroom of the Collbran House Furnishing Co. and painted the church. Her children, pictured here, went to Clover School. (Plateau Valley Historical Preservation Society.)

Cline Claim. Pictured here is the Cline Claim in Grand Mesa National Forest. The land was applied for by James W. Cline. This photograph was taken from the west side of the claim showing practically all the land within it. (Plateau Valley Historical Preservation Society.)

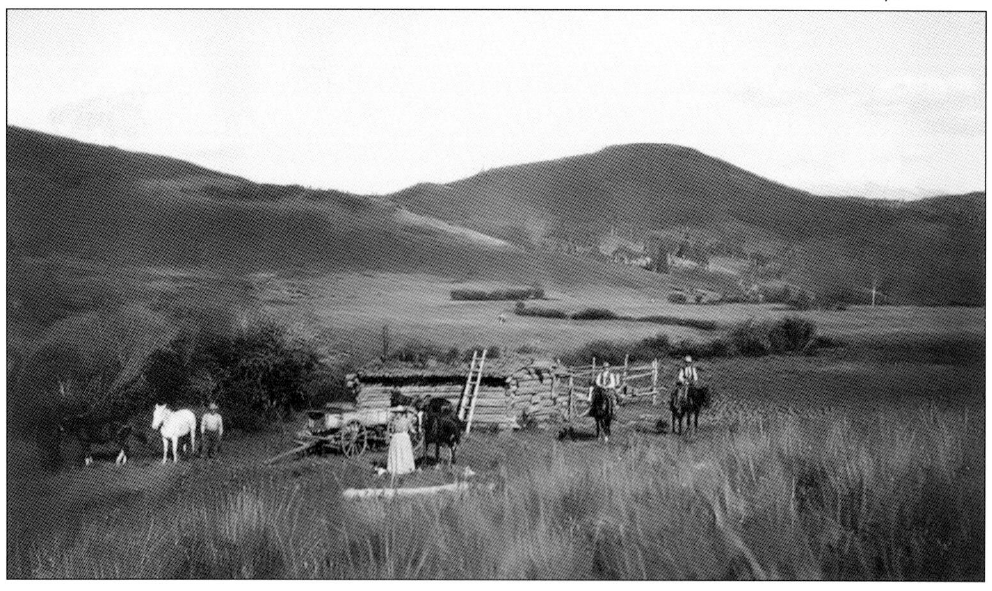

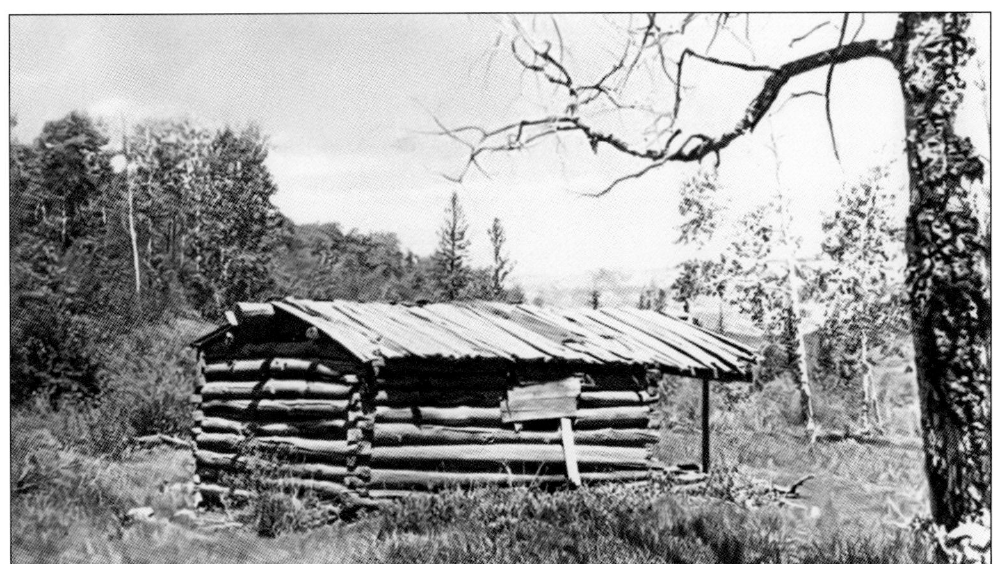

Dave Jones's Cabin. This cabin is located south of Man Mountain, along the Bonham Reservoir Road. Dave Jones was a popular thresher operator in the valley. This area is now the Twin Peaks Bible Camp, founded in 1950. (Plateau Valley Historical Preservation Society.)

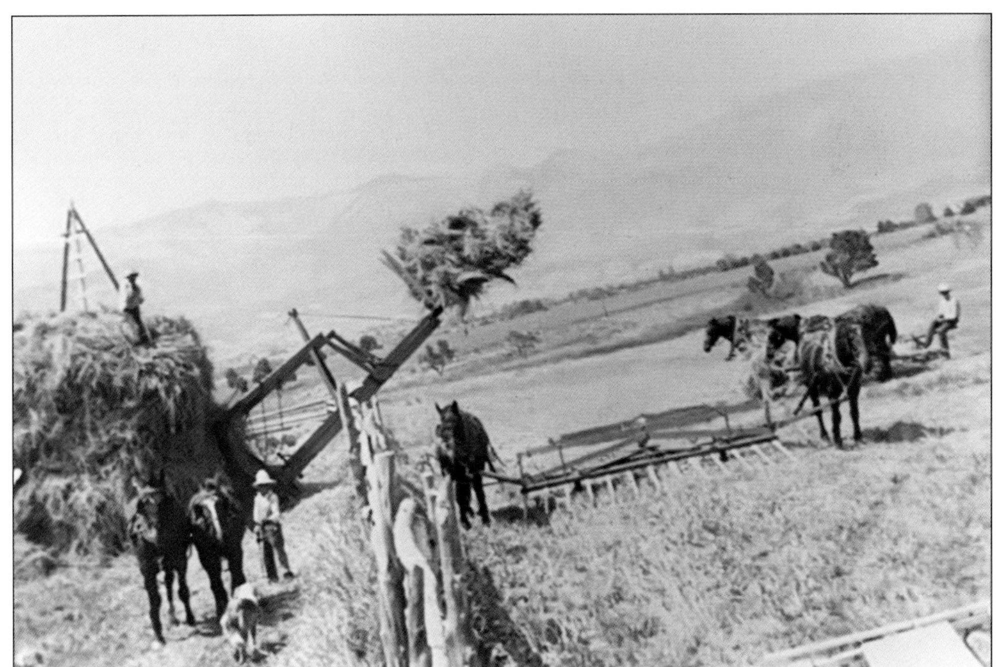

Hay Stacker. This overshot stacker is at Maigatter Ranch on Kansas Mesa. Fred Maigatter walked into Plateau Valley around 1892. He amassed 80 acres, raised cattle, and sold truck farm produce. (Plateau Valley Historical Preservation Society.)

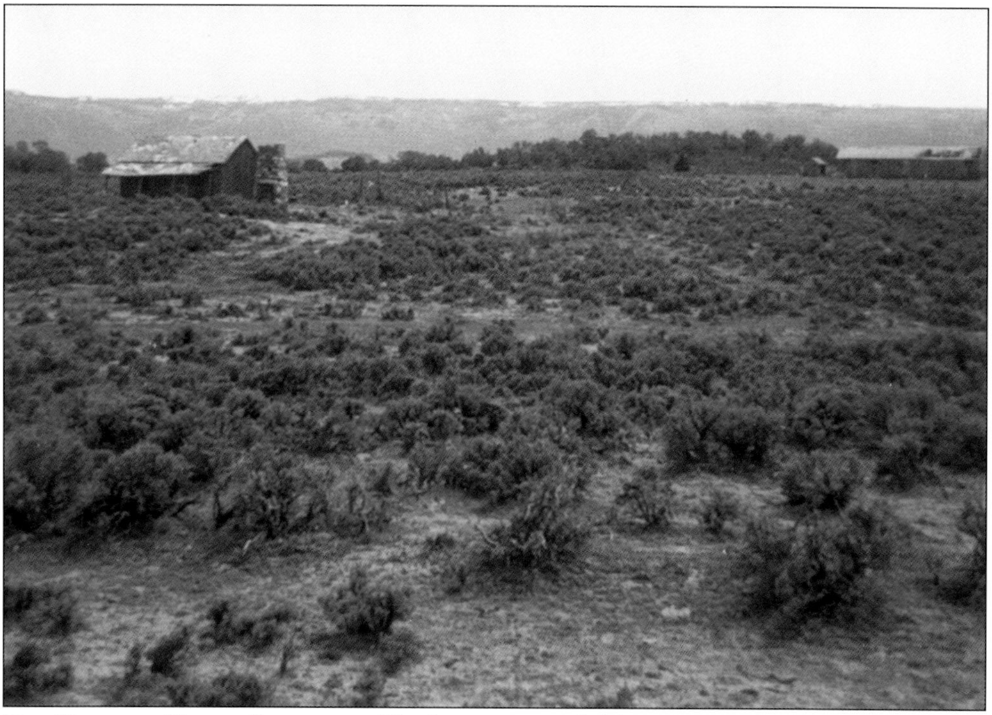

The Halfway House, Sunnyside. This house was probably constructed sometime after 1896, when the Sunnyside Road was completed, providing a route from Plateau Valley to DeBeque. The Sunnyside Road was often in frightful shape and was improved several times. The Halfway House was not an official stage stop, but almost all travelers stopped to swap news and rest their horses and often spent the night. The earliest mention of it was in 1917, when Fred A. Bloss purchased it from Mr. Hugh and Mr. Barker. In the 1920s, a Mr. Fuller purchased the Halfway House, where he grew corn, watermelons, and sorghum. Below is an unidentified wagon train. (Above, the Scott Walck collection; below, Plateau Valley Historical Preservation Society.)

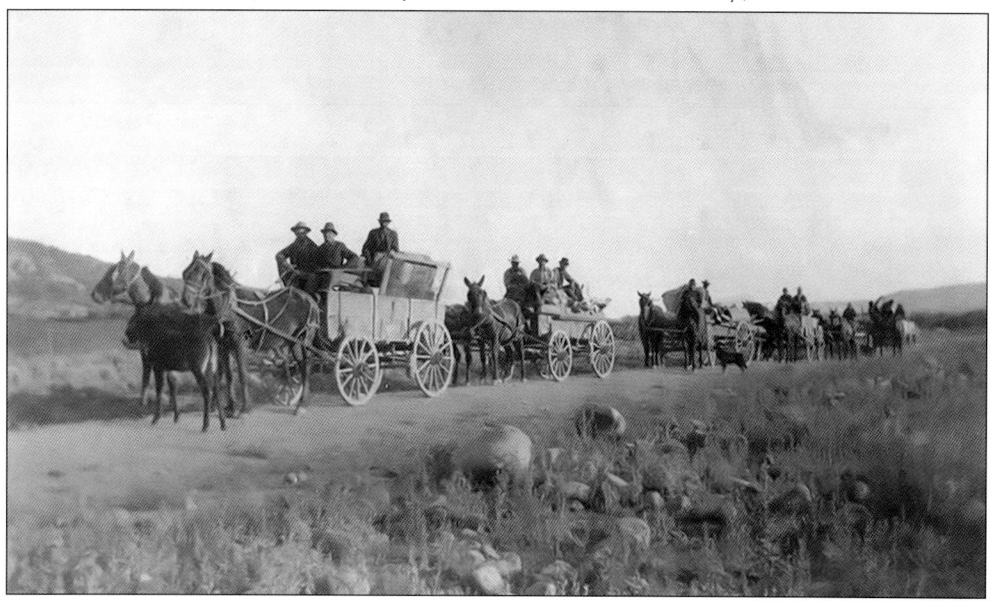

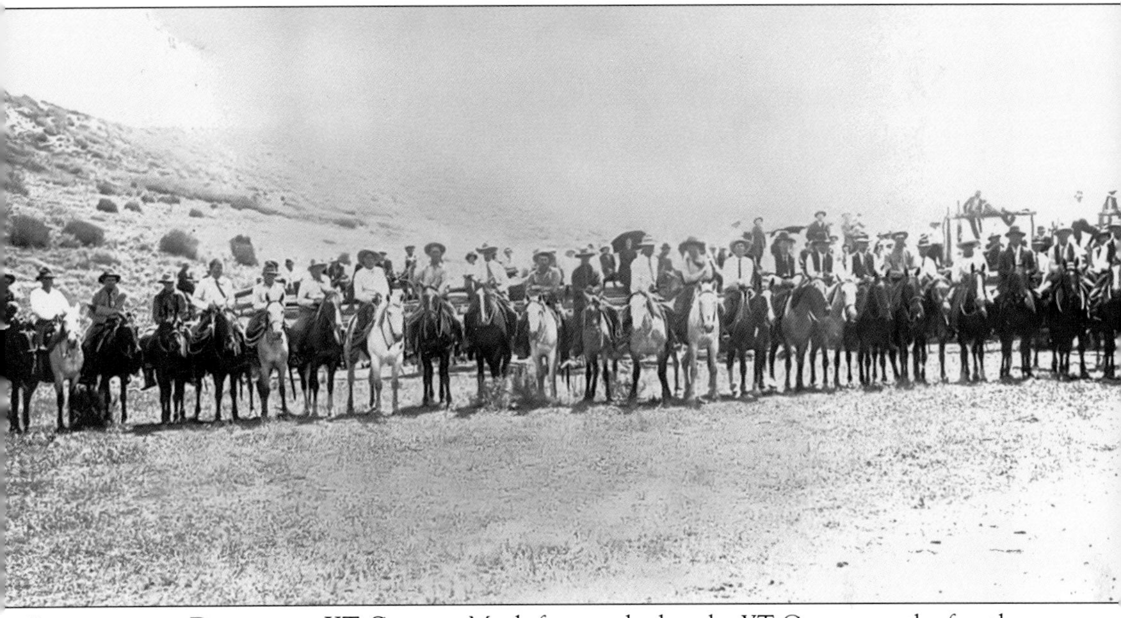

INDEPENDENCE DAY AT THE YT CORRAL. Much fun was had at the YT Camp over the fourth and fifth of July. A program advertised on July 2, 1915, in the *Plateau Voice* listed many events. Sheep roping and various races comprised the first day. A sunrise breakfast, roping and bucking contests, a band box race, a 350-yard dash, a ladies' free-for-all 220-yard dash, and a barbecue dinner made up the first half of the day. The afternoon festivities included a baseball game, and riding contests and races completed the second day's events. Cash prizes were given, as well as a Stetson hat, a pair of stirrups, a box of cigars, a pair of gloves, boxes of candy, a branding iron, a pair of shoes, a sewing machine, a bridle, a lap rope, a dozen postcards, and even a boiled ham. A grand ball at the Collbran Auditorium followed in the evening. (Plateau Valley Historical Preservation Society.)

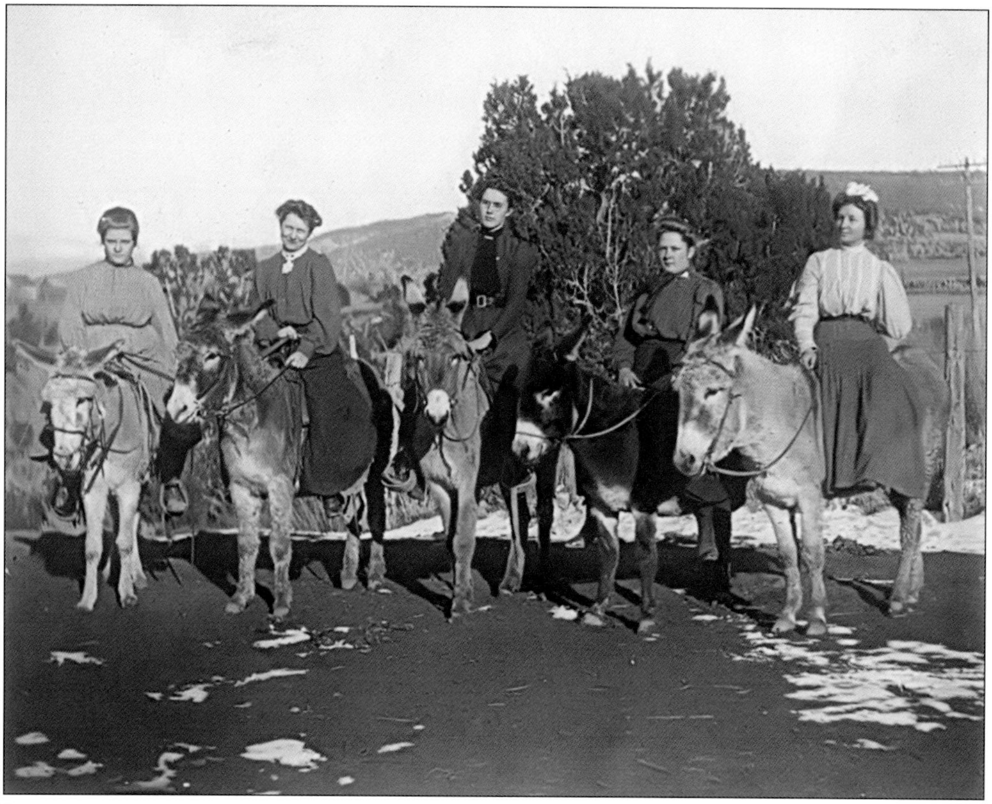

LADIES ON HORSEBACK. Pictured here from left to right are Tilla Hall, Estella Brooks, Mina Fritzler, Sadie Hall, and Hilda Severson (Ditman). (Stites Collection, Museum of Western Colorado Lloyd Files Research Library.)

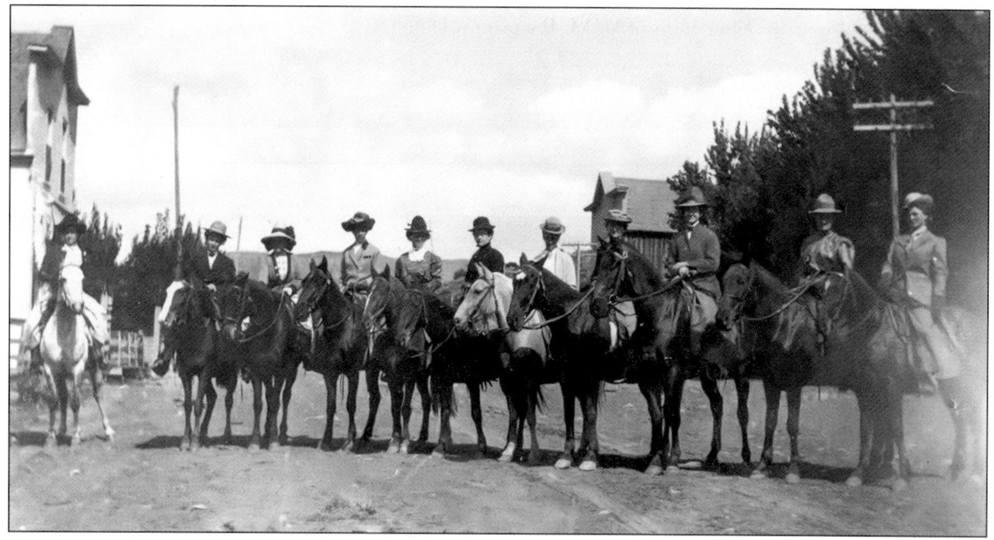

LADIES RIDING CLUB. Lucille Harris is second from the right. The riding club planned outings for the ladies of Plateau Valley. In 1911, the *Plateau Voice* reported that "The main feature of this club is that old and young, as well as fat and slim, also long and short, can become members and rub elbows with their giddy neighbors." (Plateau Valley Historical Preservation Society.)

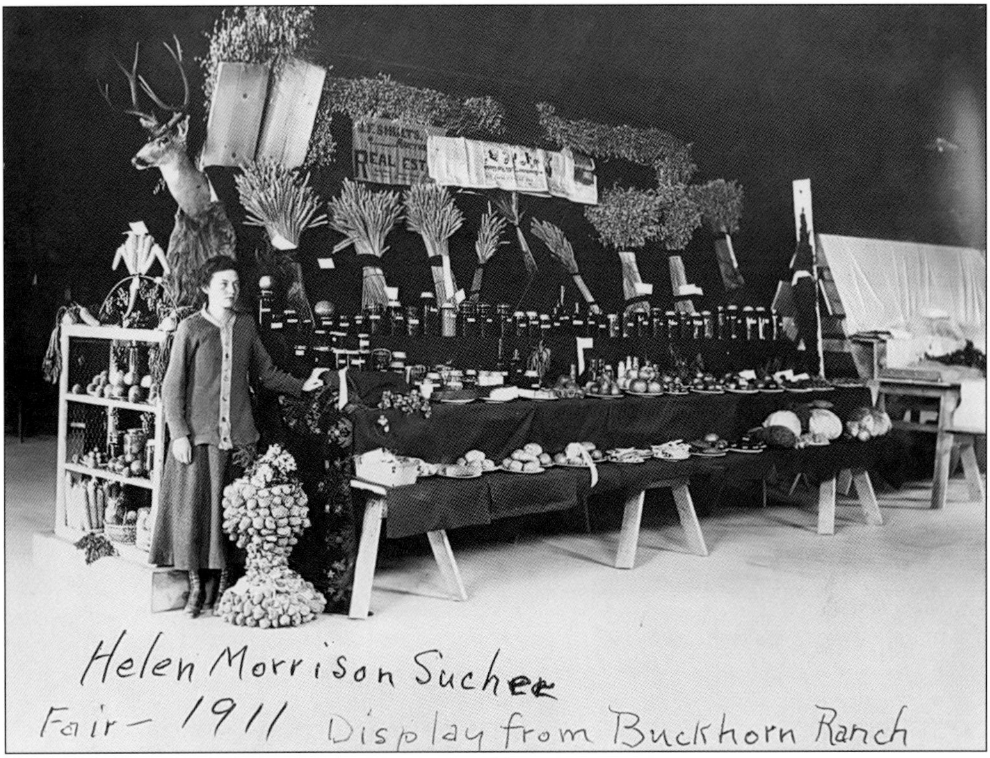

BUCKHORN RANCH DISPLAY, C. 1911. Displayed here are goods produced by the Buckhorn Ranch. In 1903, the Buckhorn Ranch was purchased by Issac Canfield. The ranch is about four miles from Collbran. Canfield, together with his wife, Imogene, and their children, Maud, wife of C.A. Morrison; May, wife of W.M. Porter; and Carl B., grew crops and produce and raised cattle. At right is a handbill for the first Plateau Valley Fair, held in 1912. The *Plateau Voice* reported, "Enthusiasm was high, but vendor turnout was much lower than expected." (Above, Museum of Western Colorado, Lloyd Files Research Library; right, Plateau Valley Historical Preservation Society.)

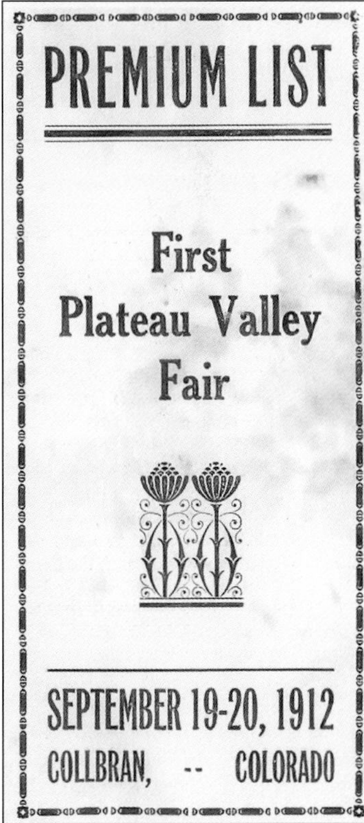

PREMIUM LIST

First
Plateau Valley
Fair

SEPTEMBER 19-20, 1912
COLLBRAN, -- COLORADO

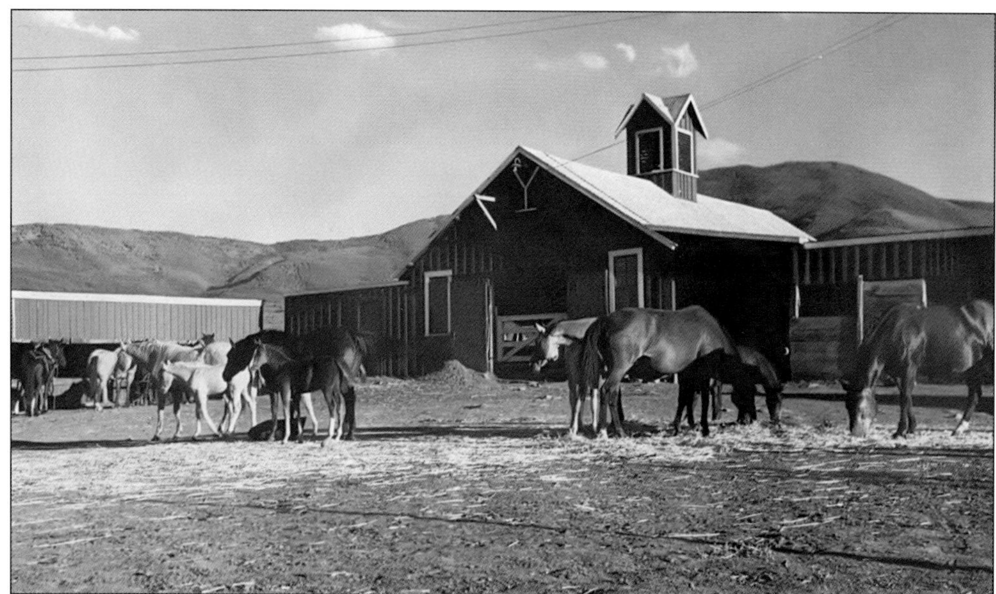

YT Ranch. Fred Rockwell and a man by the name of Needles homesteaded the area that was the YT Ranch in 1882, about five miles southeast of the town of Collbran. Several others expanded on the original ranch. In 1919, it was sold to Tom McKelvie for $140,000, including 2,080 acres and all the livestock. It was the largest land transaction in the valley at that time. The McKelvies came to the area during the Sunnyside land boom. (Scott Walck collection.)

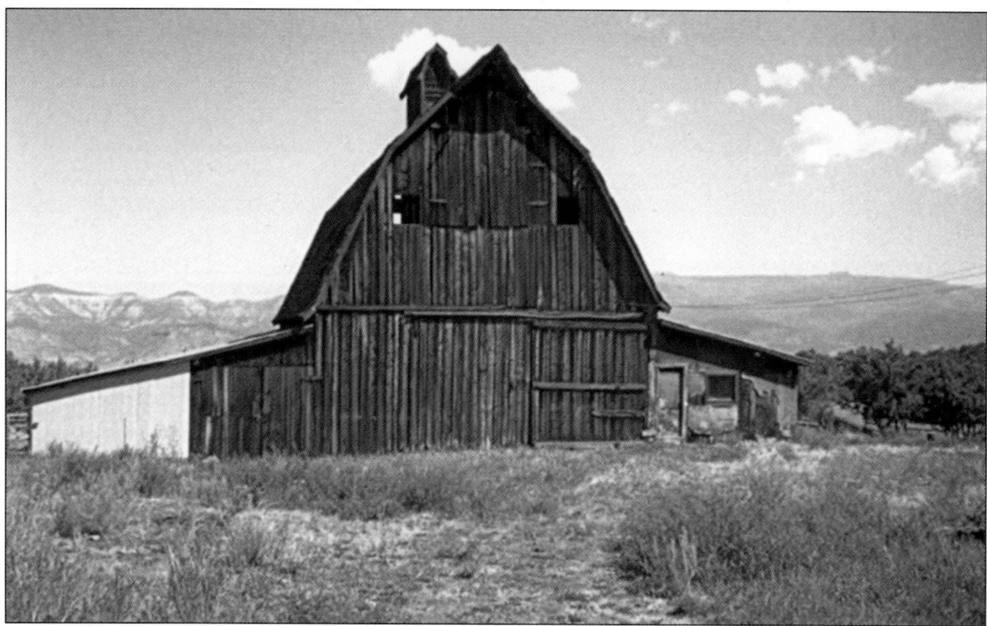

Larson's Barn. This barn was part of the Historic Barn Inventory project. This inventory was an important step in preserving a small part of the cattle industry in Plateau Valley. These Western-style barns were adapted from larger, Eastern-style barns to meet the needs of the climate, weather, and topography of the West. These styles often reflect the families' cultural heritage. This particular barn is similar to barns built in Scandinavia. (Plateau Valley Historical Preservation Society.)

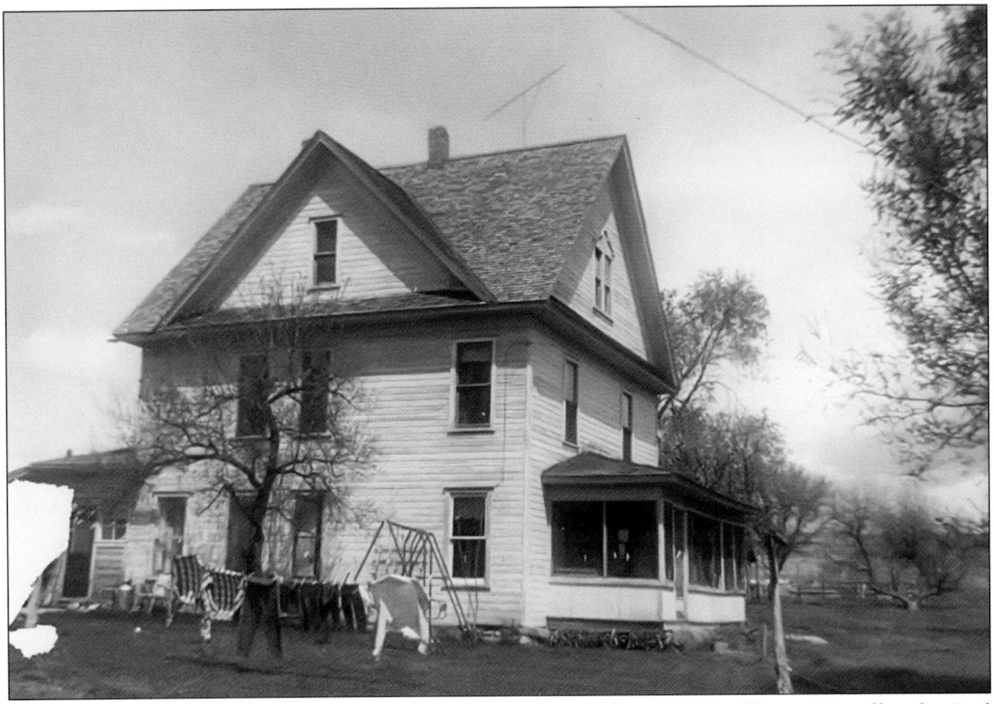

Long House, c. 1963. The Long house was constructed in 1910 by Henry Handley for Joel "Joe" Long. Joe Long was identified with the livestock business and played an important part in the organization and development of the Plateau Valley Stockgrower's Association. When the Stockmen's Bank was organized in 1916, Long was made president of the bank, a position he held until the close of 1932. (Plateau Valley Historical Preservation Society.)

Long Ranch. The "Rock Locker" brand is painted on the barn in the background. Brands and earmarks were used to identify cattle when grazing livestock on the open range, especially before fencing became commonplace. Earmarks were especially useful in large herds, poor brands, or certain light conditions. Scott Walck described how dishonest cattlemen would occasionally carry a "running iron" to change a brand to match their own for unlawful gains. (Plateau Valley Historical Preservation Society.)

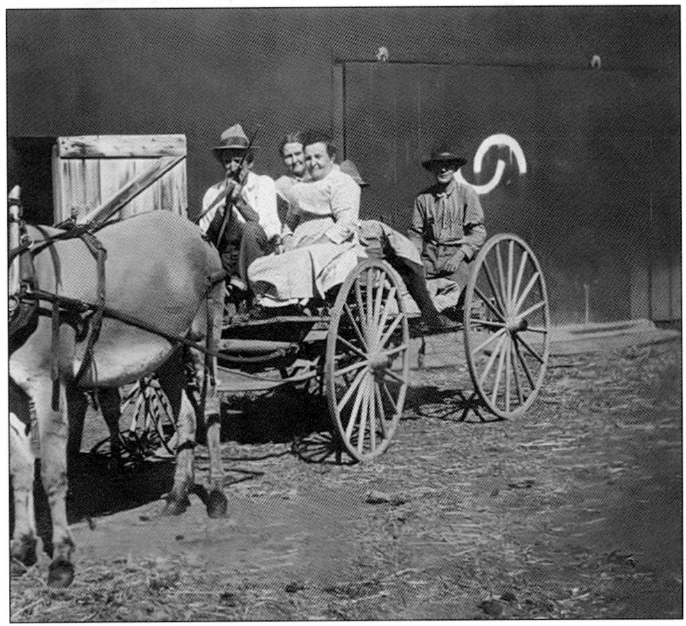

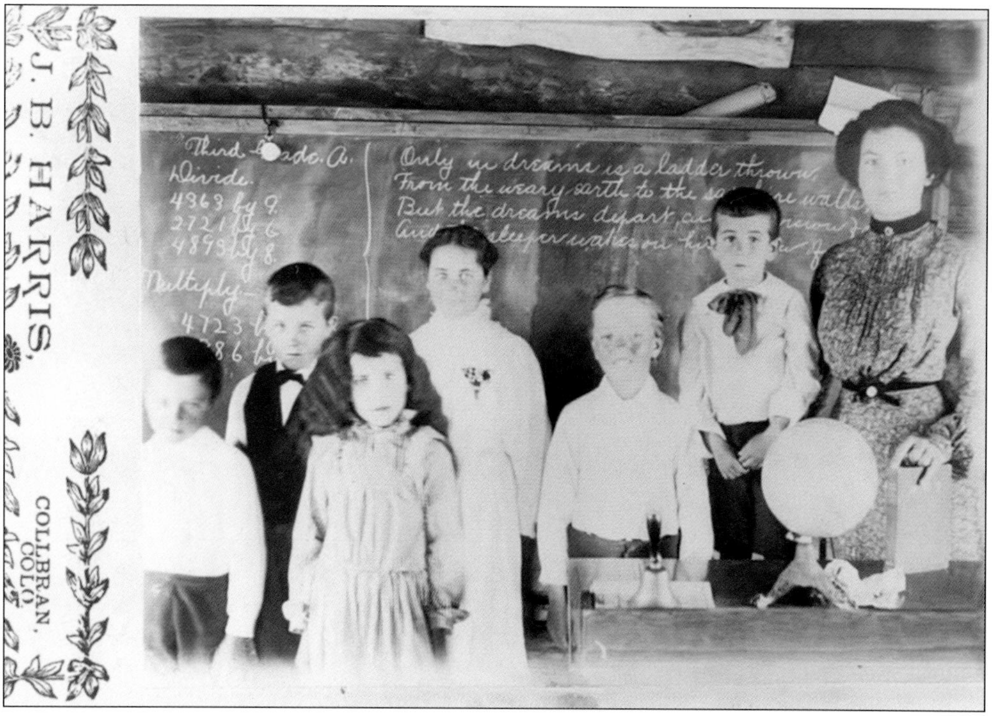

VEGA SCHOOL. Vega School—opened between 1911 and 1917 and closed in 1936—was the first school in the Heiberger District. It was a summer school held from April to Christmas. There were generally nine to twelve pupils. Ella Simmons, Della Kendall, Frances Campbell, Miriam Carrington, Mary Eddy, and Pauline Ryan were all teachers there. The school closed in 1936, after most of the families moved closer to Collbran. (Plateau Valley Historical Preservation Society.)

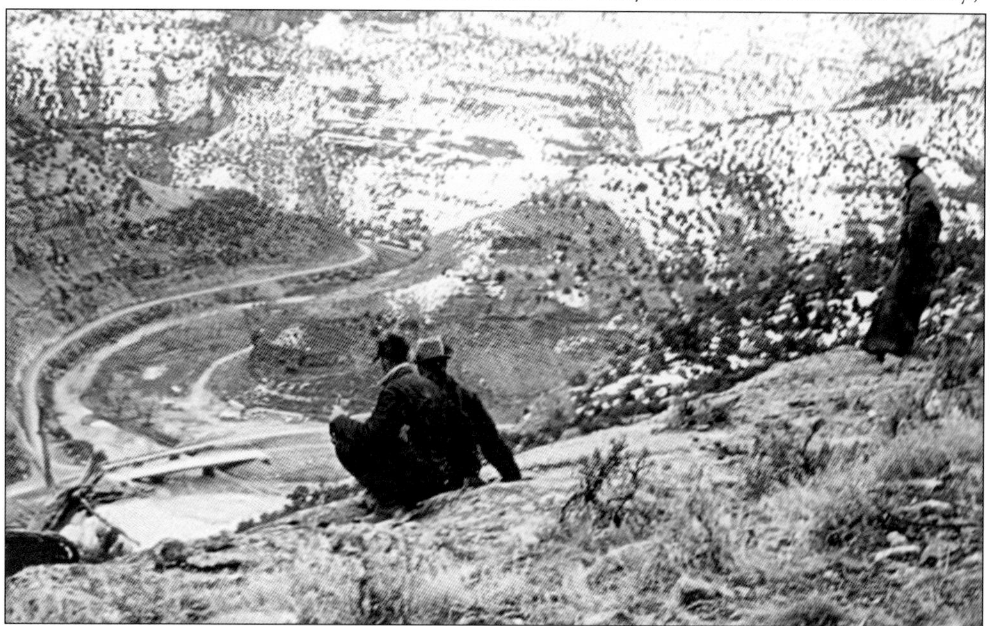

PLATEAU CREEK, C. 1930S. Pictured here are Fred Wallace and Lee Armour at a spot overlooking the mouth of Plateau Creek. (Plateau Valley Historical Preservation Society.)

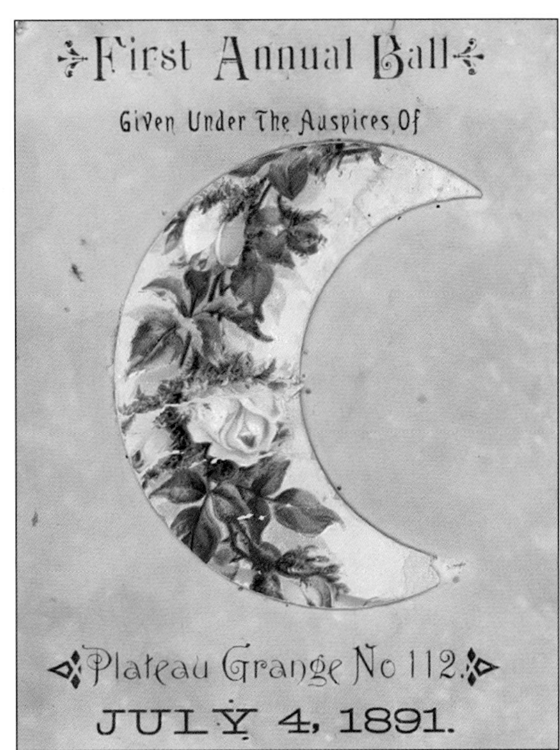

PLATEAU GRANGE, 1891. Grange organizations were founded to advance methods of agriculture and to promote the social and economic needs of farmers in the United States. The movement started in 1867 and increased in popularity during times of financial crisis. The Grange motto, "I pay for all," reinforced the idea that the farmer was the central character upon whom everyone in society relied. On the back of the program is a dance card, used by a lady to record the names of the gentlemen with whom she intends to dance each successive dance at a formal ball. (Both, Scott Walck collection.)

Programme.

Dance	
1. Grand March,	Co-Operation.
2. Quadrille,	Unity.
3. Waltz,	Gleaners.
4. Polka,	Shepherdess.
5. Quadrille,	Milkmaids.
6. Lancers,	Laborers.
7. Waltz,	Cow Boys.
8. Newport,	Haymakers.
9. Waltz-Quadrille,	Cultivators.
10. Quadrille,	Girl I Left Behind Me.

INTERMISSION.

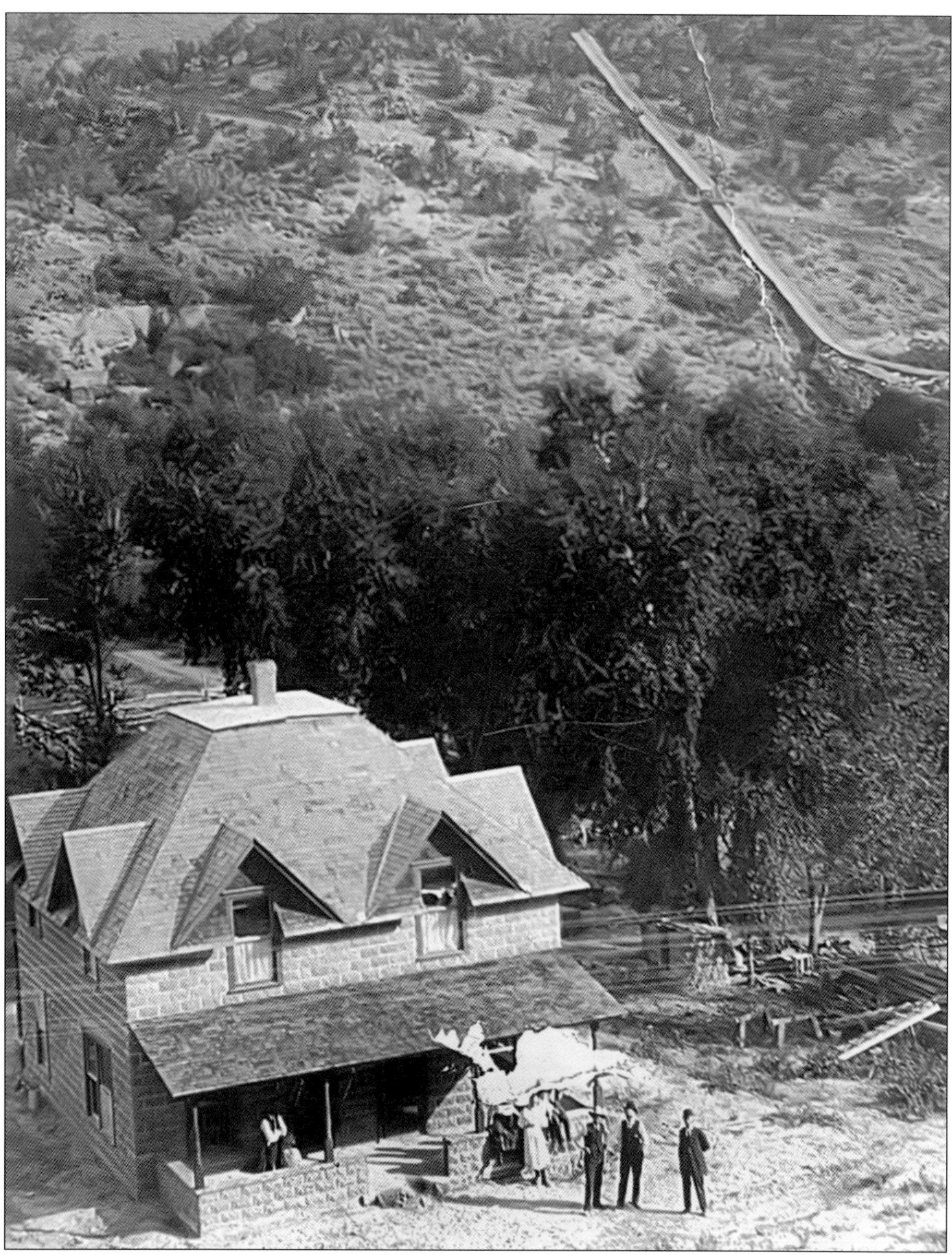

Hay Slide on Pitts Ranch. This photograph was taken about a quarter mile west of the Fuller Bridge on Highway 330 from the hillside on the north side of the highway, looking south. The house is Oliver C. Pitt's cement-block home on his family's homestead. The long structure at top right is a hay slide, used to move loose hay from a field on the top of the hill to the bottom, south of Plateau Creek. The field on the top of the hill was on the west side of Deacon Gulch, which drains into Plateau Creek south of the Fuller Bridge. The man on the far right is identified as Dr. Zinke due to his stature and Prince Albert coat, which he was known for wearing. This house was torn down in 1954. (Scott Walck collection.)

Four

The Collbran Project

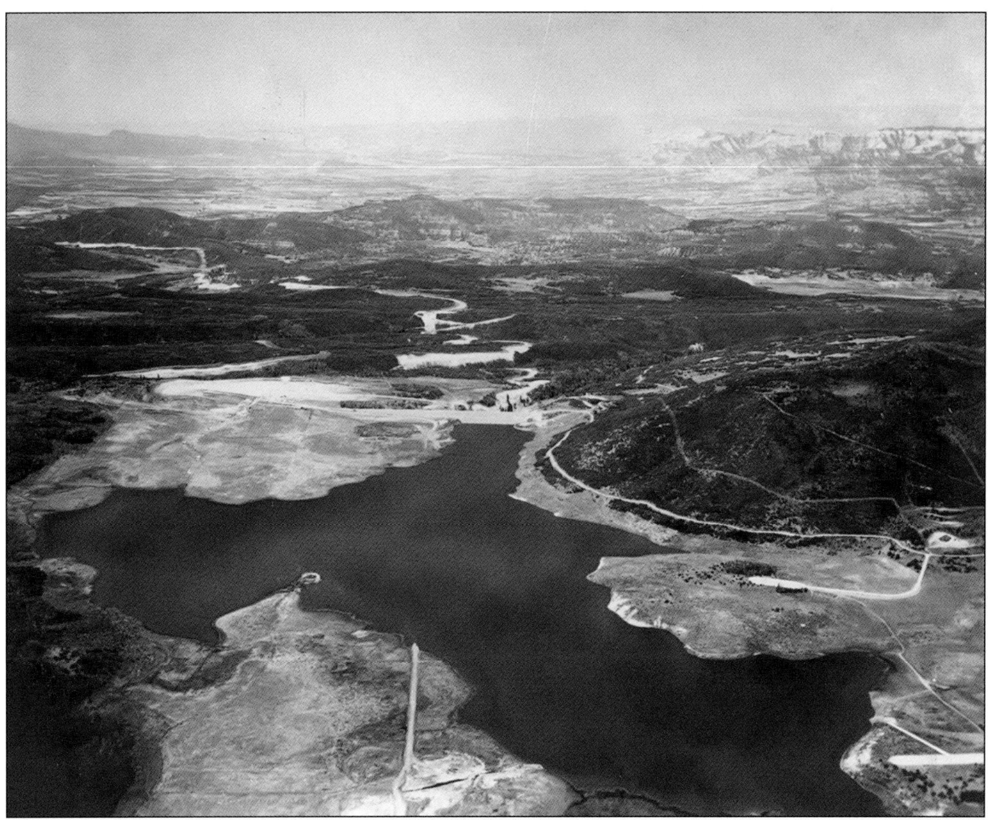

Vega Reservoir. The Collbran Project was developed to capture unused water flowing into Plateau Creek and its tributaries. The reservoir provides irrigation for more than 21,000 acres, as well as electrical energy for use in western Colorado. Major project works include Vega Dam and Reservoir, two power plants, two diversion dams, 37 miles of canal, and 18 miles of pipeline and penstock. (William H. Nelson Collection, Colorado Mesa University Special Collections.)

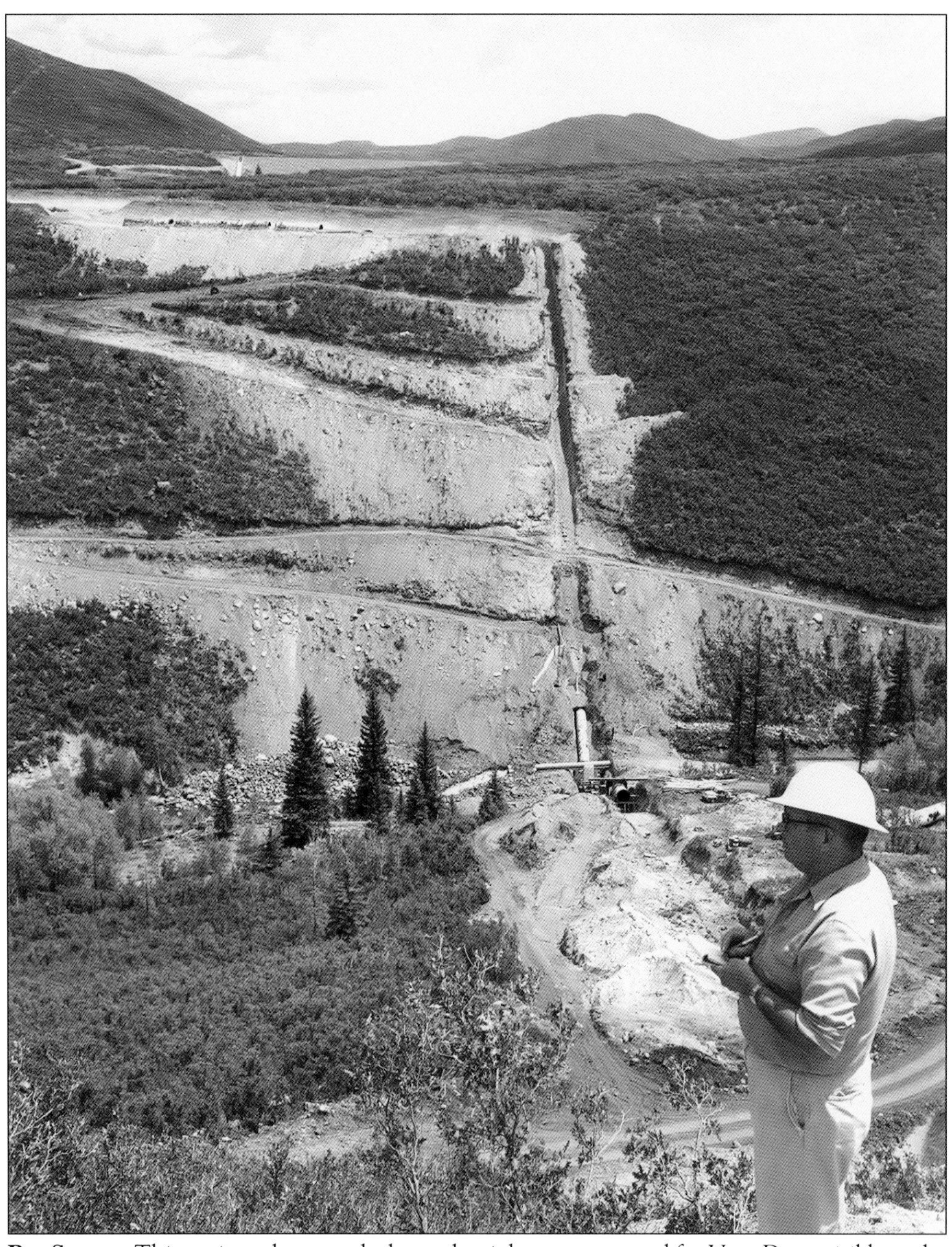

BIG SIPHON. This project photograph shows the siphon constructed for Vega Dam, visible at the top of the image. Inspector Sam Dugan is in the foreground. (Photograph by Stan Rasmussen for the Bureau of Reclamation, William H. Nelson collection, Colorado Mesa University Special Collections.)

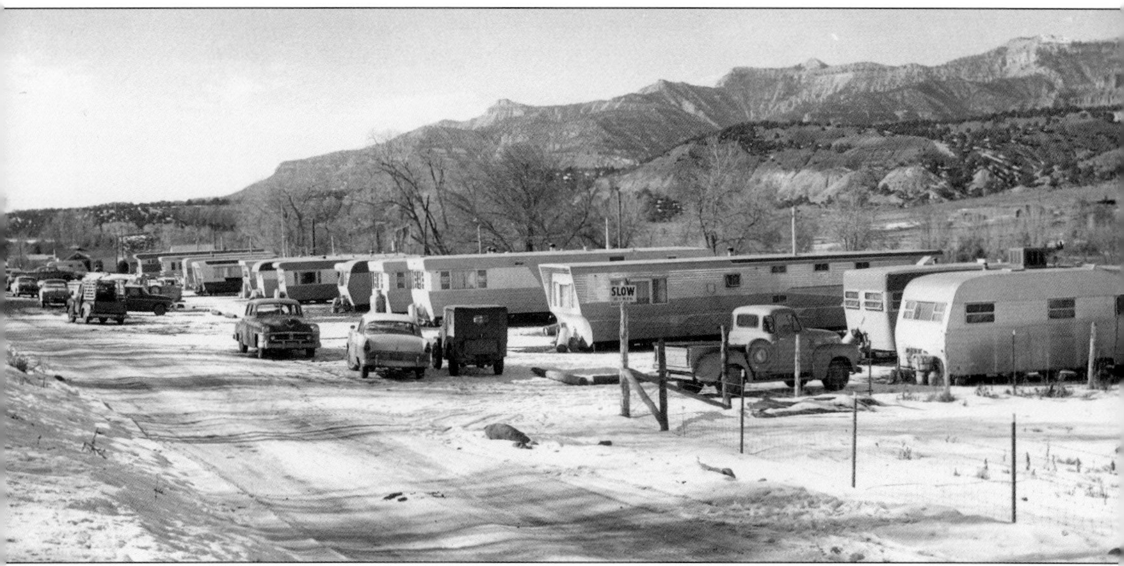

Boom Town. A small city of trailers on the west side of Collbran housed Vega Dam workers and their families. The trailers were expected to be part of the Collbran scene for several years while work on the dam progressed. (William H. Nelson Collection, Colorado Mesa University Special Collections.)

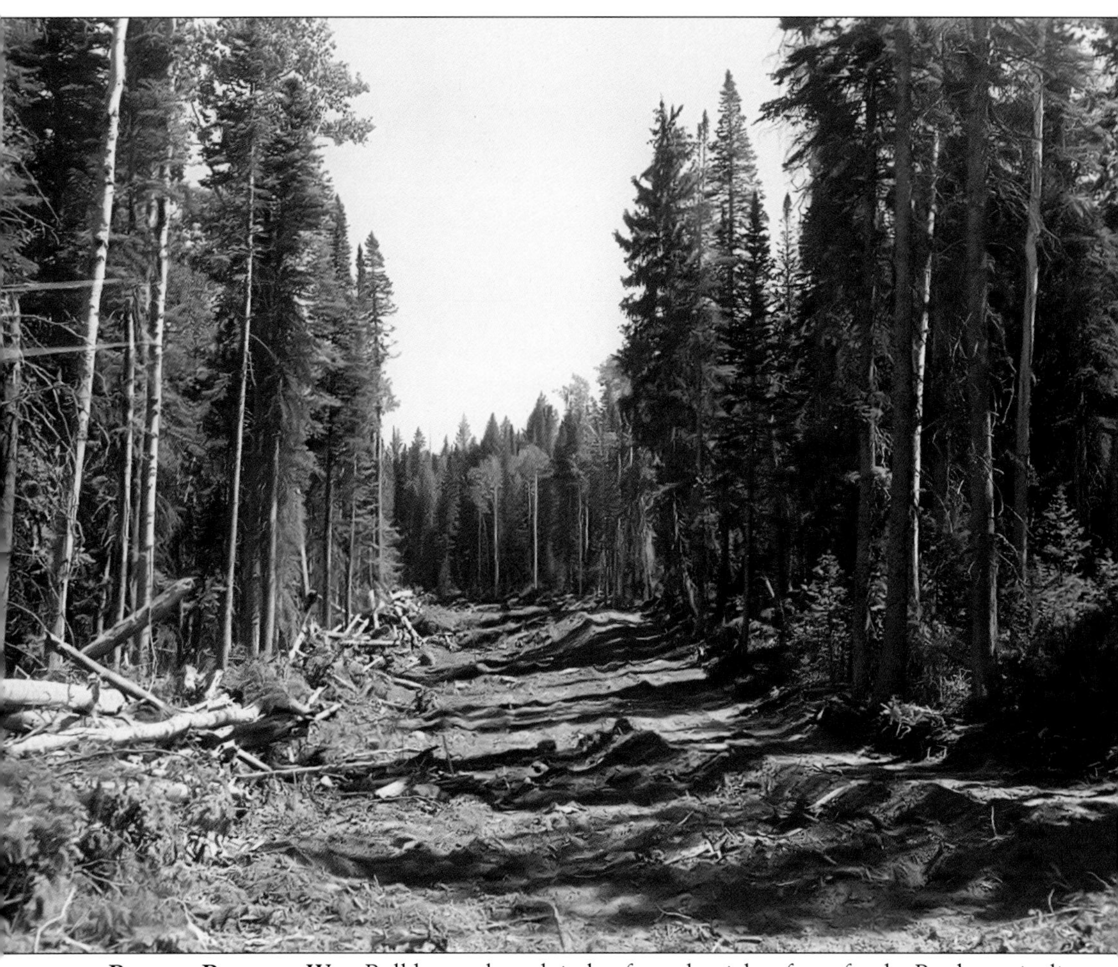

Pipeline Right-of-Way. Bulldozers cleared timber from the right-of-way for the Bonham pipeline high on the north side of Grand Mesa to pipe water to the newly constructed Vega Reservoir. Digging the trench for the pipe was the next step. The Bonham-Cottonwood Pipeline collects water from small steams and reservoirs in the watersheds of Big Creek and Cottonwood Creek and delivers it to the Upper Molina penstock. The Bonham section, 5.4 miles long, extends from Bonham Reservoir to the Upper Molina penstock. Extending about four miles from Cottonwood Reservoir No. 1 to the Upper Molina penstock is the Cottonwood section of the pipeline, which receives water directly from Cottonwood No. 1, DeCamp, and Big Meadows Reservoirs, as well as three uncontrolled stream inlets that also take releases from six other reservoirs. (Bureau of Reclamation photograph, William H. Nelson Collection, Colorado Mesa University Special Collections.)

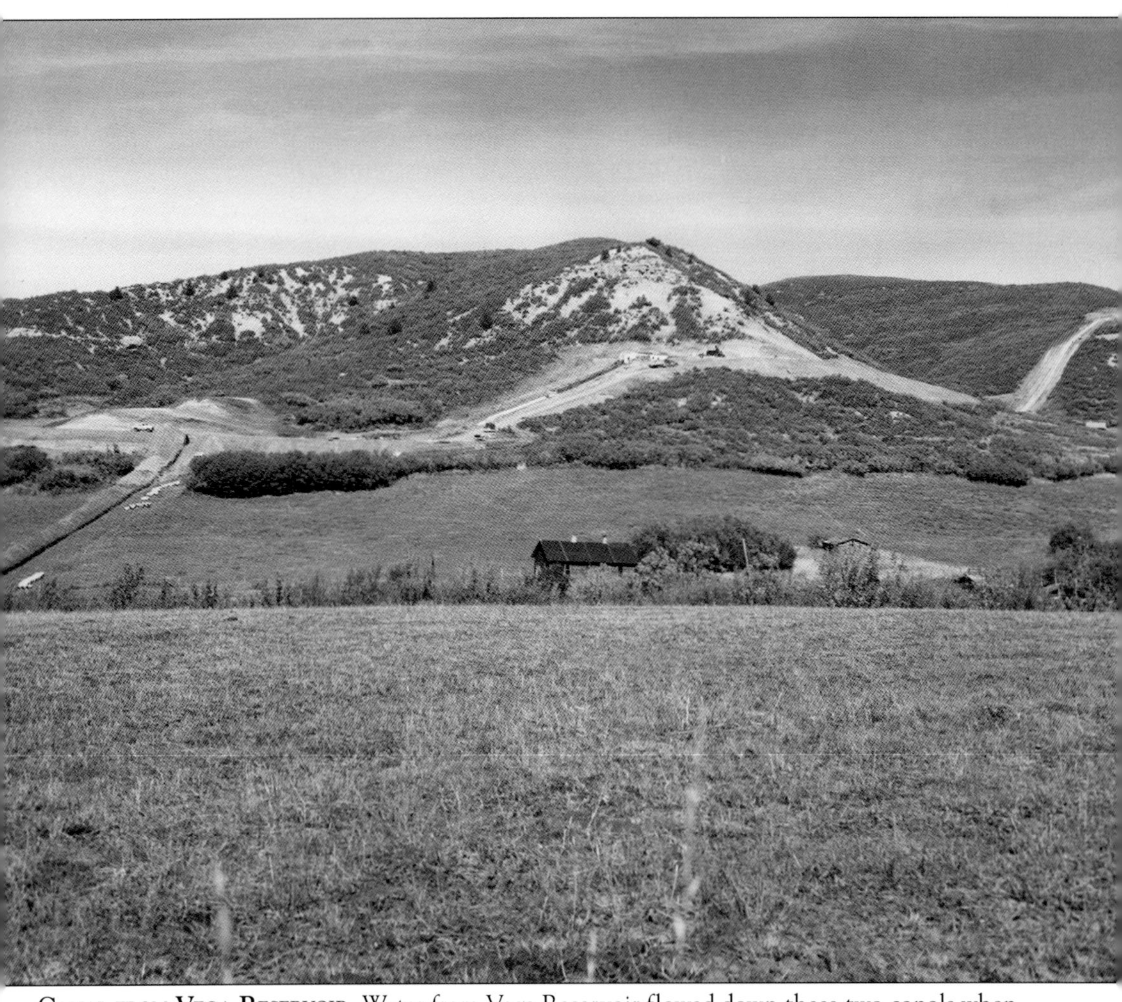

Canal from Vega Reservoir. Water from Vega Reservoir flowed down these two canals when the Collbran Project was completed. The canal appears to go up and down from this perspective, but it actually goes downhill all the way. The Leon-Park Feeder Canal conveys water from Leon and Park Creeks to Vega Reservoir. The canal begins at the Leon Creek Diversion Dam on Leon Creek and extends about two miles to a siphon under Park Creek. Water is diverted from Park Creek by the Park Creek Diversion Dam, about 1,000 feet above the siphon outlet, then combines with the Leon Creek diversions. The Southside Canal heads at the outlet works of Vega Reservoir and conveys irrigation water westward from the reservoir to project lands. The canal is 32 miles in length. Thirteen siphons carry the canal across major streams, and seven concrete chutes drop the canal in elevation. (William H. Nelson Collection, Colorado Mesa University Special Collections.)

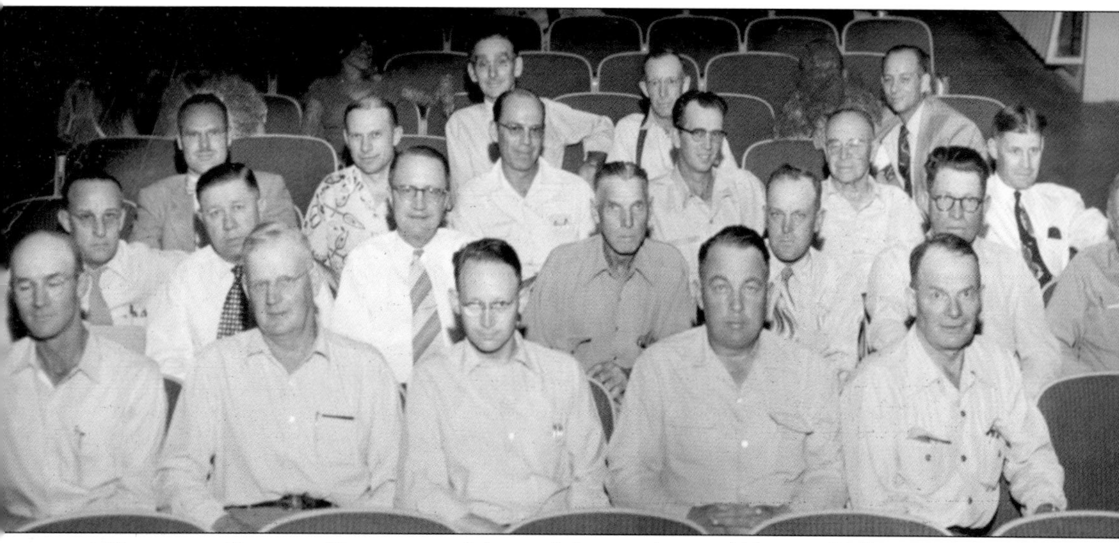

Collbran Project Committee. Many of the residents of Plateau Valley were members of the Collbran Project Committee Board. From left to right are (first row) Henry (Bill) Tupper, Collbran; Fred J. Simpson, Pomona; Dale Myers, Fruitvale; Gene Hansen, Fruitvale; and Martin Gunderson, Collbran; (second row) W.D. Toyne, Grand Junction; Oscar Hanson; Cecil Walt; Herbert Milholland, Molina; Walter R. Lloyd, Mesa; Ben Nichols, Mesa; and Erwine Stewart, Mesa; (third row) Walter E. Dalby; James K. Groves; R.B. Williams, Grand Junction; Russell Hall, Orchard Mesa; C.H. Hinman, Orchard Mesa; and Clifford Jex; (fourth row) M.L. Dilley, Clifton; R.L. Strain, Clifton; and Robert Jennings. (William H. Nelson Collection, Colorado Mesa University Special Collections.)

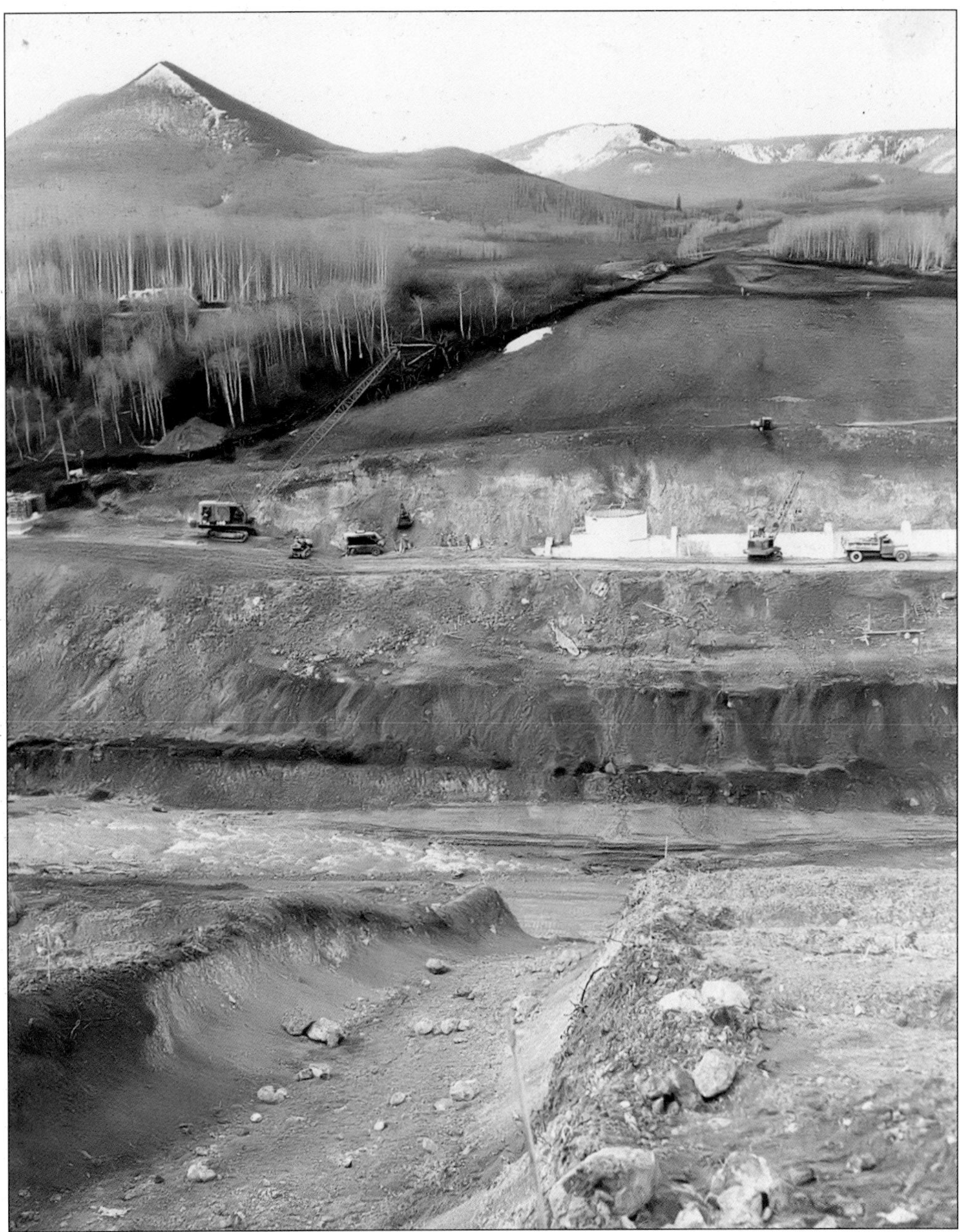

Construction of the Vega Dam. Construction of the dam was a factor in both the immediate and long-range development of the Plateau Valley. Covering the outlet works is in progress in this photograph. The trash rack is at far right, and the gate chamber is at center. A cutoff trench of the right abutment is in the foreground. The excavated area for the long dike on the left side of the dam is in the background. Water would soon be diverted from the creek through the outlet works to permit starting on the earth-and-rock-filled dam. The dam measures 162 feet high and 2,100 feet wide. Vega Reservoir has a surface area of about 900 acres and seven miles of shoreline. (William H. Nelson Collection, Colorado Mesa University Special Collections.)

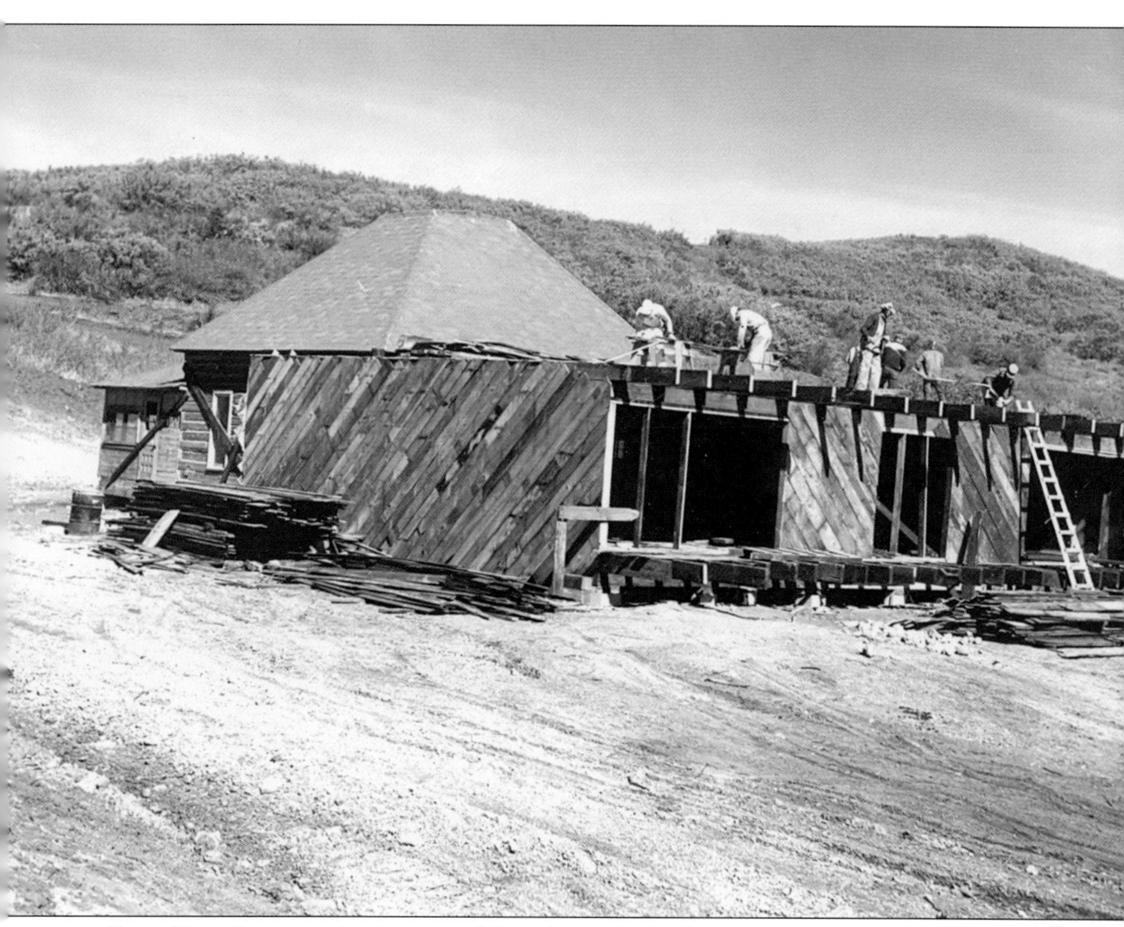

First Vega Business. Les Lupton of Grand Junction built the first commercial structure at Vega Reservoir, 10 miles southeast of Collbran. Lupton planned to put log siding on the front of the building. A log house, which was moved from the reservoir site, can be seen at the back of the building. Lupton planned for a dining room, sporting goods store, and cabins. (William H. Nelson Collection, Colorado Mesa University Special Collections.)

Five

Recreation on and around Grand Mesa

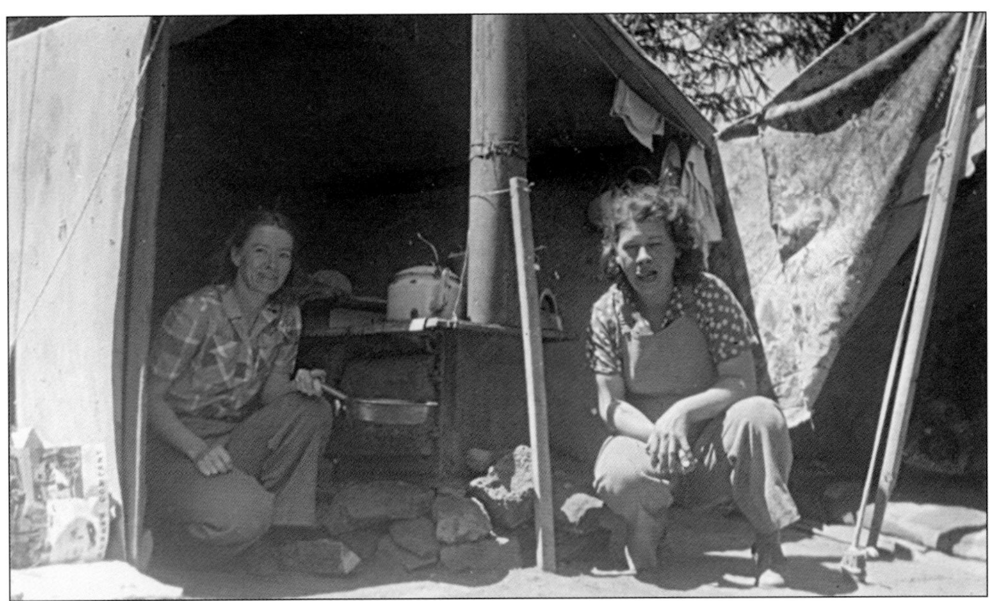

Hunting Camp on Grand Mesa, c. 1930s. Pictured here are Ethelle Silliman Raymond (left) and Evelyn Silliman. The women pose in a typical wall tent, complete with a cast iron stove, frying pan, kettle, and what appears to be an iron in the background. A wall tent from that period, complete with 10-ounce canvas, poles, and stakes would have weighed more than 40 pounds. As early as 1890, local newspapers touted the health benefits of camping on the Grand Mesa. (Author's collection.)

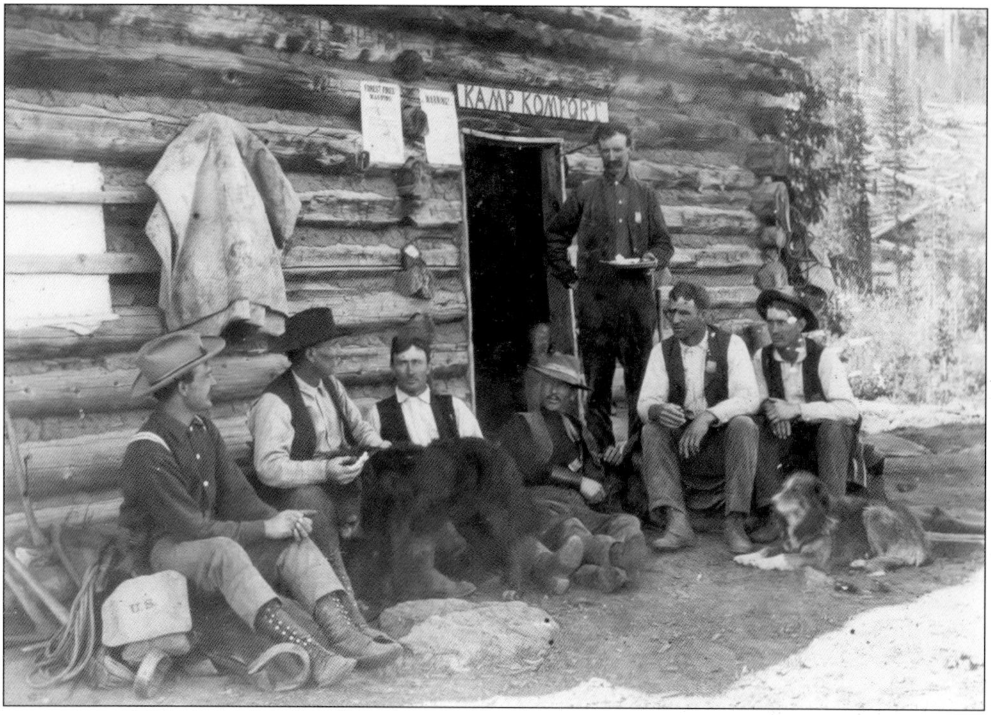

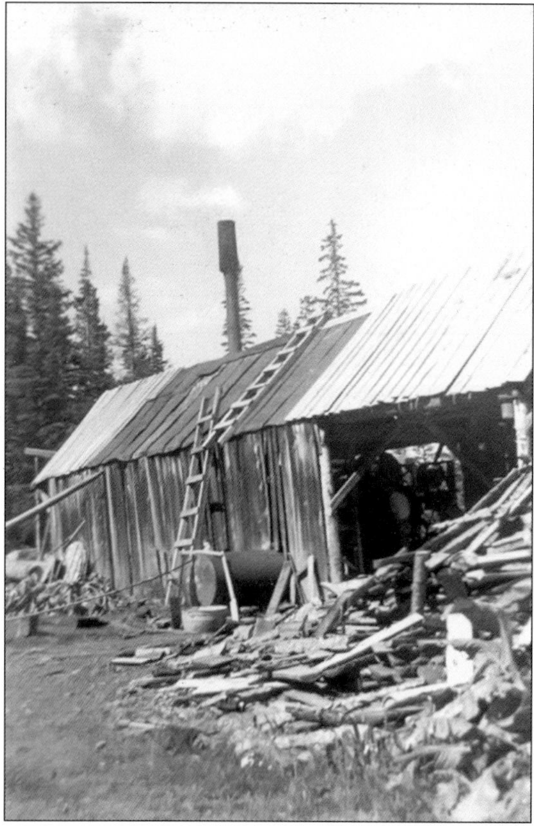

Kamp Komfort Mesa Lakes Ranger Station, c. 1905. Pictured at the national forest supervisor's office are, from left to right, W.R. Kreutzer, Dave Anderson, Henry Dingman, John W. Lowell, B.F. Jay, Frank Barnes, and James G. Cayton. William Kreutzer became the nation's "Number One Forest Ranger" in 1898. In over 41 years of service, he helped manage land in four national forests: Pike, Grand Mesa Uncompahgre, Gunnison, and Roosevelt. This management included the construction of ranger cabins on the Grand Mesa and Battlement Forest Reserve. (Plateau Valley Historical Preservation Society.)

Sawmill at Atkinson Reservoir. This sawmill belonged to George Strickland. Sawmills went into operation soon after roads were built. Most of these were powered by steam, and because steam engines were heavy, a fair road was needed to get them to the site. According to Scott Walck, Asa Palmer had the first mill in the valley on Big Creek. The last sawmill was on Owens Creek and was shut down in the late 1950s. (Scott Walck collection.)

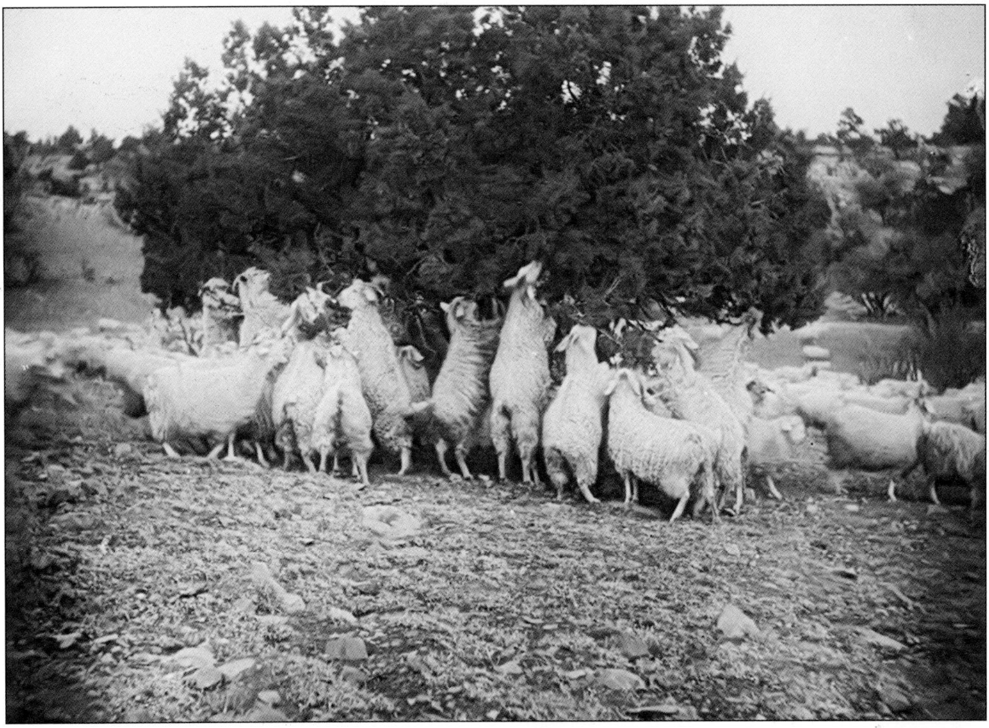

Goats Grazing, 1904. Angora goats were prized for their mohair, which was used for weaving. According to Scott Walck, the pelts and skins were tanned with the mohair on and made into chaps, which were worn by cowboys both as a fashion statement and for warmth in cold weather. Shearing technology progressed from hand shears to clippers operated by a gasoline engine. (Photograph by R.E. Benedict, Plateau Valley Historical Preservation Society.)

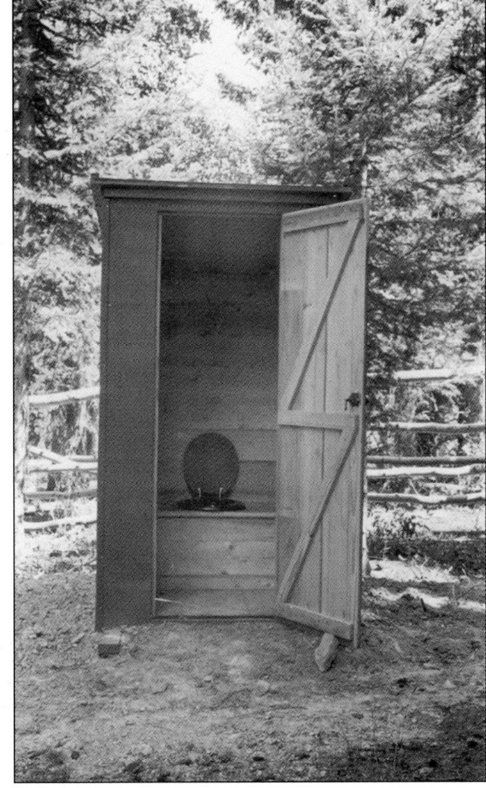

Smokehouse Campground, 1933. Pictured here is a Model A Toilet, Standard Type, commonly used on public campgrounds in the 1930s. This toilet was located at the Smokehouse Campground. (Plateau Valley Historical Preservation Society.)

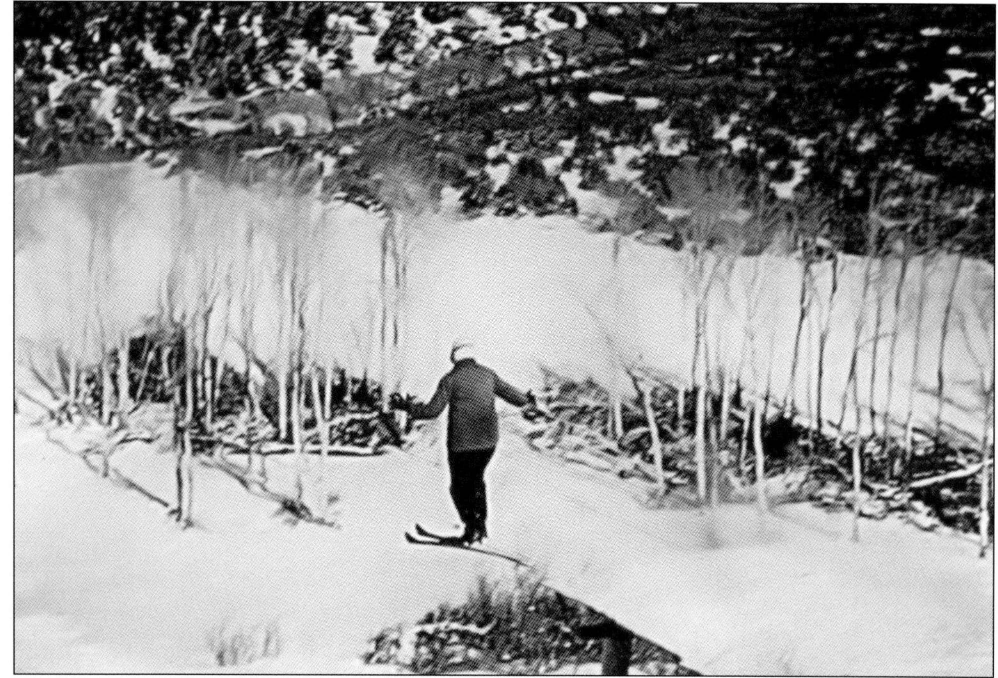

Williams Family Ski Runs. According to Verlene Dix, daughter of Paul and Cookie Williams, the Knob Hill ski run opened for business in 1948. It was owned and operated by the Williams family (Paul, Cookie, Verlene, and sister Jean) and was a half-mile west of their home. A 600-foot rope tow conveyed skiers to the top of the hill, powered by a Buick sedan. Cookie Williams sold sandwiches, doughnuts, coffee, and hot chocolate. The ski run was open for 11 years. In 1960, the family opened a new ski area, the Williams Ski Course, which had two rope tows. The first began outside the front door of the Williams home and took skiers 500 feet upslope. Skiers could ski down a short distance and catch a second rope tow, which was 850 feet in height. Tractors powered both rope tows. The ski area closed to the public in 1963. (Both, Verlene Dix.)

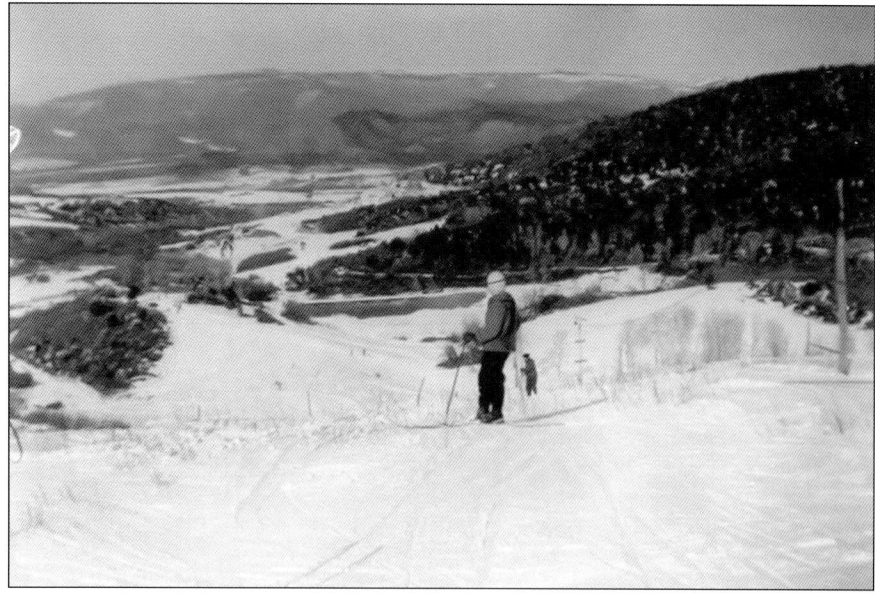

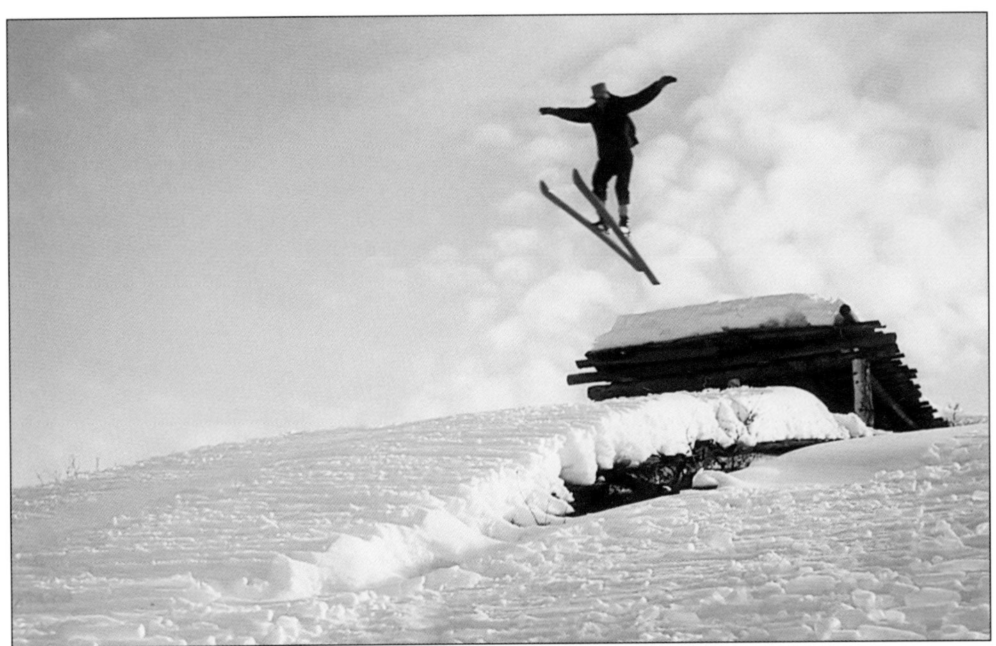

Williams Family Ski Jumps. Jean Williams is shown here on a ski jump around 1960. Local newspapers reported: "There is little or no danger in skiing, and it is one of the most thrilling and enjoyable of winter sports. Perhaps the outstanding thrill of skiing is the jump; the sensation is probably somewhat similar to one a diver gets from a very high diving board. It is, however, greatly heightened by the tremendous speed and by the skill required in making the 'sats' and landing. A sensation very much like falling may be obtained on very steep courses. The joy one gets from successfully riding such a course is another sensation—and the fall gives still another. The most pleasant of the mild thrills attached to skiing will be obtained on long, smooth, gentle slopes where no effort is required to stand erect while slipping along at a rapid rate." (Both, Verlene Dix.)

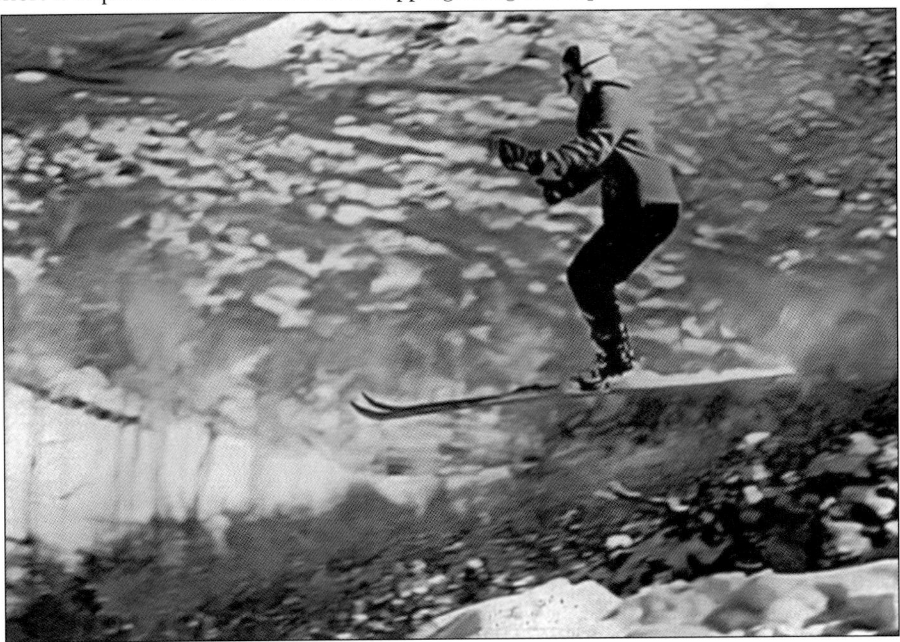

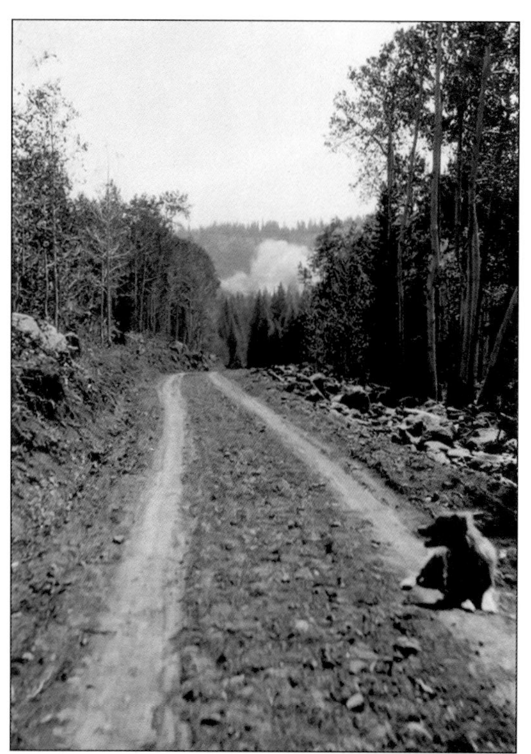

Mesa Lakes Road. In the spring of 1920, forest supervisor J.W. Spencer announced plans for construction of an automobile road from Mesa to Mesa Lakes. This was the first in a system of roadways that would connect the communities of Plateau Valley with the top of Grand Mesa. Using a construction crew that averaged eight men, a 40-foot right-of-way was cleared. Oak brush was removed, and large boulders were blasted with TNT. Spencer was anxious to make the forest an ideal summer resort for people. It was his desire to keep the numerous lakes and streams well stocked with fish. Pictured below is the road survey around 1916; at left is its construction around 1920. (Left, Museum of Western Colorado, Lloyd Files Research Library; below, Plateau Valley Historical Preservation Society.)

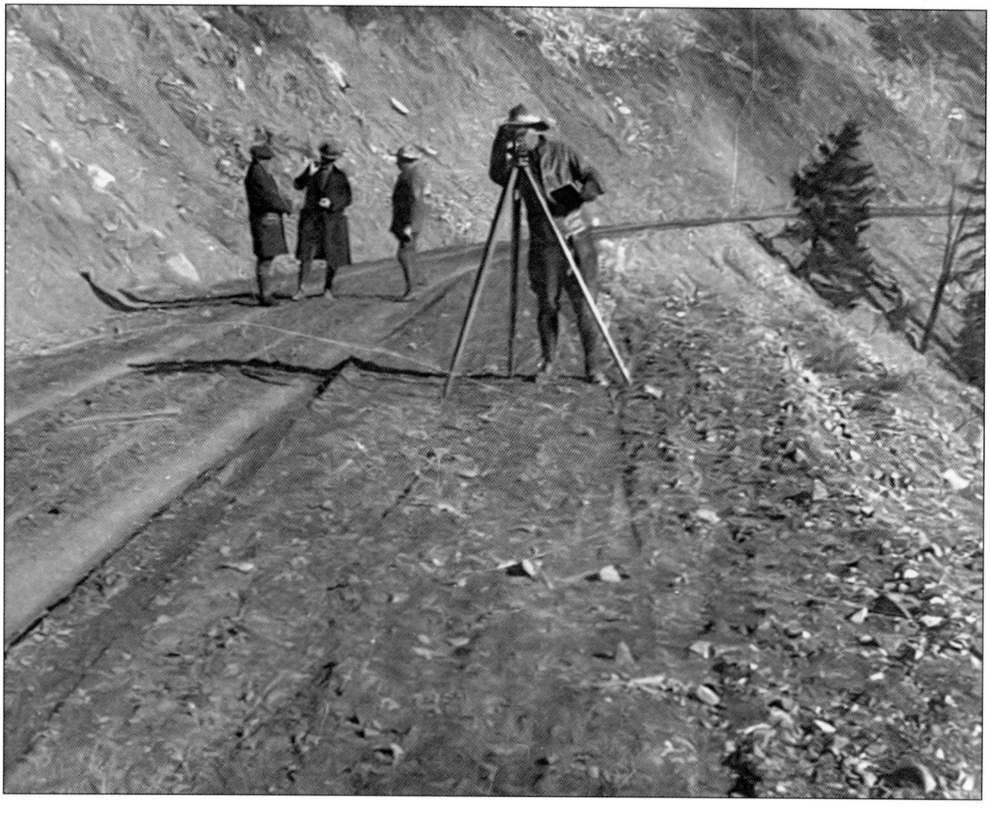

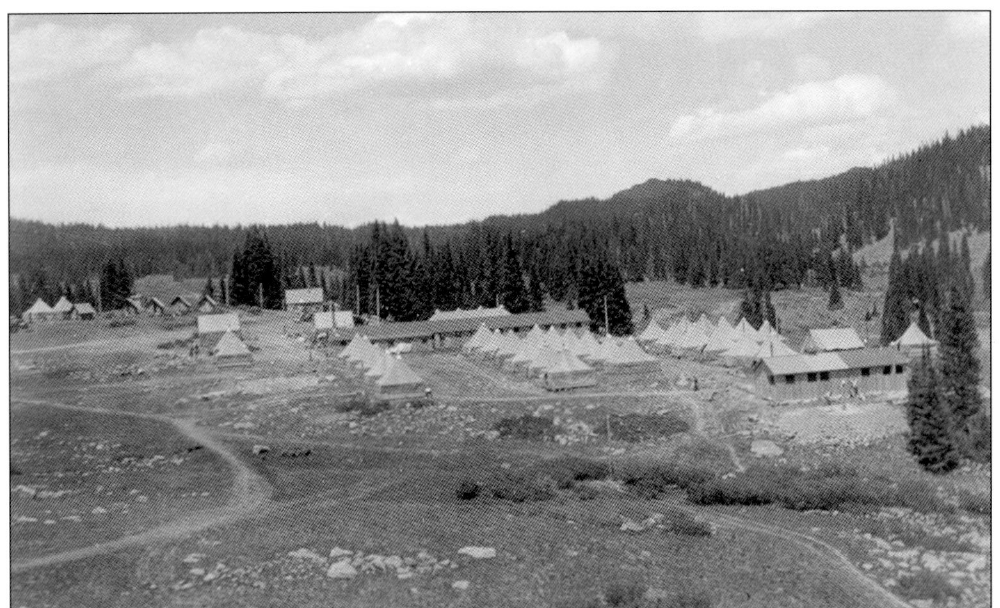

Coon Creek CCC Camp. The Civilian Conservation Corps was formed as a New Deal governmental program to combat the poverty caused by the Great Depression. The Coon Creek CCC Camp was operated as a side camp from 1937 to 1940 but was used as a base camp between 1940 and 1942. Coon Creek Camp was administered by Superintendent W.R. Haynes. (Plateau Valley Historical Preservation Society.)

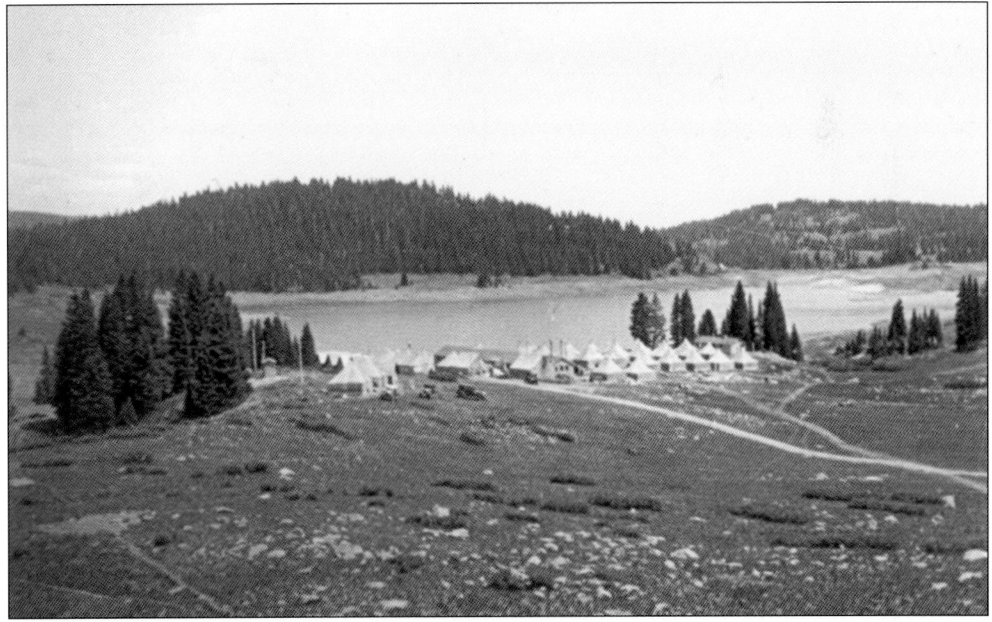

Coon Creek Camp Projects. Projects completed by the camp include the construction of Mesa Lakes (Cedaredge) and Ward Lake Ranger Stations, the Grand Junction Administration Office, and the Mesa Lakes Ski Area. The camp may have been utilized as a staging area for highway construction in the 1950s. (Plateau Valley Historical Preservation Society.)

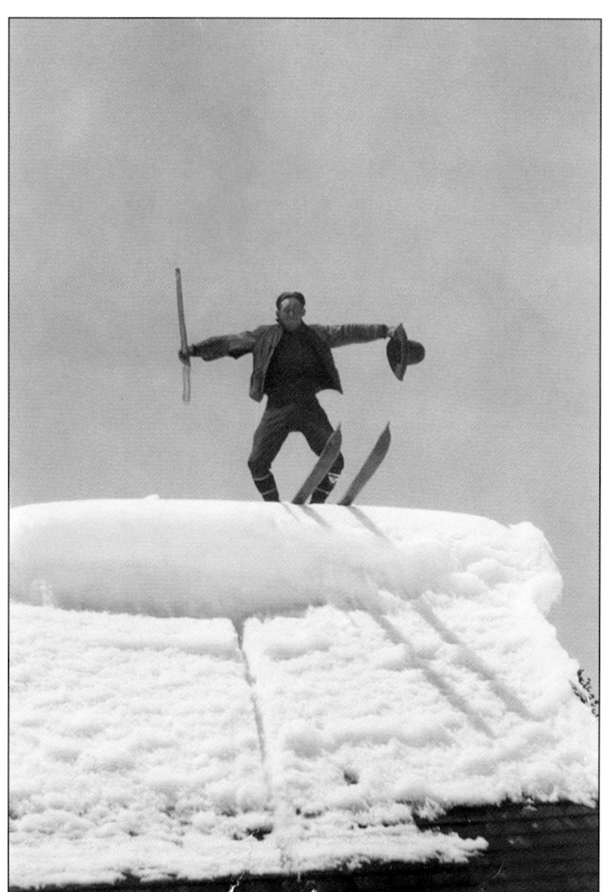

Ward Lake Ranger's Station, 1925. Pictured here is Harry Smith. The photograph was taken while Roscoe Bloss was the ranger. Bloss was born in Kansas but was living in Collbran by 1920. He was a farmer in addition to his duties as a forest service ranger. (Plateau Valley Historical Preservation Society.)

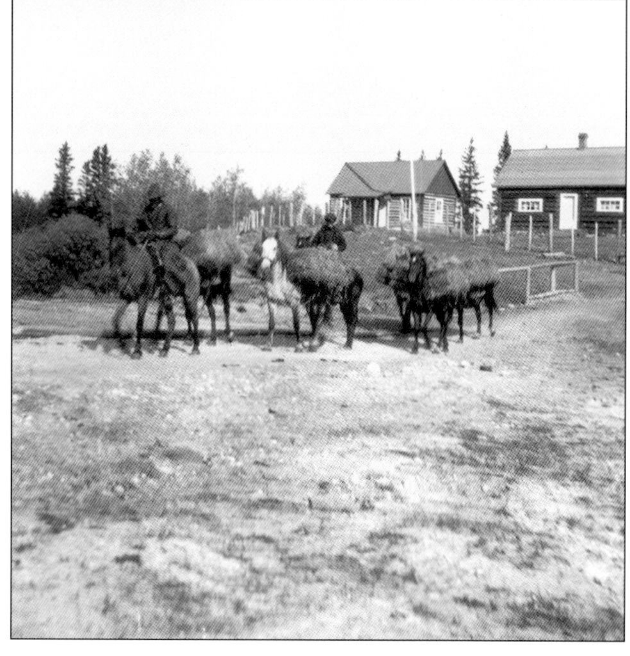

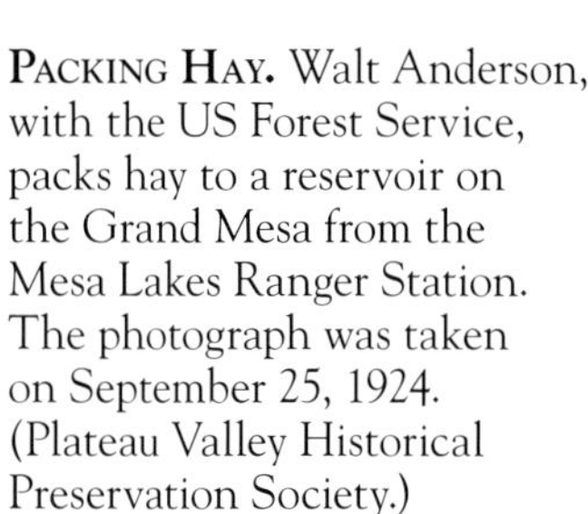

Packing Hay. Walt Anderson, with the US Forest Service, packs hay to a reservoir on the Grand Mesa from the Mesa Lakes Ranger Station. The photograph was taken on September 25, 1924. (Plateau Valley Historical Preservation Society.)

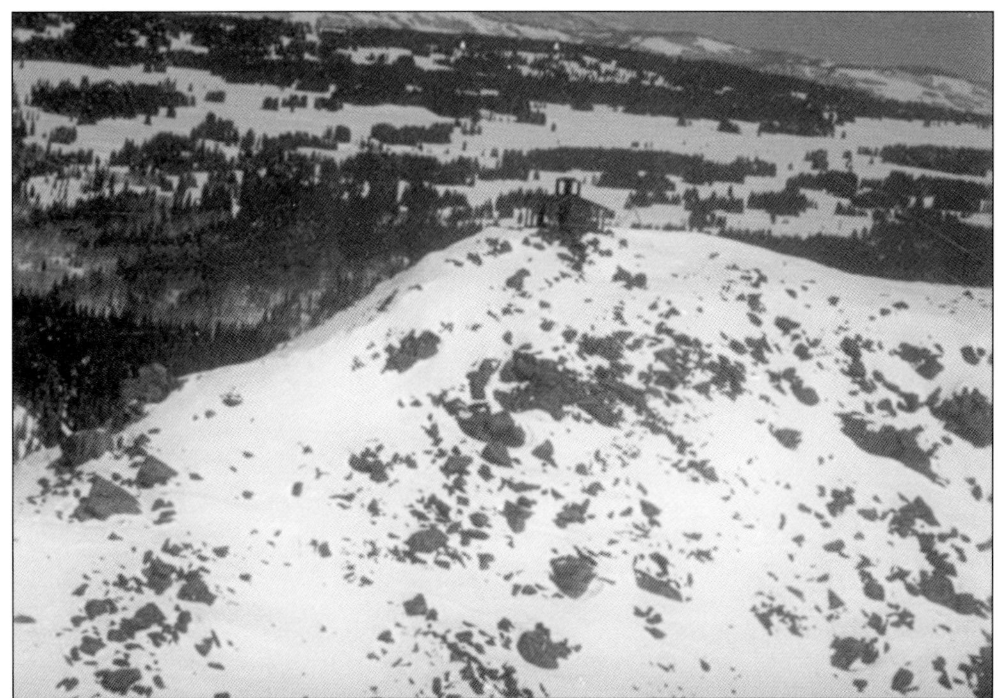

Leon Peak Lookout Station. Forest ranger Roscoe Bloss and his family lived out of a tent and used it as a headquarters in the summer and fall for two years, in 1914 and 1915, after which it was deemed unprofitable and abandoned. (Plateau Valley Historical Preservation Society.)

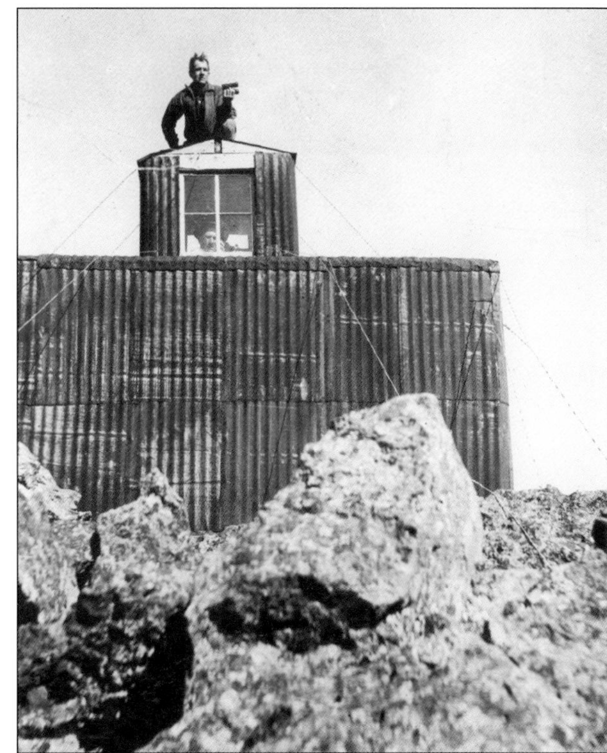

Leon Peak Lookout Station, 1914. According to a history written by Goldia Bessie Kruh Stites, Barnard "Barney" Duffy was appointed forest ranger of a large district in the valley in 1901. He built the Leon Lookout Station on Leon Peak. He carried materials by pack horse as far as possible, then carried them the rest of the way on his back. (Plateau Valley Historical Preservation Society.)

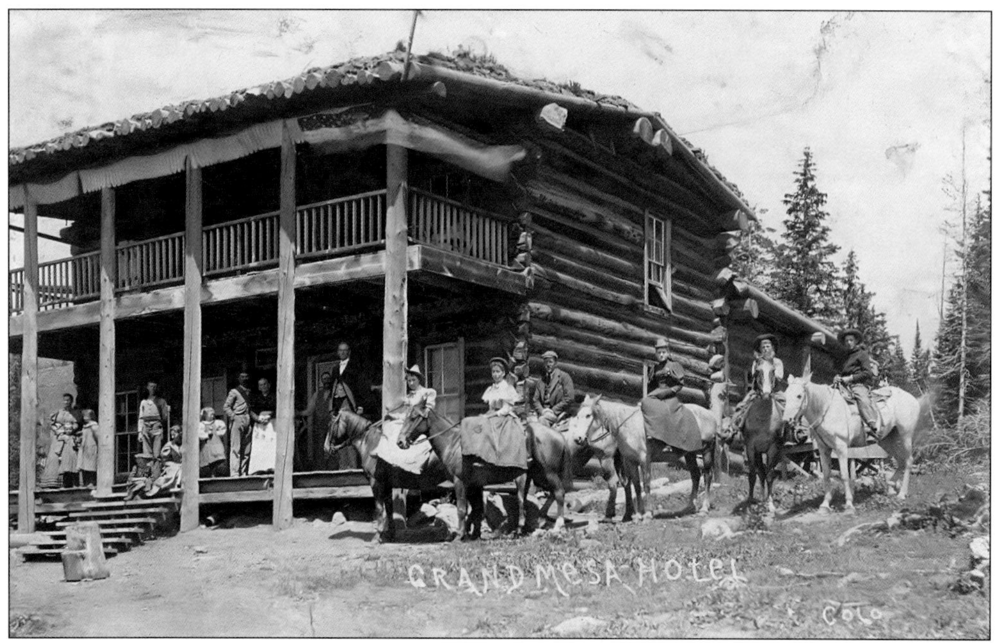

Grand Mesa Resort. Water from Alexander Lake was appropriated in 1886, when the Surface Creek Ditch and Reservoir Company was formed. William Alexander, one of the original directors, filed a preemption claim on 160 acres of land on the Grand Mesa that included Alexander Lake and the Twin Lakes. In 1890, he partnered with Richard Forrest. Alexander Hotel (also known as Grand Mesa Hotel) was opened for business in 1891. William Alexander disappeared in 1892, and Richard Forrest sold the lake properties to William Radcliffe in 1895. (Above, Frost RV and General Store; below, Museum of Western Colorado, Lloyd Files Research Library.)

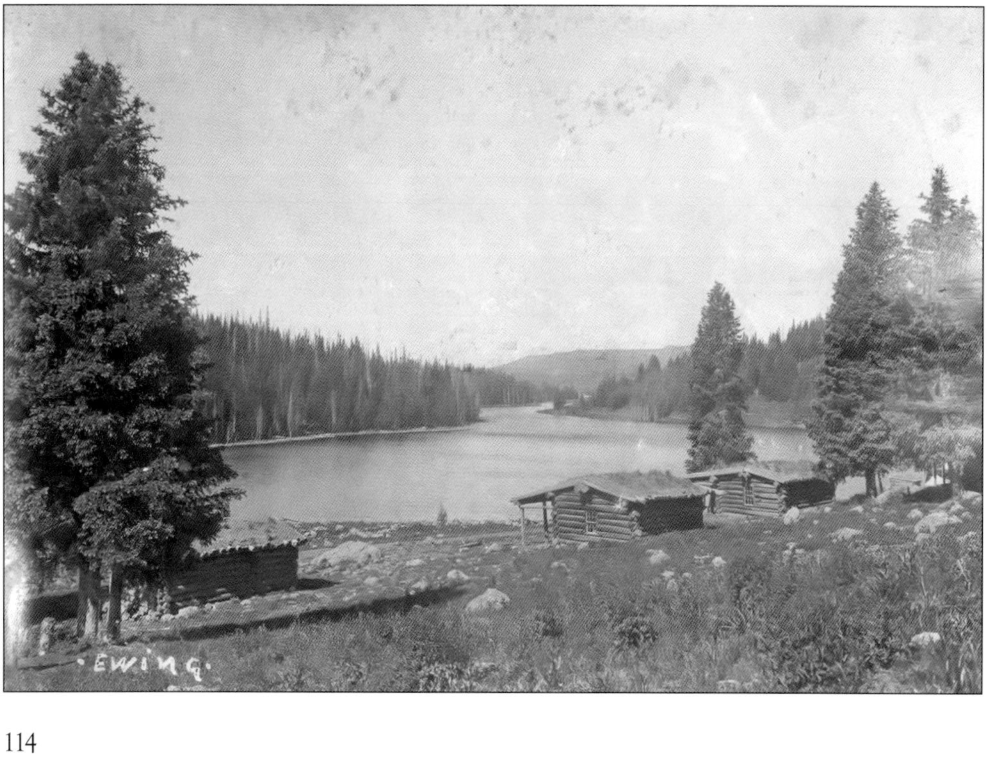

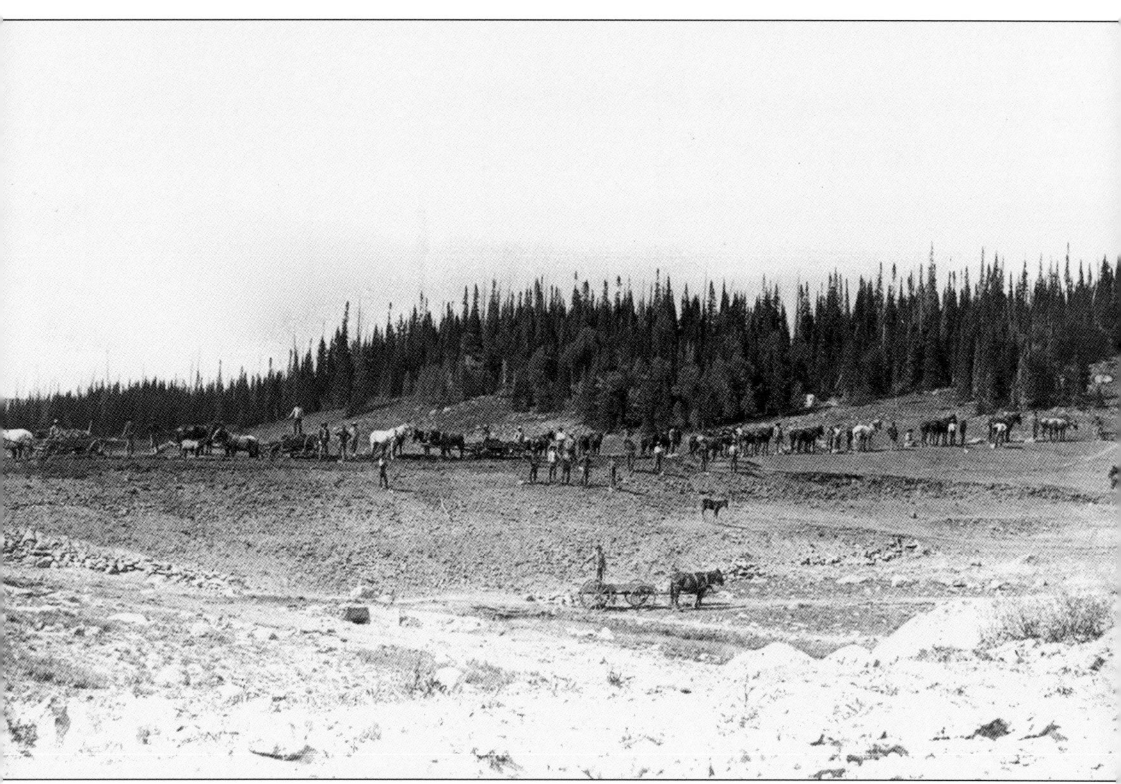

Bonham Reservoir. According to *Skin and Bones*, the Big Creek Reservoir Company was started in 1888. David Bonham, John Stites, Charlie Arkinson, and Chris Lude Sr. built the Bonham and Atkinson Reservoirs. Other men became interested, and a chain of reservoirs were planned to empty into Big Creek. Bonham, Atkinson, Number One, Silver Lake, and Forty Acre Reservoirs are part of this chain. By 1902, there were six reservoirs, but in 1911, the Atkinson dam went out, and the shareholders were forced to pay damages to the residents down Plateau Canyon. Shown here is the construction of Bonham Reservoir. (Plateau Valley Historical Preservation Society.)

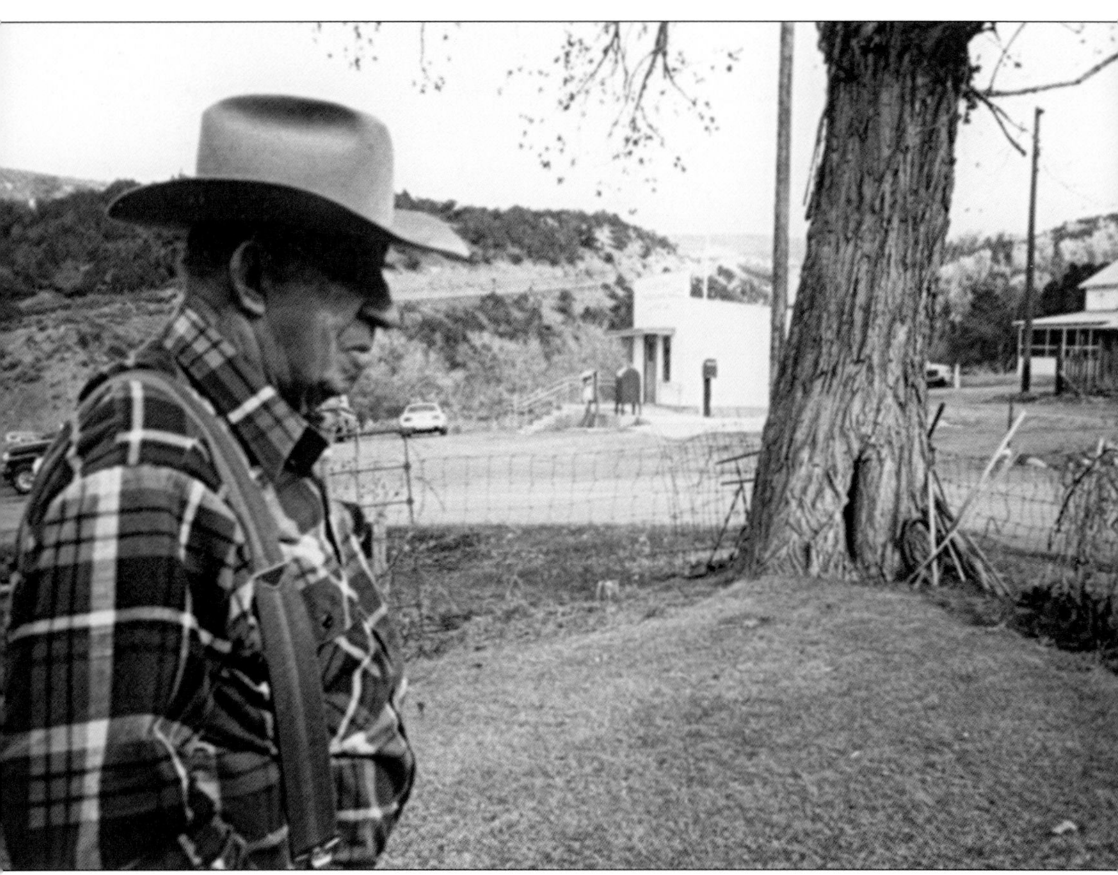

LOUIS KITSON. Louis Kitson likely held the job as pool rider longer than anyone else in the valley. He was also selected as "Range Man of the Year" by the Forest Service. A pool rider was tasked with caring for all the cattle in a particular allotment. A good pool rider who understood cattle, grass, and the range could hold and control cattle by the placement of salt. He also had to be a diplomat to get along with all the permittees and the Forest Service rangers. (Plateau Valley Historical Preservation Society.)

Louis Kitson at Kitson Reservoir. Water feeds into T.E. Kitson Reservoir from Cottonwood Creek. Water for the reservoir was appropriated in 1911, which was likely the year of its construction. (Plateau Valley Historical Preservation Society.)

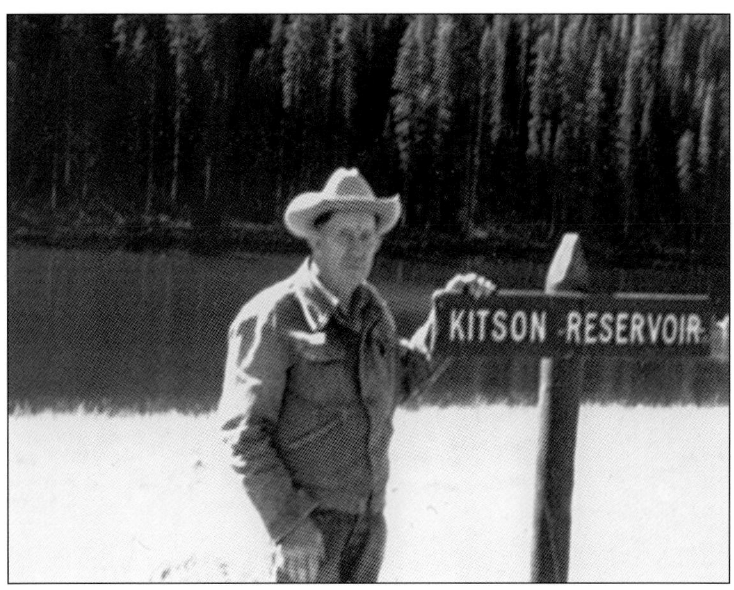

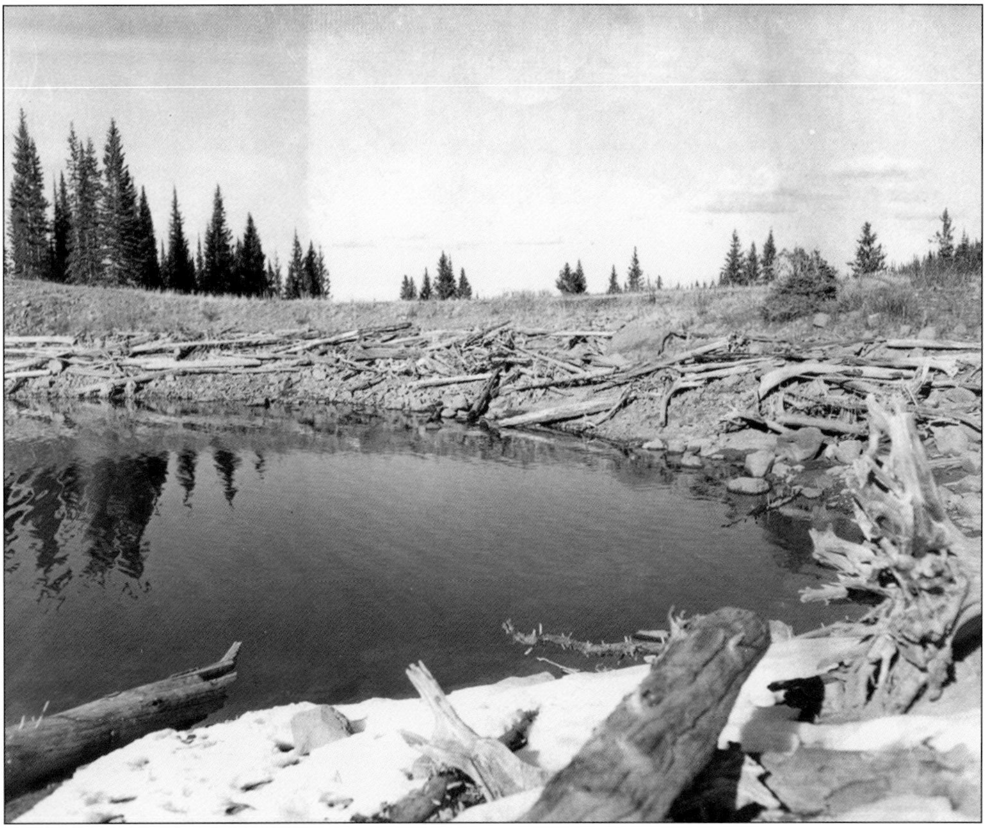

Leon Lake Ditch and Reservoir Company. Water for Leon Reservoir was appropriated on October 5, 1898. (Plateau Valley Historical Preservation Society.)

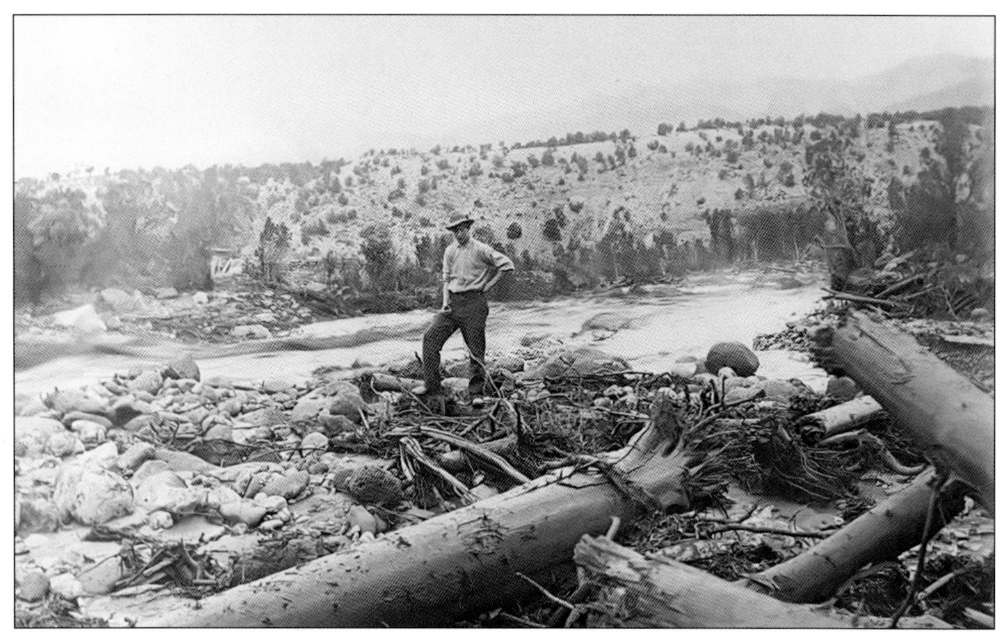

ATKINSON RESERVOIR, BIG CREEK FLOOD. The dam was breached in 1911. The *Plateau Voice* reported, "The places in the Canyon were ruined. Mr. Hutton says there was so much debris you could not see any water. The bridges went by riding like ferryboats. Took out a lot of the convict road that will not have to be rip-rapped. No major buildings were taken, but water was in the houses." (Both, Museum of Western Colorado, Lloyd Files Research Library.)

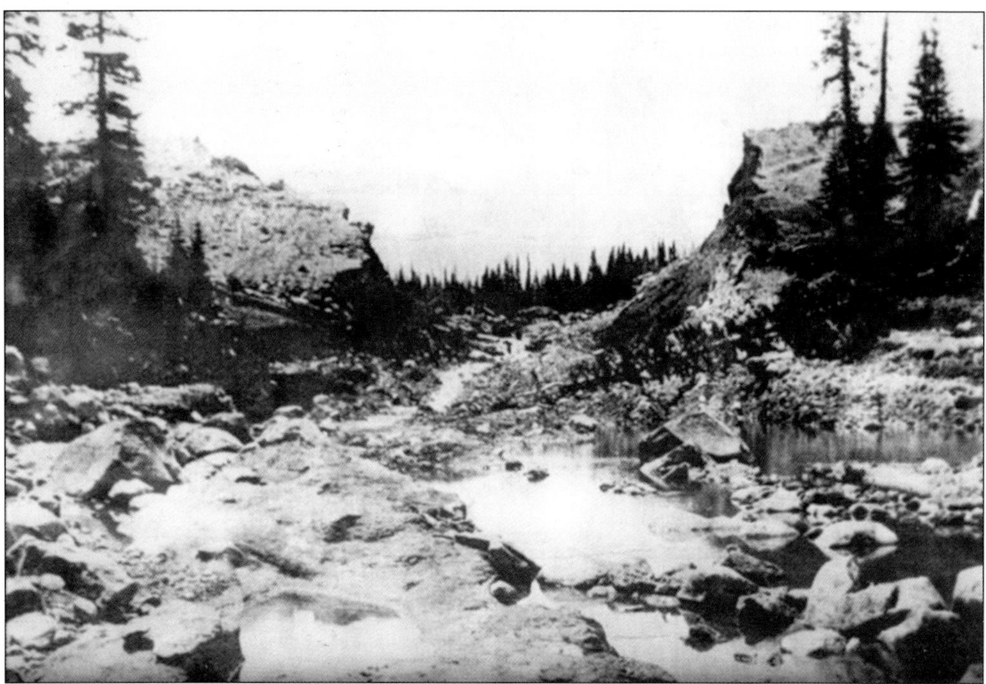

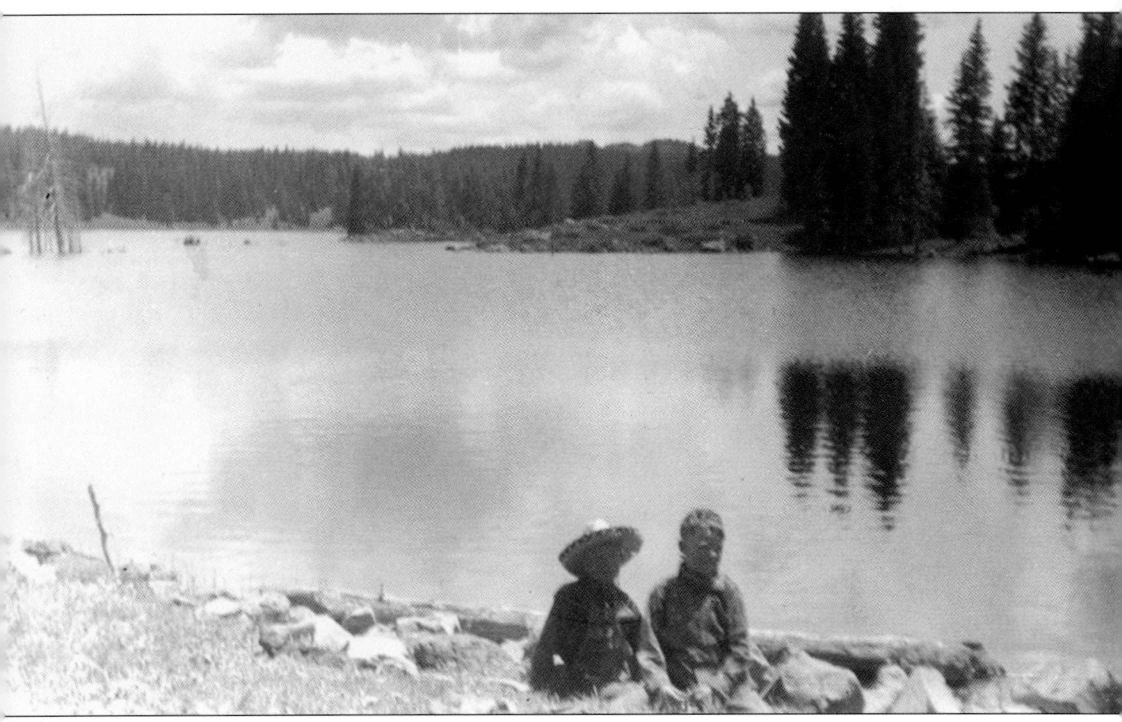

GRAND MESA LAKE. William "Billy" (left) and Robert "Bobby" Raymond sit at the edge of one of more than 300 natural and man-made lakes on the top of Grand Mesa. The Battlement Mesa Forest Reserve was established in 1892 and withdrew nearly a million acres to serve as a public benefit. The proposed reserve included the entire surface of the Grand Mesa and the slopes almost to the range of available agriculture lands. The intention was not to withdraw the reserve absolutely from occupation or use, but rather to increase its usefulness and the sum total of the productiveness of the territory by making each acre do its utmost for the benefit of the people. Some of the purposes set forth were to minimize the destruction of forest areas by fires and wasteful use, to maintain and increase the lumber industry by permanent and continuous yield of forest products on nonagricultural lands, and to guard and protect rivers and lakes and continue their flow for the benefit of the people at large. (Author's collection.)

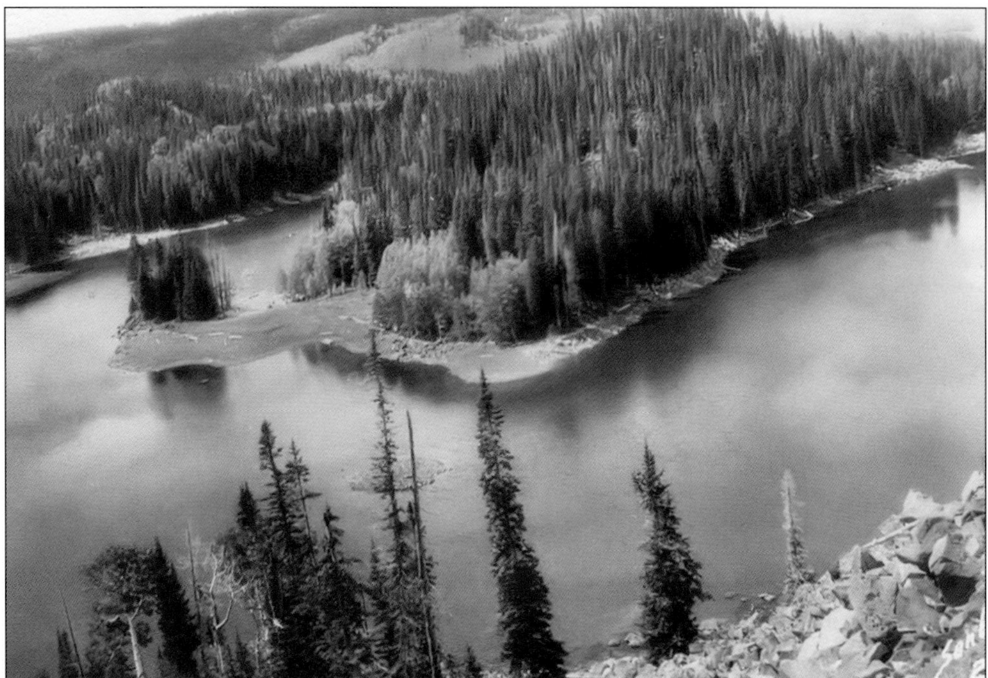

Mesa Lake. A local newspaper reported on the condition at Mesa Lake in an 1892 article: "The lake is filled with trout, covered with boats, and all around it are abundant forests through which dash and splash innumerable mountain streams. There is a good hotel, a herd of fresh milk cows on hand, and cabins already built and plenty of timber for more. There is every convenience for enjoying a good rest and regaining strength and vigor. The water is perfectly pure, coming right out of the hills. As a summer resort, no better place can be found." Above is a postcard of Mesa Lake. Below, people enjoy an unidentified lake on Grand Mesa (Above, author's collection; below, William H. Nelson Collection, Colorado Mesa University Special Collections.)

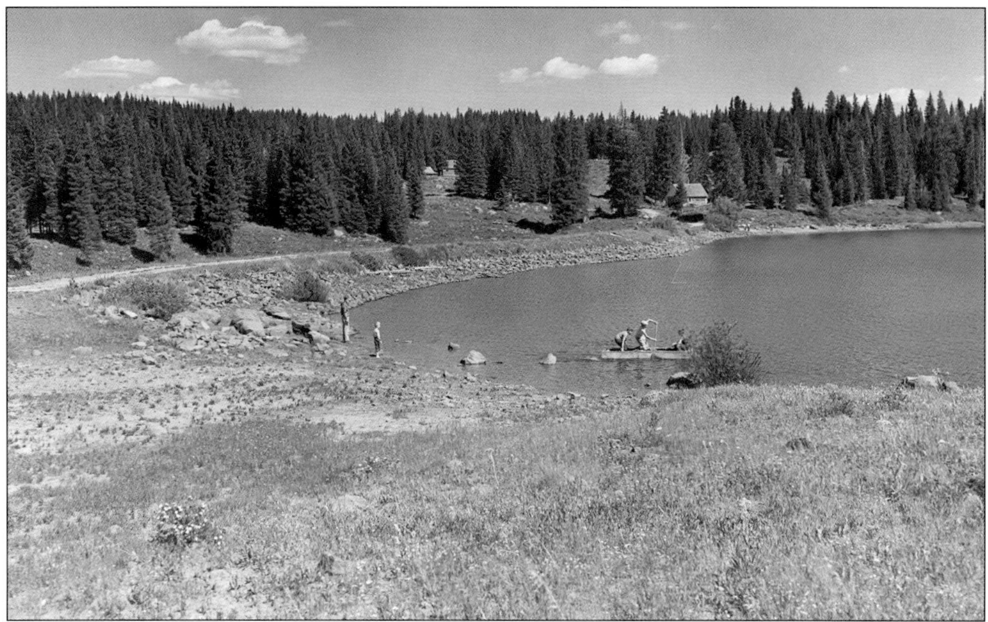

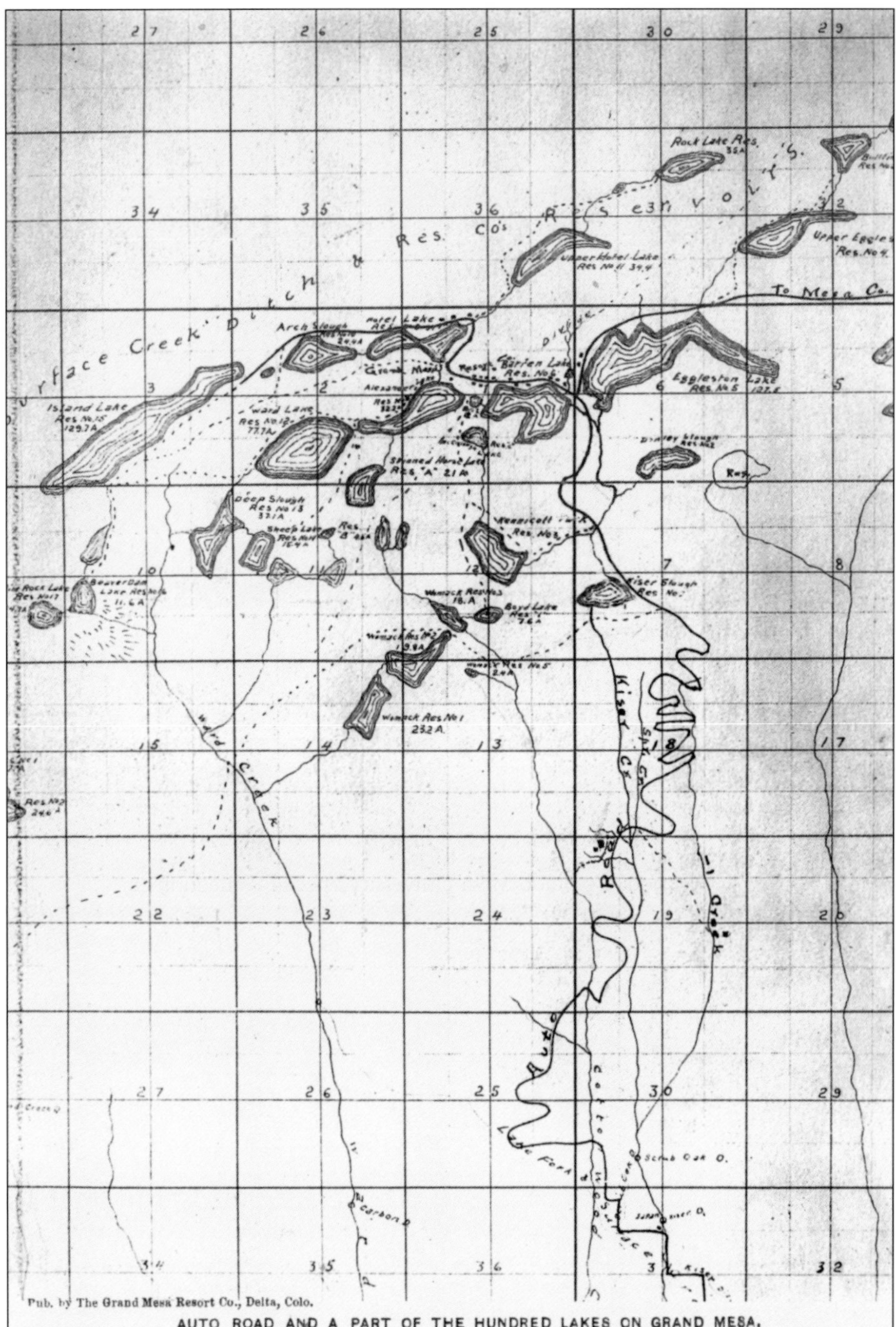

Automobile Road. Grand Mesa Resort Company published this postcard showing a portion of the lakes and automobile routes over the Grand Mesa. Fifteen men, most of whom were business leaders in Delta County, Colorado, founded the Grand Mesa Resort Company in 1893. Until the advent of the automobile, residents of Mesa County generally frequented the north side of the Grand Mesa, whereas the area south of the divide was explored and settled by residents of Delta County. (Museum of Western Colorado, Lloyd Files Research Library.)

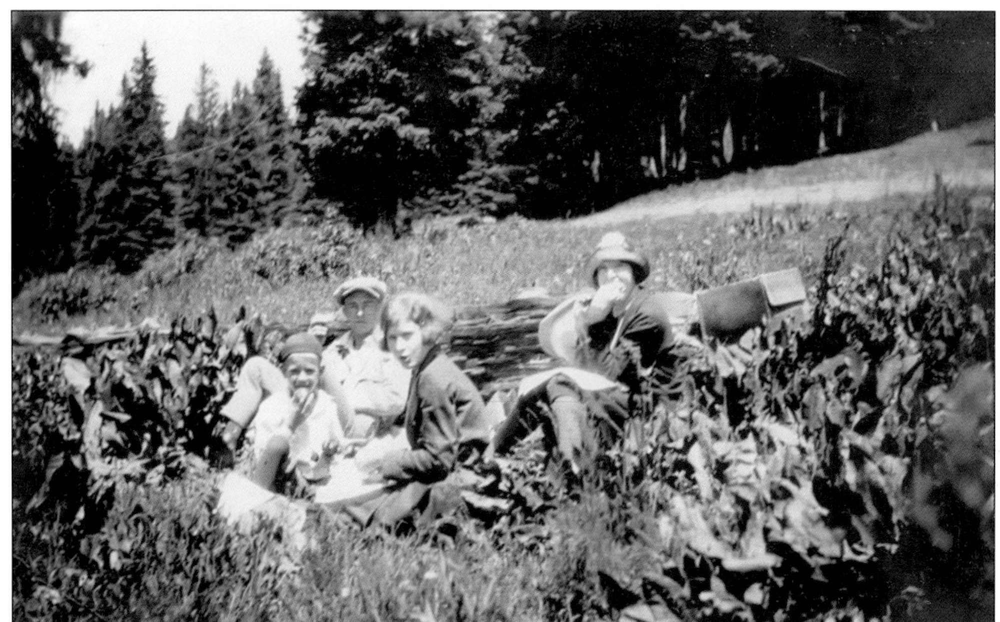

PICNIC ON GRAND MESA. Pictured here are Ethelle Silliman Raymond, George and Esther Silliman Knowles, and their son. The Grand Mesa was a destination for locals who enjoyed the outdoors. In 1913, the *Plateau Voice* reported that fishing at Alexander Lake by Grand Mesa Resort was free, pasture for horses cost 10¢ per horse per day, camp sites were 50¢ regardless of the length of stay, and a cabin was $1 for the first day and 75¢ thereafter. (Author's collection.)

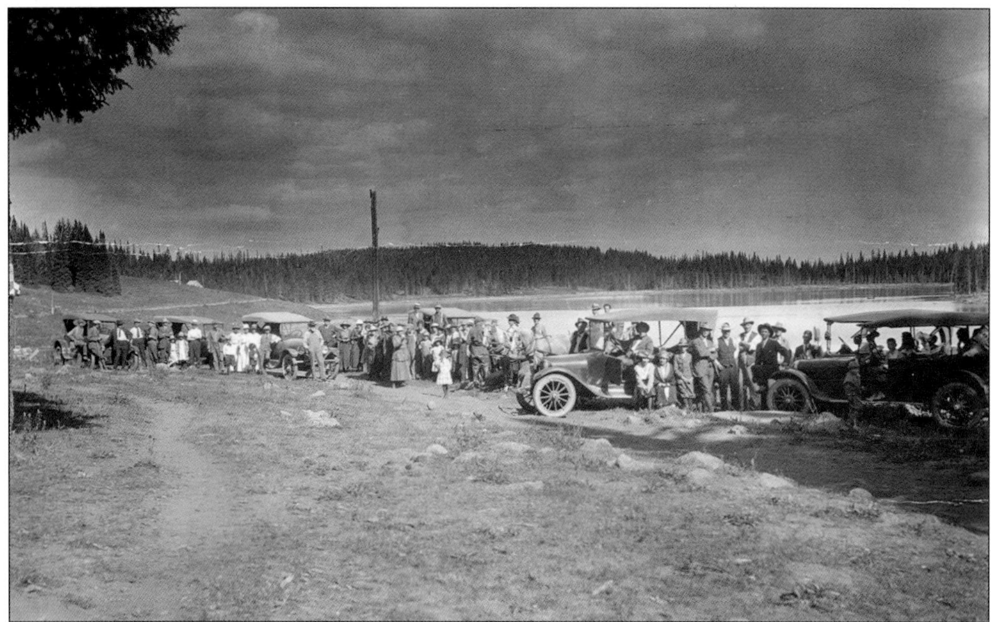

ALEXANDER LAKE. A celebration was held for the completion of the automobile road to Alexander Lake Lodge. According to the note on the back of this photograph, "the building of the road was called a graft by the mossback element." Although it appears it was not supported by everyone, tourism to the area increased by the thousands after the roads were complete. (Museum of Western Colorado, Lloyd Files Research Library.)

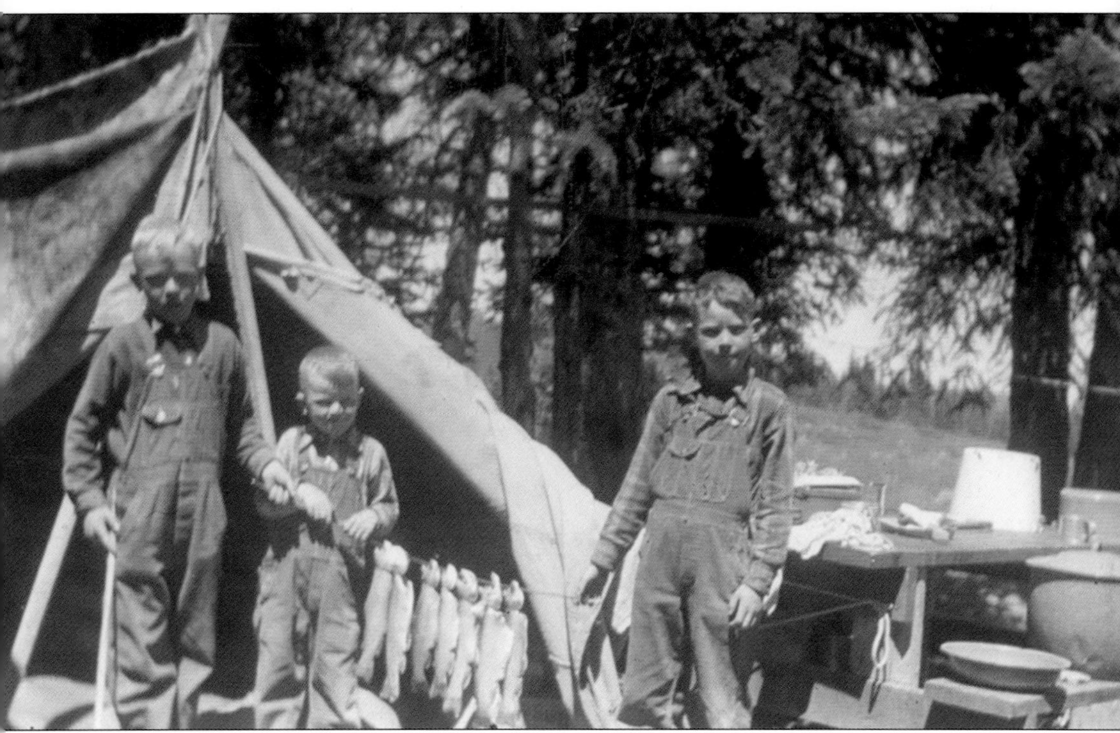

TROUT FISHING. From left to right are Billy, Darrell, and Bobby Raymond showing off their catch from one of the lakes on Grand Mesa. Automobile routes made camping and fishing expeditions more comfortable for families. The average annual number of visitors to the Grand Mesa numbered 10,000 prior to completion of the roads. In 1939, the Forest Service reported more than 40,000 visitors. The Masons and the Odd Fellows each had large blocks of lots that they subleased to members. Permits were issued for over 200 summer home lots, and three resort hotels were in operation at that time. (Author's collection.)

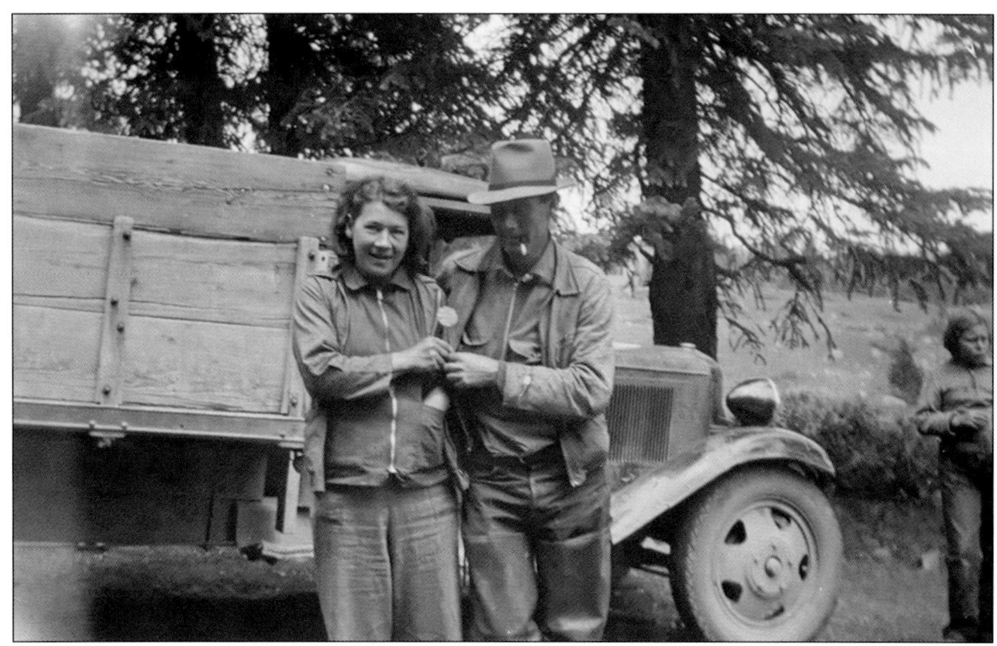

Recreation. Above, Rupert Raymond presents his wife, Bette Raymond, with a freshly picked wildflower. They are likely camping at Bonham Reservoir. Below, a hunting party poses for a picture. Only Wilbur and Ethelle Raymond (back left) are identified. They are with friends who were visiting from out of state. (Both, author's collection.)

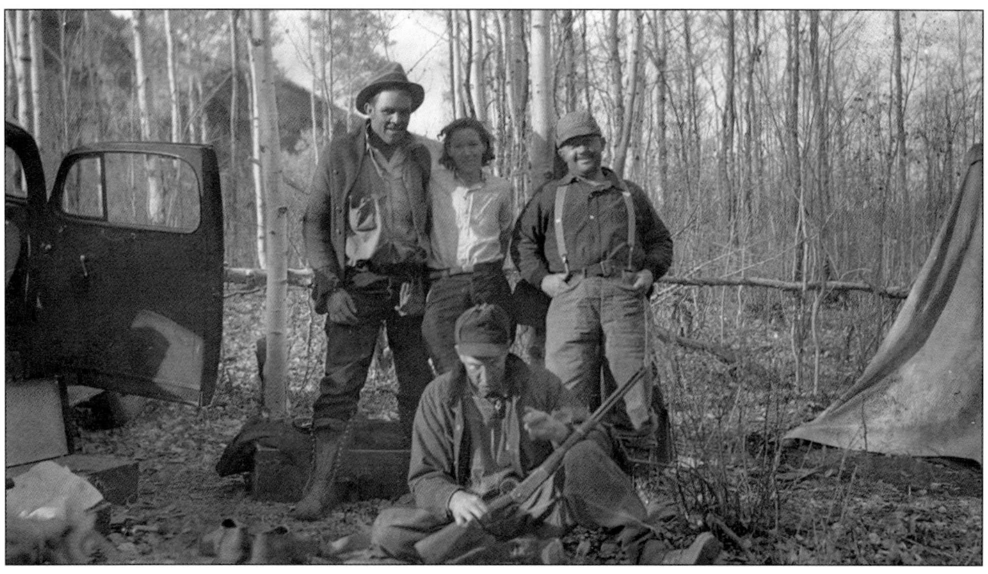

Odd Fellows Cabin, c. 1920s. An unidentified woman is shown at the Odd Fellows cabin at Alexander Lake. (Frost RV and General Store.)

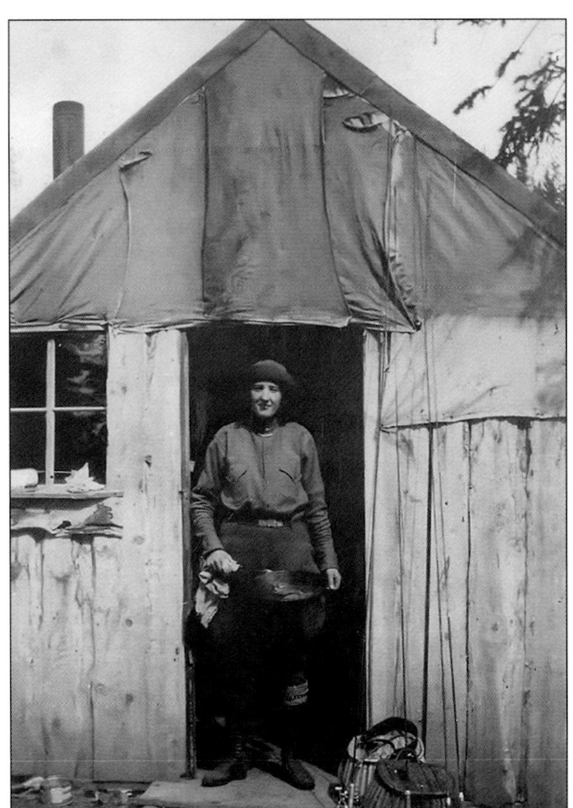

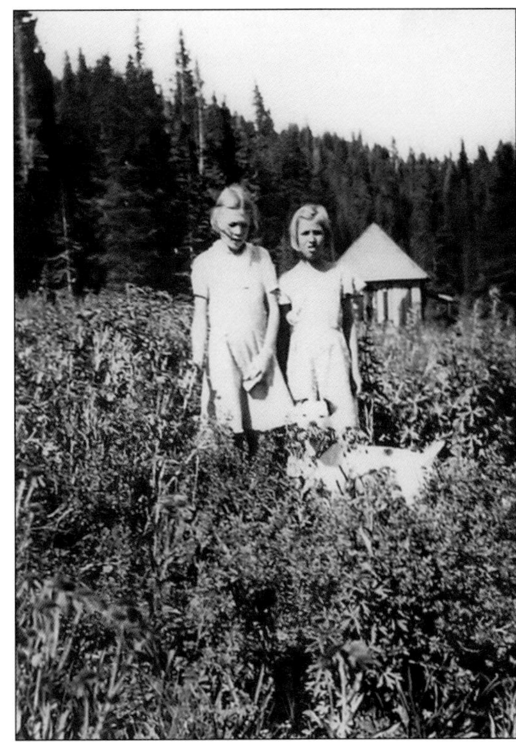

Barren Lake. Young girls pose for the camera sometime in the 1930s. While some lakes on Grand Mesa contained native trout, others had few fish, and some, like Barren Lake, had no fish at all. (Frost RV and General Store.)

Bibliography

Hawxhurst-Young, Helen. *The Skin and Bones of Plateau Valley History*. Grand Junction, CO: Wilson and Young Printers, 1976.

Pitts, Reuben. *The Bull and the Bees or The Facts of Life in the Plateau Valley*. Grand Junction, CO: Mesa County Historical Society, 1997.

US Forest Service. *Grand Mesa and Plateau Valley History*. Collbran, CO: US Forest Service, Collbran Ranger District, 1997.

Walck, Dean. *I Donated My Life to a Cow*. Inkom, ID: Arcon Publishing, 2008.

Walck, Scott. *The Way She Were Back Then: A Cowboy's Memoirs*. Grand Junction, CO: Lifetime Chronicle Press, 2014.

Wetzel, James K. *Murder and Mystery on the Grand Mesa: A Fishing Feud Begins*. Montrose, CO: London Publishing, 2011.

About the Plateau Valley Historical Preservation Society

We promote history, facilitate historical literacy, and educate about the history of the Plateau Valley by identifying, collecting, organizing, storing, interpreting, disseminating, preserving, and displaying historical information and artifacts from within and about the Plateau Valley area in Western Colorado.

Plateau Valley was settled in the early 1800s by strong, hardworking families that have endured good and bad times, war and peace, birth and death, and many types of weather. They planted their roots and loved this valley. If you are interested in any of your local family history, we may be able to help you with photographs or stories that you will enjoy.

Come help us identify photographs and landscapes of the valley and keep our history of Plateau Valley alive.

Consistent with our mission to preserve history on a local level, this book was printed in South Carolina on American-made paper and manufactured entirely in the United States. Products carrying the accredited Forest Stewardship Council (FSC) label are printed on 100 percent FSC-certified paper.

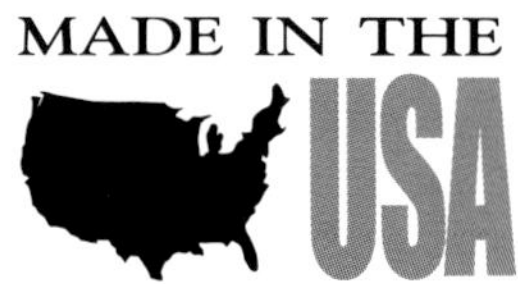

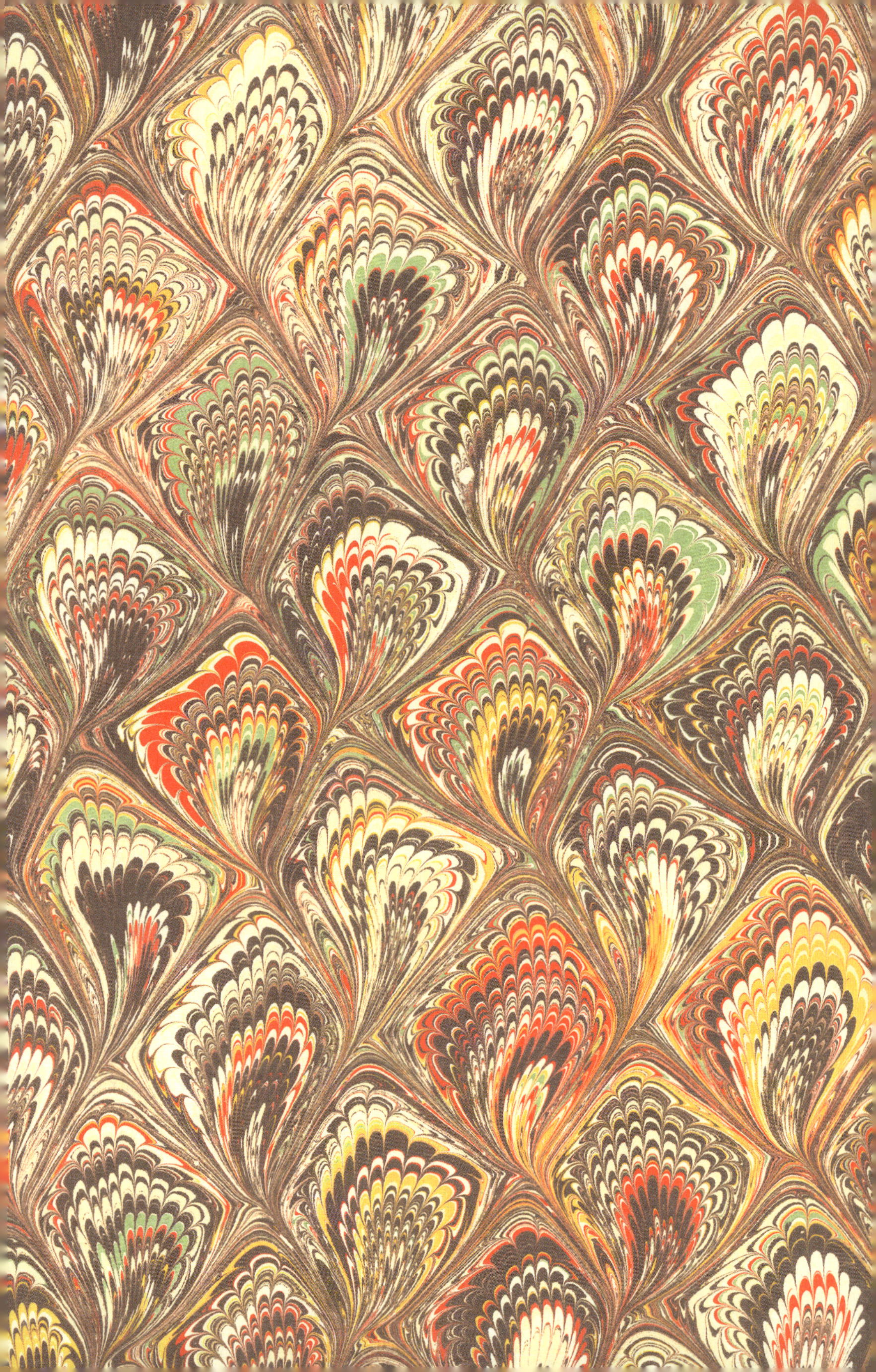